SCOTTISH ARCHAEOLOGY:
NEW PERCEPTIONS

D1354984

SCOTTISH ARCHAEOLOGY:
NEW PERCEPTIONS

edited by
W.S. Hanson and E.A. Slater

ABERDEEN UNIVERSITY PRESS

Member of Maxwell Macmillan Publishing Corporation

First published 1991
Aberdeen University Press

British Library Cataloguing in Publication Data

Scottish archaeology: new perspectives.
I. Hanson, W. S.   II. Slater, E. A.
936.11
ISBN 0 08 041212 2

Typeset by Hewer Text Composition Services, Edinburgh
Printed by BPCC-AUP Ltd

CONTENTS

FIGURES

PLATES

Contributors

Mr. J.C.Barrett, Department of Archaeology, University of Glasgow, Glasgow, G12 8QQ.

Dr. D.J. Breeze, Historic Scotland, 20 Brandon Street, Edinburgh, EH3 5RA.

Dr. D.V. Clarke, Royal Museum of Scotland, Queen Street, Edinburgh, EH2 1JD.

Dr. S.T. Driscoll, Department of Archaeology, University of Glasgow, Glasgow, G12 8QQ.

Dr. S.M. Foster, 25 Sloan Street, Edinburgh, EH6 8PN.

Mr. S.P. Halliday, RCAHMS, 54 Melville Street, Edinburgh, EH3 7HF.

Dr. W.S. Hanson, Department of Archaeology, University of Glasgow, Glasgow, G12 8QQ.

Dr. J.R. Hunter, Department of Archaeological Sciences, University of Bradford, Bradford, BD7 1DP.

Dr. R. Lamb, Orkney Archaeologist, 48 Junction Road, Kirkwall, Orkney, KW15 1AG.

Dr. Lesley Macinnes, Historic Scotland, 20 Brandon Street, Edinburgh, EH3 5RA.

Mr. R.J. Mercer, RCAHMS, 54 Melville Street, Edinburgh, EH3 7HF.

Mr. C. Richards, Department of Archaeology, University of Glasgow, Glasgow, G12 8QQ.

Dr. E.A. Slater, Department of Archaeology, University of Glasgow, Glasgow, G12 8QQ.

Mr. J.B. Stevenson, RCAHMS, 54 Melville Street, Edinburgh, EH3 7HF.

Ms. V. Turner, Shetland Archaeologist, 22–24 Lerwick Road, Shetland, ZE1 0NQ.

Mr. P.A. Yeoman, Department of Economic Development and Planning, Fife Regional Council, Fife House, Glenrothes, KY7 5LT.

PREFACE

As we enter the last decade of the twentieth century there is a natural tendency to look forward to the end of the millennium as a significant milestone, and beyond that into a new era. But changes are already in evidence, at least in terms of personnel. The last two years have seen the retirement of three influential Scottish archaeologists: Iain McIvor as Chief Inspector of Ancient Monuments, Scottish Development Department; John Dunbar as Secretary of the Royal Commission on Ancient and Historical Monuments of Scotland; and most recently, in September 1990, Leslie Alcock as Professor of Archaeology at Glasgow University. It was in such a mood of change that this book was formulated, with the intention of providing a reassessment of the current state of Scottish archaeology and some thoughts on its future.

The aim of this volume is to demonstrate to a wider audience, some of the depth and breadth of Scottish archaeology not merely the excellence of its surviving remains, but also the advances made in approaches to, and understanding of, that data. The focus is forward-looking and the scope wide-ranging. However, whilst the particular situation in Scotland provided the major impetus, and the main area of focus, the issues raised have a broad relevance within archaeology; just as Glasgow, as European City of Culture for 1990 and a focus of activity and attention across a wide spectrum of the arts, has been able to demonstrate the relevance of the particular Scottish dimension to the broader European picture.

All the authors are specialists in their particular fields and have been brought together with the remit of assessing new directions in specific areas of study. Time will judge the validity of their approaches. Certain themes have emerged: the high degree of archaeological survival in some areas, the current threats to that survival, and the strategies necessary to deal with the situation; the impact of aerial photography in enhancing the database; the challenge posed by the variable geology, topography and contrasting landscapes of lowland, highland and islands, and the role of more theoretical aproaches to the data.

We are grateful to all the authors for accepting our invitation to contribute; to Aberdeen University Press for producing the volume with such speed; and to Aberdeen Archaeological Surveys (Plate 6.1), Historic Scotland (Plate 4.1) and the Royal Commission on the Ancient and Historical Monuments of Scotland (Plates 4.2, 5.1, 5.2, 5.3, 5.4, and 5.5) for kind permission to reproduce a number of the photographs which enhance the volume.

We would like to dedicate the volume to Leslie Alcock. The strength of the Department of Archaeology at Glasgow owes much to his efforts and that strength is reflected in the number of contributors who have close links with the Department. We wish him well in his retirement and look forward to his continuing contribution.

W.S. Hanson and E.A. Slater
Glasgow

1

SIR LINDSAY SCOTT: FORTY YEARS ON

Elizabeth A. Slater

In 1951 Sir Lindsay Scott published a paper in the *Proceedings of the Prehistoric Society* on the colonisation of Scotland in the second millennium BC (1951). As he was operating within the pre-radiocarbon chronology, the period under discussion was the Neolithic and Early Bronze Age, and one of the main issues addressed in the paper was the possible influence of natural resources on the location of settlement dating from that period. He discussed topography, river systems and other geographical factors that might have been important, but the main focus of much of his argument was the distribution of lithic and metalliferous raw materials, the possible utilisation of these resources and the influence they may have exerted. He also examined the distributions of lithic and metal artifacts, and explored their contexts and the patterning and location of Neolithic and Bronze Age sites.

In much of this he followed conventional archaeological approaches, considering typology, discussing artifacts in terms of context and under the classification of utilitarian or ritual etc, but in many ways this was also a pioneering paper. It was somewhat ahead of its time in the use of ethnographic observations on the nature of trade and exchange, and in moving away from the idea that the final patterning of artifacts could be explained solely in economic terms. Thus the importance of social contact and relationships in the distribution of material goods were highlighted. When market forces and economic factors were introduced, distribution was not viewed as a purely spatial phenomenon and the relative costs of transport via land or water, for instance, were considered.

However, whilst the paper shows several interesting lines of approach, its underlying rationale was still a discussion of the colonisation of Scotland in the Neolithic, and an explanation for the routes followed by the incomers; these being colonists who owed their ultimate origins to the Aegean. As this basic concept has been revised the paper would normally have become little more than an historical document giving an insight into archaeological approaches in the early 1950s. It is, though, still cited; not as part of the history of archaeology, but as a source of primary information on the natural resources of Scotland and the exploitation of those resources. Scott presented data culled from geological records on the geographical

1

distribution of potentially useful lithics, native metals and metallic ores, and the paper remains a convenient reference for these. However, there are also problems because he made positive statements on the exploitation of these resources, and these statements may still be quoted. But not all have stood the test of time. The study of archaeological artifacts as material entities has developed very strongly over the last few decades, and the aim of this paper is to compare Scott's conclusions on resource exploitation with current perceptions. The overall conclusion, depressing to some but invigorating to others, is that in many instances 40 years of further study have simply removed Scott's certainties and replaced them with doubts.

Historical and technical framework

For Scott, the distribution of natural, geological resources and the influence this might have had on the nature of colonisation and the location of settlement was a central theme to be addressed. In this he followed the general assumptions of the time by implying that the ability to recognise potentially useful raw materials might have required an initial, external stimulus, but that once that stimulus had been received, local resources would probably have been exploited. The product would then have been distributed in the immediate area, with long-distance movement of materials only into areas without their own resources. Therefore, by considering artifact deposition and potential sources, the actual sources used could be identified. On this basis, Scott used the location of archaeological artifacts to indicate which sources would have been known at a specific time, and a circular argument then developed. The discovery of, say, Bronze Age metalwork near a copper ore deposit meant that this ore was known and, if known, it must have been used to produce the metalwork found nearby. Thus we have 'The principal source of gold was the streams running down from Leadhills . . . The Leadhills streams were certainly worked, three of the seven Scottish lunulae and a gold twisted-ribbon armlet came from the goldfield itself and two other lunulae from not very far away' (Scott 1951, 37). So Scott was still very much a man of his time. He was prepared to consider various mechanisms that might influence trade and the circulation of finished artifacts, but continued with the idea that simple economics and questions of expediency would govern the primary production of those products.

This was not a concept originated and fostered particularly by archaeologists, but often came from the perceptions of scientists working with archaeological material. Many of them saw early technology as an expedient technology, based on experience and experimentation rather than any theoretical, scientific knowledge. Where a technological element was allowed was in the mode of production, and this was seen to change, if it changed at all, in some logical way and with the assumption that it would probably move in the direction of increased efficiency. This approach was very much influenced by modern analogy and practice, and some scientists working in the 1960s and 1970s seemed to view prehistoric technology simply as a precursor to modern western European systems. It is almost as if they assumed that those involved in the prehistoric metal industries, for example, saw the formation of British Steel or General Motors as their ultimate goal.

It is mainly archaeologists and anthropologists who have forced a reassessment of the very simplistic and, admittedly, attractive idea that people in the prehistoric periods merely operated within the landscape, automatically utilising the natural resources in that landscape, with the only restrictions being the time and effort involved in procuring raw materials or a lack of technical expertise to convert them into a useable commodity. It is an attractive idea because it seems to offer an explanation for the many instances when local resources did predominate. But it really offers no explanation because use of any resource, local or otherwise, must be a positive choice and the exercise of that choice still requires explanation from within that specific context.

For the two types of material discussed most extensively by Scott, lithics and metals, the changes in perception have been at different levels, and the main reason for this is that different processes are involved in the production of artifacts of these materials. Lithic objects can be worked direct from naturally-occurring pieces of rock or mineral, and so some of the points of interest from the material standpoint are the geological source of the material, whether the material has particular properties, whether these properties appear to have been recognised, the form of the artifacts and the context of their final deposition. All these points may be equally important for metal artifacts, but there is also a far greater technical dimension, and the 'lack of technical expertise' mentioned above has long been considered a potential limiting factor.

Many hundreds of papers have been written on prehistoric metallurgy and metal artifacts, and it is impossible to attempt to summarise them here or give an assessment of current ideas on the nature of innovation (eg van der Leeuw and Torrence 1989). But it is reasonable to examine some of the technical aspects of metal use, working and production; not because these are necessarily prime factors, but because they have often been seen to be determining factors. Thus Scott, in the spirit of his time, did not have to consider any indigenous elements influencing the appearance of metal in Scotland. With the assumptions that the idea of using metal was brought in from outside, that the production of metal was technically complex, and that expertise also had to appear from outside, the only question was the origins of those who introduced these innovations. Then, though the introduction of metal marked a technical advance, once sufficient technical experience was available, metal would continue to be produced and used as part of some logical system.

This was Childe's static Neolithic society, incapable of scientific innovation, which gratefully received and absorbed new ideas. Because the introduction of metal was so strongly linked in some quarters to a 'technological trigger', so the general discussion had a technical bias.

Scott was, therefore, merely reflecting a general concept that metal working, and particularly metal ore smelting, was a process that could not have been developed independently in Britain, or even Europe. With diffusionist models holding sway, both metal use and metal ore smelting were thought to have been 'invented' in northern Mesopotamia and then transmitted through Anatolia into Europe via colonists, traders or other entrepreneurs.

Despite the concentration on technical factors above, it would obviously be wrong to suggest that these models and archaeological frameworks were developed in a vacuum. Much archaeological evidence, and cultural and social perspectives, were presented in discussion and marshalled in their support. Nevertheless, technical data were also used and this caused problems because often no clear distinction was made between the use of metals and the production of metals. There are two main types of source material for metals; the native metal (eg gold, silver, copper, lead and meteoric iron) and metalliferous ores. Native gold has always been the main source of gold, but as supplies of all native metals are somewhat limited, it is normally assumed that the use of smelting to yield metal from ores was a necessary prerequiste for the large-scale use of other metals. This has produced a rather complex picture because, on the one hand, smelting is a technical process and so the use of any metal, whether native or smelted, has been often presented as involving some technical expertise and, on the other, smelting is seen as a difficult process and is not one that even all metal-using societies would find easy to 'invent'.

So we have two lines of argument being followed, often at the same time. In the first, in an echo of the Three Age System, the first appearance of metal of whatever form marks a major divide. It is this first use that is significant because after that metallurgy develops with experience and proceeds along a simple path through to the present day. The other line of argument sees smelting as the great divide, with the use of metal not necessarily leading through into smelting, and information on the early exploitation of metals in areas outside the Near East and Europe used in its support. One such example, often cited in support of the technical difficulties associated with smelting, was that of the North American Indians who used native copper derived from the Lake Superior deposits but never developed copper ore smelting. However, despite being continually repeated, this is not a useful analogy.

The reason why neither of the two lines of argument mentioned above are very compelling, and why an example of the use of native copper not followed by the development of smelting offers no insight into prehistoric practices, is because different processes are involved. 'Use of native copper', 'copper working' and 'copper production via smelting' are not synonyms, neither are they part of some logical progression which was completed in the Near East but only partially achieved in North America. The shaping of native copper, lead or gold indicates 'metal use', and in some areas this is the form that the first use of these metals takes. However, if merely hammered to shape using techniques akin to those employed in working lithics, this cannot be seen to mark a major technical advance nor to require any new range of technical, as opposed to practical, expertise. It cannot also be seen necessarily to indicate true 'metal working' if, as seems reasonable, this is taken to mean that the specific properties of the particular metal were recognised and exploited.

Properties like colour and form would have been noted, but just as for the lithics, it is to other physical aspects that one looks for properties that are specific to the metals or present at a different level than in materials previously encountered. Native copper, lead and gold are, in general, more ductile than lithics, and gold and lead very much more so; and any craftsman must have recognised this. Even then, it is question of degree. Copper becomes embrittled when worked, so the forming of a small pin from a piece of native copper does not necessarily mean more than metal use, whereas the repeated hammering of a gold nugget to yield a very thin sheet of metal may be seen as metal working, as the continued ductility of the gold is being exploited. Enbrittlement in some metals can be reduced by the process of annealing in which the solid metal is heated to a temperature between one-third or one-half of its melting point (c. 450° C for pure copper) so that the stresses introduced by working are removed. The use of annealing would thereby demonstrate that this specific quality of the metal had been appreciated, but this can only be determined if a section from the object is examined metallographically. Few early metal artifacts have been examined in this way and so little data are available.

Where there is no doubt that advantage is being taken of a particular property of a metal is when it is melted and cast; and there is little difficulty in recognising cast objects. This ability to melt at a reasonable temperature, but not one reached in normal domestic activities (melting points of 1,063° C and 1,083° C for pure gold and copper respectively), is clearly one of the major differences between these metals and lithics, ceramics, jet, wood, bone etc. Why casting of metals should be adopted at any specific time, or where the idea came from, is a matter of conjecture but, in the absence of anything more concrete, one just has to fall back on ideas like general curiosity or experimentation with heat. It is possible to look outside at other materials and processes, such as the firing of pottery, but much as a link is sought by those seeking a single pyrotechnological revolution and unity between processes, the hardening of clay when heated scarcely offers a useful parallel to metal casting. The main problem is that there is often no precedent. What other melting processes would have been observed: ice into water, fats melting? What is certain is that there is no reason why familiarity with native copper or gold should automatically lead to the casting of these metals.

As far as smelting is concerned, this opens up a further new area. A strong practical framework can be established; what is often lacking is the archaeological perspective. For the framework, the types of ore mineral that will yield a particular metal can be identified and the chemical processes they must undergo can be determined on theoretical grounds. The specific conditions necessary vary between ore types and between individual samples of ore, as much experimental work has demonstrated

(Craddock and Hughes 1985), but general systems can be established. For copper, for example, the final treatment of the ores should involve a reducing atmosphere and a minimum temperature of around 800°C, or over 1,000°C if the metal is to be molten at any stage, with charcoal or other carbonaceous fuel mixed with the ore to provide both heat and a reducing atmosphere rich in carbon monoxide. These are the principles, but it is very difficult to translate these requirements into actual processes without some archaeological input in terms of furnace remains, ores known to have been used or the smelting product.

The problems produced by the paucity of direct data from Bronze Age Scotland are discussed below, and the main point to be considered here is the nature of the smelting process. Smelting is totally different from melting, and the differences are as much conceptual as practical. In the case of copper, a powdered green malachite ore, powdery blue azurite or shiny yellow pyrites ore, plus charcoal or coal, eventually yields metallic copper. A transformation of form and colour that finds no parallel in copper melting; just as it finds none in lithic working, hide processing etc. The only advantage of a previous knowledge of metal would be that the metal produced during smelting might be recognised as a potentially useful material.

Forty years ago the study of prehistoric metallurgy was mainly confined to typological classification of metal artifacts. Various typologies emerged, with much discussion on what they represented, but the artifacts were somewhat divorced from their production. For the European Bronze Age they were the products of 'the metal industries', industries that converted metal into artifacts with various controls on the form and shape of these objects. Behind this was the primary extraction and production of the metal itself, and this was seen as part of a different system. That there was far less discussion on this is hardly surprising because there was little direct evidence of where native metals were extracted, which particular ore bodies were used or the smelting processes involved. To assume that some basic industrial system was in place, and to consider prehistoric metal production as a simplified version of current industrial practice, with the product being a valued commodity produced to fulfil some need and the processes evolving through experimentation and cumulative experience, was seen to be as good a model as any when there was almost no evidence to permit more detailed examination.

The situation for the Bronze Age is now more complex, with metal seen as operating within a series of specific social and economic frameworks; at one point a utilitarian material, at another a symbolic or economic commodity, at another all three. There is far more emphasis on the nature and form of final deposition, the role of the craftsman, the control of resources, the variability of patterning through space and time etc. In short, everything from geological sources through to modes of recovery is under consideration.

One of the major factors prompting a reassessment of the nature of all facets of early metallurgy in Europe was the use of radiocarbon dating which, revolutionary at the time (Renfrew 1973) but now almost peripheral, suggested that the first use of metal in Europe was earlier than previously postulated, and that smelting might have been developed independently in Europe. It is now generally accepted that the diffusionist model for the introduction of metallurgy into Europe is inadequate, and that there were at least two, or perhaps more, independent centres of metal working and production in Europe. However, whilst it provided the chronological framework that prompted reassessment, what radiocarbon did not do, and does not do, is offer any explanation.

When diffusionist views held sway, metal use, working and production were all given a single origin and only one explanation was needed. Thus it was assumed that metal use came about though access to native metals and that the introduction of smelting in northern Mesopotamia could be attributed, in technical terms, to very long experience in metal use and working, or from exposure to a range of pyrotechnological processes involved in the production of plasters and ceramics. Neither explanation has received universal acceptance, and these models are not particularly convincing if transferred to Europe. Other models have been adduced for the origins of metal production in south-east Europe, an area where independent innovations seem to have been demonstrated, and these models include discussions on changes in social systems, pyrotechnological experience, the movement of settlement into areas rich in ores etc (Sherratt 1976). The net result is that we have abandoned the stable, universal and positive position of Scott for a series of problems, questions and putative explanations that vary from area to area.

Much has now been written on the nature and organisation of metal use, working and production in Bronze Age Europe, but there is still no totally compelling, simple explanation for the first appearance of metal in many areas. However, it may be that this is no longer an important issue, with far more interest in the use of metal and its impact than in the origins of the technology. It must be for archaeologists to decide if these questions are worth addressing, and perhaps too much has been written by scientists looking for answers solely within the technology of processes. From the materials point of view, do we not often appear to be trapped in the Three Age System? Not seeing the past as a continuum, but more as series of static periods marked by significant boundaries delineated by aspects of the working of lithics and metals? What is certain is that histories of technology should emerge from archaeology and not be separate studies running along side it, and that scientific studies of archaeological materials should be viewed within their own terms. Such studies do have their limits, and limitations. Where they can have a specific value is in providing at least part of a basic framework.

As far as the Neolithic and Bronze Age periods of Scotland are concerned, as for almost any area in any period, major components of this framework are material resources, and this was highlighted by Scott. He presented an assessment of the natural lithic and metalliferous resources of Scotland; how much we now know of the actual use of these resources is discussed below.

Lithics

Two of the main factors involved in the use of any type of lithic must be availability and specific properties, although, however favourable these factors might appear to be in allowing use, neither of them could actually dictate it. Artifacts are produced because they are required, all the other factors can do is influence how that need is satisfied. In Scotland as in many other areas, some types of lithic resource have only a very limited distribution or only a few natural deposits are known, and so it has been possible to provenance some artifacts of these particular lithics back to potential natural sources. This can be very useful, of course; distribution patterns emerge and explanations are sought. But it can also be rather dangerous if all the unprovenanced material is forgotten — and this means the vast majority of the artifacts. Therefore, to give a map showing the location of the sources that can be identified, either because they are so few or have particular characteristics that make them easy to recognise, and present this as a record of lithic resources as currently known is extremely misleading. Just being able to demonstrate that these sources were used does not make them any more significant than the myriad sources that have so far not been identified.

When dealing with lithics it often has to be recognised that it will never be possible to link all artifactual material back to a specific source. There may be many reasons for this: because the artifactual material represents a general type of lithic, but has no particular diagnostic feature to link it to any one of several possible deposits; or because potential deposits have not been recorded; or potential deposits cover an extremely large area etc. But in areas like Scotland that have suffered glaciation there is the additional point that much lithic material may have been removed and redeposited via glacial action and other natural agencies far from the original primary formations. All primary deposits and most secondary accumulations now known have been recorded in geological surveys, but small accumulations can go unnoticed, or those available at times in the past may have been further distributed or are no longer extant. Therefore, as most of the rocks and minerals within the primary geology of Scotland are suitable for exploitation in some form, and secondary and tertiary accumulations may have been deposited over parts of the land area, a more honest assessment of lithic resources in Scotland available at any particular period would probably be just a map of the total land mass at the period in question. The main variations to be seen through time would then be changes wrought by glaciation and the influence of post-glacial sea level variations on access or visibility. As material could also have been brought to Scotland from external geological contexts by both human and natural agencies, the possible locations of the resources available to the inhabitants of Scotland in some periods might also have to include parts of Ireland, England and continental Europe.

Beyond availability, attention naturally turns to the chemical and physical properties of raw materials that might have influenced use. This is often thought to be particularly informative when some choice seems to have been made between different raw materials, but should be just as relevant if no apparent selection has been made. Seemingly expedient utilisation is equally a result of choice. Unfortunately no two pieces of rock or mineral ever have identical physical and chemical properties, so only broad, general categorisations can be attempted. Also the properties normally thought worth investigating amongst lithic artifacts of both utilitarian and non-utilitarian function are ease of working, ability to be shaped to the form required and behaviour during use, plus the colour, form and appearance of the material. This raises a further problem as the properties seen as significant today may not be those seen as important at the time the material was being used.

The basic distinction between minerals and rocks is that a mineral is a naturally occurring substance with a fixed chemical composition whereas a rock is an aggregate of grains of one or more minerals, with most rocks composed of one to four main minerals and up to six minor ones (Kempe 1983). Once formed geologically, minerals and mineral aggregates are subject to erosion, chemical breakdown and other forms of weathering. Only the most resilient will survive unchanged as reasonably large blocks of material, or will remain in their original form even if the surrounding matrix erodes away. Some of the more stable and chemically unreactive minerals are silicon oxide (silica) and various silicates, and it is therefore not surprising that many of the lithics exploited as raw materials in the past are silica minerals and rocks containing silicates. Amongst the former are quartz, the cherts — flint, chert, chalcedony, bloodstone, plasma, jasper etc — and the natural volcanic glasses such as obsidian and pitchstone. All these silica minerals have a fairly similar chemical composition, with silica as the prime constituent, but they have acquired separate names because of their different modes of formation or, particularly in the case of the cherts, because they differ markedly in appearance. They also show variations in their detailed structure and this, in turn, produces some variation in physical properties.

The natural glasses are of volcanic origin and form when a magma erupts at or near the Earth's surface. The magma separates into various fractions on solidification, and the normal result is a series of crystalline mineral phases. However, as with man-made glasses, if the magma has a chemical composition that allows the formation of a particularly silica-rich fraction, and this fraction cools extremely rapidly, a natural glass rather than crystalline phase may result. This glass will retain the random arrangement of particles seen in the liquid, and it is on the basis of this vitreous structure, very different from the ordered arrangement seen in crystalline materials, that it is classified as a glass.

This structure also gives natural glasses some specific physical properties which may have influenced their use as artifactual materials. Like all glasses they tend to be brittle and comparatively easy to fracture, but they do at least fracture in a relatively controlled manner. If struck a sufficiently heavy or sharp blow, a small crack will form at the surface and the stress concentration at the tip of the crack will tend to make the crack grow and spread through the material. In a crystalline material there are lines of weakness between the individual crystal grains and so any crack will tend to follow these grain boundaries, but in a flawless piece of glass there are no such lines of weakness and the direction the crack takes is far more influenced by the force and direction of the original impact than it is by the material it is passing through. The net result is that, in theory, volcanic glasses are easy to flake and that the size and shape of the flake removed can be controlled externally; although the corollary of this is that artifacts of natural glass tend to crack under stress. However, as with almost any type of natural material, this can only be a theoretical assessment of behaviour because the properties of a specific piece of pitchstone or obsidian will depend on the structure of that piece, and this in turn is influenced by size, the degree of vitrifaction and the presence of flaws.

The cherts are a far less homogeneous group of materials in almost all respects, and one where even the nomenclature is not clear-cut. Sometimes the word chert is used for a specific mineral, sometimes chert is seen as a particular rock type or, as here, chert is used as a collective term for a whole group of crypto-crystalline materials that have silica as their main component. Silica is always the major constituent, but forms where the other components are negligible are considered minerals while others with a high level of secondary constituents are sometimes called rocks. Here they are all referred to as minerals. They have diverse geological origins, with most of the highly coloured varieties (eg jasper, bloodstone, carnelian) solidifying in cavities within igneous rocks and others, like the flint in the cretaceous chalk deposits of England, forming as nodules within sedimentary rocks via the redeposition and aggregation of silica.

What these minerals do have in common is a crypto-crystalline structure, with small crystals of silica arranged in a fine network, and this distinguishes them from the volcanic glasses with a vitreous structure, and from the macro-crystalline varieties of quartz where the crystals are larger and in a more regular array. The crypto-crystalline silicas are, in general, less brittle than the glasses but they do show the same conchoidal fracture pattern. Though any crack generated during working will follow the crystal boundaries, they can still be flaked with some degree of control because the boundary network is very fine and so a large number of routes is possible. Again, the overall result is that the direction the crack takes, and thus the form of flake removed during working, is controllable by the knapper to some degree. However, it cannot be stressed too strongly that the behaviour of any particular piece of material in both working and use is specific to that piece and the study of any lithic assemblage should not be approached solely on theoretical grounds but should be sufficiently detailed to allow any variations in technique to emerge. If no questions are asked, none will be answered and there will be little progress in this aspect of lithic studies.

Much as the crypto-crystalline silicas are somewhat diverse in form, behaviour and appearance, the properties of rocks cover a far wider range. The general definition is extremely broad — rocks are aggregates of minerals — and the properties of an individual piece of rock depend on the types of mineral present, the relative proportions and distribution of each phase and the mode of formation. Working properties and behaviour in use therefore vary considerably, from the very soft steatites, for example, through to hard, tough jadeites. In general, and it can only be at a very general level, the igneous rocks which form an appreciable component of many prehistoric lithic assemblages in Scotland tend to be hard, tough and fairly resilient; and certainly more so than the volcanic glasses and poor quality cherts that are also represented. As with the crypto-crystalline silicas, fractures in rocks tend to follow grain boundaries and if these boundaries are very pronounced they will influence the direction the crack takes. Therefore, if these rocks are worked by flaking it is difficult to control the shape of flake removed, and so they were probably worked by flaking, chipping, grinding and pecking, either singly or in concert. As would be expected there is some evidence that the ability to be worked by a particular technique, possibly associated with the related aspect of behaviour in use, had some influence on the types of rocks used for particular purposes. For example, an experimental and petrological analysis of perforated stone tools from Scotland showed that rocks were favoured that are not too difficult to drill and tough enough not to have been weakened too much by the presence of a shafthole (Fenton 1984).

All lithic artifacts can be classified on the basis of their material in some way, even if it is only into the types of rocks and minerals represented, but to move beyond this into provenance work is more difficult. Then all potential sources must be identified, including all secondary accumulations, and there must be a specific characteristic that is reasonably homogeneous within a source, but at a different level for each individual source. These variations can then be used to link artifactual material back to a specific deposit or demonstrate that it could not have been derived from any of the known deposits. For archaeological material the results are often of more value if the potential sources are discrete and the geology variable so that any provenance identified can be narrowed down to a reasonably small area. Despite some successful projects, the basic requirements for provenance work are rarely achieved and much lithic material from sites in Scotland has been identified down to lithic type but still remains unprovenanced beyond attribution to sources within a large geographical area or to a number of alternative sources.

Geological examination of archaeological lithic material has a very long history and in the 1930s it was recognised that the geology of the British Isles was sufficiently variable to make a systematic petrological study of British Neolithic rock artifacts worthwhile. Several thousand artifacts have been examined and the work still continues. The results so far and conclusions to date — the classification of some of the artifacts into 31 petrological types; the identification of potential source regions for all these groups; the association of seven of the groups with 'axe factories' in these areas; and the recognition of putative distribution systems — have been much discussed (eg Clough and Cummins 1979; 1988; Cummins 1983). However, it is worth stressing that over half the British material examined so far still falls outside the groups because it is either too individual or is not sufficiently distinctive petrologically; that the classifications are being modified as more material is examined; and that whilst the source areas for primary deposits of the grouped materials have been identified, some of the raw material for the artifacts in these groups may have been obtained from secondary deposits rather than the primary locations. Therefore, whilst this programme of petrological analysis has produced some worthwhile results, much of the interpretation at the detailed level still has to be done.

Small in number as they are, and therefore presumably representative of only one aspect of resource procurement, more detailed work than in the past in the areas of the known 'factory sites', asking the questions we would ask today, would also be of value. However, this is only possible in practice at Great Langdale and two Scottish sites because the other factory sites are now no longer extant or have little working debris still recognisable. Recent work has been undertaken on some of the working areas at the 'factory sites' in Great Langdale associated with group VI material (Bradley and Edmonds 1988). Whilst this was only a preliminary survey, and more needs to be recorded before visitor pressure in the area increases much further, some interesting points have emerged. It would appear, for instance, that both surface collection and quarrying were used, that some of the extraction sites are in very inaccessible positions and that various working sequences were followed. The detailed chronological picture has still to emerge, but it is clear that it is no longer possible to talk of the 'axe factories' at Langdale as if they operated as a single entity. Carrying this work forward, Edmonds has recently conducted a similar field survey at Killin in Perthshire, and there are other lithic deposits in Scotland that show some indication of working that would also merit further investigation.

Rocks

Although systematic programmes of petrological analysis of Neolithic stone artifacts started in the 1930s, most of the early work related to English material, and Scott in 1951 could only refer to a few examples of axes in Scotland identified as coming from the 'factories' at Great Langdale in Cumbria and Graig Lwyd in Wales. Otherwise he said 'Of the sources of axes and other implements of stone we know little that is precise' (Scott 1951, 42). Visual and petrological examination did continue, and when Ritchie produced a paper in 1968 on current knowledge on the stone implement trade in Scotland in the third millennium (Ritchie 1968), artifacts of porcellanite from County Antrim had been identified as far north as Shetland, archaeological material had been linked to riebeckite felsite outcrops on Shetland and working sites of possibly early date had been found associated with calc-silicate hornfels at Killin, Perthshire. Further petrological analysis of Scottish material since then has confirmed the fairly widespread distribution in Scotland of artifacts of group IX material from County Antrim, and material from Killin (now petrological group XXIV) has been found on archaeological sites. The Shetland riebeckite is now also recognised as a distinct group, group XXII, but of more use as all artifacts of this material recovered so far have come from Shetland. Five new petrological groups, groups XXVII–XXXI, have also been identified following petrological examination of Scottish battle-axes and axe-hammers (Fenton 1984).

Identification via petrological examination involves an assessment of the texture of the rock and the nature, form and distribution of the constituent minerals. No two samples of rock will have exactly the same characteristics and so a classification into groups, as in the archaeological programmes, involves some assessment of the degree of similarity between samples. Biases can be introduced if the number of samples is small and there should always be the possibility of reclassification as new data appear. For example, once the hornfels at Killin had been identified as a potential raw material and its characteristics were established, a small group of artifacts within group V that were originally ascribed a Cornish provenance have been seen to be more akin to the Killin samples and their provenance reassessed (Clough and Cummins 1988). Equally, as soon as the raw material at Killin was recognised as very similar in appearance to that of group VI from Great Langdale doubts have been expressed about any artifacts assigned to group VI on the basis of visual examination alone.

Reliance on visual characteristics is decreasing as more Scottish artifacts are examined petrologically and, whilst the work on even the Neolithic material is far from complete, data are accumulating and further insights into the use of rock in Scotland are appearing as these data are assessed (Ritchie pers. comm.).

Certainly the picture is becoming more complex. Not all the material examined falls into the groups recognised so far, the range of rock types identified within archaeological material is increasing and the importance of raw materials derived from secondary deposits is manifest. As Fenton says of the perforated axes: 'The petrologies are diverse . . . virtually every major rock type in Scotland that is suited to the manufacture of these implements is represented . . . any rock-type that looked suitable and was readily at hand was exploited' (Fenton 1984, 218). Thus the bulk of the material came from cobble deposits, with a very wide range of possible locations for each rock type, rather than primary outcrop or scree sites which might possibly be more readily identified. This fits well with current, overall perceptions that where there were secondary deposits that could be utilised they would be used, particularly as such deposits often contain suitably sized blanks that require a minimum of preparation. Many of these accumulations are mixed and yield a range of rock types, but as coarse-grained rocks that can be worked by chipping or pecking rather than flaking tend to predominate in the primary geology of Britain, they also form the bulk of these deposits. This means that where fine-grained, flakeable rocks were needed it might have been necessary to turn to primary outcrop or screes, and if these were seen as good quality sources, such as Great Langdale, they may well have been worked extensively. Thus there are two basic sources of raw material — the primary deposits that retain evidence of working and are now seen as particularly important because of the large quantities of artifacts from broad distribution areas that have now been linked to them, and the secondary deposits that are hard to pinpoint but may well have provided the bulk of the material.

The polished jadeite axes of Neolithic or Bronze Age date found in Scotland and other parts of Britain still remain outside this general picture of resource utilisation, because jadeite is seen as an extremely tough material that is difficult to work, and no source of jadeite has yet been found within Britain that could have supplied the raw material. The nature of the material and its non-indigenous origins have both been used to support the idea that these objects have a particular significance. Chemical and petrological analysis of samples from some European artifacts has indicated the particular forms of jadeite involved, but no firm conclusions on the source of the raw material could be made (Woolley 1983).

In direct contrast to the tough, resilient jadeites are the very soft steatites that are very easy to carve in their natural state, although they do harden or can be hardened by heating. This softness and ease of working almost certainly influenced their use, and vessels and other objects carved from steatite are known from many areas from the prehistoric periods onwards. In Europe the use of steatite is particularly associated with Scandinavia and, no doubt having some influence on this apparently northern bias, natural deposits are concentrated in northern Europe. In Britain the main deposits are in the Shetland Isles, and steatite artifacts have been recovered from Neolithic and Bronze Age sites on both Shetland and Orkney. Scott made few direct comments on the use of steatite, other than saying 'Trade in steatite, of which the main source of supply is Shetland, is not reliably evidenced', although he does imply that some objects from Bronze Age sites in Orkney might be of Shetland origin. The situation is little changed.

As a metamorphosed rock with a fairly limited suite of constituent minerals, steatites are not particularly amenable to petrological analysis because their textures and petrological characteristics reflect the processes they have undergone and are both too limited and too varied to be of diagnostic value. However, work on steatite and related rocks in north America and other areas outside Britain has suggested that rare earth element concentrations determined by chemical analysis could aid provenance. Therefore, when Moffat and Buttler (1986) were looking for a method to link the archaeological material from Shetland to possible geological sources, they analysed samples from separate outcrops on Shetland to determine if chemical composition would be diagnostic. Unfortunately it proved to be too variable for material within a source and too little different between sources for this to seem a viable approach. Therefore, in the absence of any evidence to the contrary, the material for the prehistoric objects from Shetland, Orkney and nearby areas is assumed to derive from sources on Shetland.

Pitchstone

Pitchstone is a natural volcanic glass composed predominantly of silica, akin to the other major form of volcanic glass, obsidian, but with a somewhat higher water content. Like all glasses, natural and man-made, pitchstone has a non-crystalline, vitreous structure and, whilst the properties of any particular sample will be influenced by the presence of flaws, good quality pitchstones show the brittleness and conchoidal fracture pattern typical of these vitreous materials. Therefore, if the raw material is selected with care, natural glasses tend to be relatively easy to work by flaking, and flake in a controlled manner, and evidence for working and use has been recovered from archaeological sites in many parts of the world.

This is not a world-wide phenomenon because natural deposits only occur in certain geological environments, but it is not very helpful to talk of obsidian and pitchstone being used in 'areas with access to supplies' because artifacts have been recovered several thousand kilometres from the geological source that provided the raw material. There are numerous examples of long-distance trade or distribution of obsidian and pitchstone, but they are brittle glasses with a limited range of functions, and rarely form more than a small component of the total lithic assemblage. They have, though, been studied extensively, mainly because they are easily recognisable, there are only limited natural deposits to provide the raw material and archaeological material can often be linked back to a specific source.

There are no records of workable deposits of obsidian in Scotland but intrusions of pitchstone do occur in specific geological environments, those of most archaeological interest being related to the British Tertiary Volcanic Province running through western Scotland and north-west Ireland. Surface deposits that yield workable blocks of raw material, and could therefore have served as sources of artifactual material in the past, have been recorded on the islands of Arran, Mull, Eigg and Raasay, in County Antrim in Ireland and in Ardnamurchan on the Scottish mainland. There are few reports of pitchstone from other locations, but as there has been no systematic survey of secondary sources there is always the possibility that there might be small deposits elsewhere.

The geological outcrops of pitchstone have long been known, as has the presence of artifacts of pitchstone and working debris on archaeological sites. The linking of artifacts back to potential sources also has a long history because as early as 1897 John Smith (Ritchie 1968) suggested that the petrographic characteristics of worked material from Shewalton in Ayrshire indicated that it came from a source on Arran. Mann (1918), in a broader study of pitchstone use in Scotland, also considered Arran was the main natural source of the raw material. This was the position followed by Scott, but by the 1950s there was far more information available from the Geological Survey on the petrological characteristics of Scottish pitchstones, and at least two separate forms had been identified on Arran, and many more archaeological artifacts had also been examined petrologically. Thus Scott notes that whilst 'natural deposits of pitchstone occur from Mull to Skye' most archaeological material had by then been attributed not just to Arran but to deposits of one particular type of Arran pitchstone, Corriegills type. Some identifications were by petrological analysis, but most made on colour alone — 'the typical greenish colour of Corriegills material'. Colour is not always a very reliable guide, but seems to have been sufficiently diagnostic in this case because the importance of Arran pitchstone has been confirmed by an extensive programme of chemical and petrological analysis of Scottish pitchstones and pitchstone use in northern Britain.

Williams Thorpe and Thorpe (1984) sampled 13 geological outcrops of good quality pitchstone which they thought might have served as sources of raw material during the prehistoric periods. The samples from sources on Mull, Eigg, Raasay and Ardnamurchan could be distinguished from each other and the Arran sources by trace element content, and the Arran samples from three locations (the Corriegills, Tormore and Glen Shurig areas), although very similar in trace element content, could be separated from each other via petrographic characteristics. As this satisfied two of the basic requirements for provenance studies — that all potential sources had been identified as far as possible and that samples from these sources could be distinguished — Williams Thorpe and Thorpe then extended their work to cover archaeological artifacts and examined 28 samples of material from 22 Neolithic and Bronze Age sites on Bute, Arran, Jura and the Scottish mainland. A comparison of petrological and chemical data indicated that all these artifactual samples were of either Corriegills or Tormore type pitchstone from Arran. Many of the artifacts were from sites or at least areas mentioned by Scott and, whilst not all were linked to Corriegills, the general, historical attribution to Arran still stands.

However, not all is as it was in 1951. There are now over 1,800 pitchstone artifacts or pieces of pitchstone recorded from over 100 prehistoric sites in northern Britain, and these sites range in location from the Ord North chambered tomb in Highland Region to Carlisle in Cumbria (Williams Thorpe and Thorpe 1984). Few of the sites have been excavated but the dates they have been given range from the Mesolithic through to the late Bronze Age, and it would be hard to imagine that any single pattern of resource procurement would have persisted over that time span, even if there ever was one single system. This makes it all the more surprising that the results so far show than only the Arran resources were exploited. However, the 28 samples examined by Williams Thorpe and Thorpe represent less than 2 per cent of the archaeological material so far recovered and as more samples are examined scientifically perhaps more will be revealed. For example, it is suggested that pitchstone recently found within sites on Rhum, Eigg and at Archarn opposite Mull (Wickham-Jones 1990, 52 and 155) might have derived from Eigg, but as no chemical or petrological analysis had been carried out Arran as the source was not ruled out either.

Just as further scientific work may change the picture, the excavation of more Mesolithic and Neolithic sites in Scotland using modern techniques might well also yield new insights, and information from sites near the pitchstone sources would be of particular interest. The potential is there, as shown by recent excavations of a Mesolithic site on Arran. Only part of the site was examined, but over 400 pieces of pitchstone were recovered (Affleck *et al.* 1988), and this throws into relief the small quantities recorded from other sites. The quantities may be small because the material was never there or, as would seem possible for a number of sites, it was not recovered. However, numerous as they may be in relation to the total quantities of pitchstone recorded elsewhere, the 400 blakes and flakes from the Arran site still comprised less than 10 per cent of the overall lithic assemblage, suggesting that pitchstone was not a prime, utilitarian resource even for sites near sources. The dating of this site, and the other evidence for Mesolithic activity on Arran, is of particular interest because there was no evidence of Mesolithic activity on the island itself when it was first suggested that pitchstone artifacts assumed to be of that date were of material derived from Arran. This did not mean that either the date of the artifacts or the source attribution was necessarily incorrect, but this evidence for activity near the sources does strengthen the idea that any pitchstone found on Mesolithic sites away from Arran might have been transported there by human agency.

Cherts

The scientific work on pitchstone has been discussed at some length because firm conclusions have been reached in answer to certain questions, but the total number of pitchstone artifacts from sites in Britain is still less than 2,000. The number of artifacts of chert must be more than a thousand times greater, but there is far less information about provenance. The main reason for this is that it is far more difficult to link artifacts of chert back to a geological source. The cherts have a very fine-grained, crypto-crystalline structure with silica as the main mineral constituent, and this means that petrological analysis is not particularly informative. Any distinction rests on the texture and the distribution of minor components, and there can be as much variation in these within a single sample as between samples. This means that there are only two further characteristics that can be used to group cherts and possibly relate the groups back to source — appearance and chemical composition.

Many of the highly coloured cherts, such as red carnelian or banded agate, have a very distinctive appearance which makes objects of these materials easy to recognise, and often means that potential sources have been noted. If only one possible source is known, provenance can obviously be done on appearance alone and it has been long considered that this was the case for bloodstone in Scotland. 'True' bloodstone is green with very distinctive red spots. The material reported from archaeological sites was assumed to derive from a well-known source of this material, Bloodstone Hill on the island of Rhum, and this was certainly the view adopted by Scott. However, recent excavations of Mesolithic and later sites on Rhum have produced small quantities of bloodstone and this prompted a reassessment of potential sources of this material (Clarke and Griffiths 1990). Two sources are now recognised on Rhum itself, Bloodstone Hill and Fionchra, with other, smaller outcrops recorded within the Tertiary Volcanic Province of western Scotland and odd nodules of material reported in beach deposits.

Geological samples from the Rhum sources, locations on Mull and from the mainland at Port Appin, Kerrera, Kinlochewe, Shieldaig and Strontian were examined visually and compared with archaeological material from Rhum and other sites in western Scotland. Little of the archaeological material was the 'true' green/red bloodstone, with many other colours being represented, and this aided identification because it was assumed it would all have come from the same source. The overall conclusion for the archaeological material from Rhum was unchanged, only the material from Bloodstone Hill or the associated scree or gravel deposits had the required characteristics.

Jaspers, other highly-coloured chalcedonic silicas and some types of European flint may also be easily recognised and classified by appearance but, unfortunately, most chert from geological deposits and archaeological sites is visually undistinctive. It is usually grey, brown, white or red, with several different shades even within a single nodule and the underlying colour often obscured by weathering and staining. Thus appearance alone will not aid classification or provenance, and attention has turned to chemical analysis. With silica as the main component, it is variations in minor and impurity elements that have been examined, and this approach has been used to examine flint resources within Britain. As with most analytical programmes, the first requirement was the identification of potential sources and then tests to ensure that each source did have, at least in part, a characteristic chemical composition that could be used to separate sources and thereby link archaeological material to a specific one. Locating potential sources was relatively easy because *in situ* deposits of flint can be found in the Cretaceous chalk of southern and eastern England, and the well-known Neolithic flint mines mark the location of at least some of the extraction sites. Samples were taken from these sites, and the analytical results showed that the flint was very inhomogeneous, with large variations in composition within a single nodule and across a deposit. With a broad compositional range for an individual deposit, often following almost the full range of possible compositions for flint, there was also considerable overlap between sources (Aspinall and Feather 1972). Some further discrimination was achieved via statistical techniques, but an examination of provenance by comparison between data from the flint mines and chemical composition of some Neolithic artifacts was still problematic (Craddock *et al.* 1983).

If attribution to a source by chemical analysis is so difficult when at least some potential sources are known, it would be well nigh impossible in Scotland where the source material is much more variable. As far as flint is concerned, there are no *in situ* deposits known, but Scott did not see sourcing as a problem. He said 'The only important source of flint in Scotland is at Buchan', and noted a substantial number of flint axes from the surrounding areas which he assumed were of Buchan material. These gravel deposits of flint and quartz, that extend for about 10 km inland from the north-east coast north of Aberdeen, contain as much as 90 per cent flint in places and are still recognised as a potentially important source of flint in prehistory (Wickham-Jones 1986), although the pits and working areas described by Scott and ascribed by him to the Neolithic have still not been securely dated. Scott did mention other flint deposits, but his overall conclusions were that Buchan was the main source of supply, and that Buchan flint could be recognised by its characteristic red/yellow colouration. These two conclusions can now be questioned on two grounds: that there are a number of other gravel and beach deposits that yield flint and might well have been less, more or equally important depending on circumstance; and that red or yellow coloured flint is not restricted to the Buchan deposits.

The recent revival of interest in lithic resources and utilisation within Scotland during the prehistoric periods owes much to the work of a few individuals — Williams Thorpe and Thorpe on pitchstone, Ritchie, Fenton and others on the petrological examination of rock artifacts and Wickham-Jones and colleagues at the Artifact Research Centre in Edinburgh on various aspects of resource procurement and use. The various programmes of field survey, excavation and artifact analysis have all served to highlight the differences between southern and northern Britain, with nodular flint and rock dominating in southern parts but a far broader range of raw materials being used in Scotland. These materials include not only rock and flint, but also a whole spectrum of other forms of chert, mudstone, quartz, pitchstone etc, and by concentrating on flint Scott tended to ignore this diversity. Possible sources of a range of lithics have been documented (Wickham-Jones 1986; Wickham-Jones and Collins 1978), and, whilst new deposits are continually being recognised, the overall picture provided by Wickham-Jones and Collins in 1978 is still valid.

> There are no known sources of flint nodules *in situ* in Scotland, but several deposits of flint gravels are well known. These are most abundant in the Buchan district . . . There are other sources in the north, notably Orkney and Caithness as well as in the east in Berwickshire and Fife. In the west sources have been recorded mainly on Mull . . . In addition to these mapped sources flint is plentiful on many beaches . . . Chert is more abundant in Scotland than flint and, unlike flint, not all of the sources are derived pebble sources . . . It will be noted that chert is most abundant in the Borders although there are deposits along the west coast on both islands and mainland and also in Orkney and the Elgin area. Similar to flint, chert may also be collected from both beaches and riverine deposits.

Flint and chert mines may be lacking in Scotland, and it remains as difficult as elsewhere to follow the detailed resource pattern for the use of flint and chert, but this does not mean that we are seeing an expedient technology in relation to these lithics. As Wickham-Jones (1986) says: 'As techniques develop, however, the variety of methods employed to utilize lithic resources is revealed and a sophisticated pattern of exploitation throughout prehistoric Scotland is emerging.'

Metals

This is the area in which Scott was most positive, and it is the area in which we now have to be most cautious because of both the lack of direct information and changing circumstances. In 1951 Scott assumed that local resources had been exploited, and used the geological framework and the distribution of artifacts known at that time to support his arguments. There were no mines or smelting furnaces, but a very strong theory to hold things together. Just about all that now remains unquestioned is the basic geology of Scotland that can be used to indicate possible locations of native metals and metallic ores.

Copper-based metal

In the 1950s in Europe there were no smelting furnaces that could be dated unequivocally to the Bronze Age, and the only direct evidence on resource exploitation came from the mining complexes in the Alpine area (Pittioni 1951). Since then, but after radiocarbon dating had already suggested that there might have been early centres of metal working and production in Iberia and south-east Europe, Bronze Age mines for the extraction of copper-bearing minerals have been identified in Spain, Yugoslavia and Bulgaria. As far as the British Isles are concerned, early working for copper ores has long been recognised at Mount Gabriel in Ireland and, despite various vicissitudes in the dating, it is now generally accepted that some of these can be firmly placed in the Bronze Age (Jackson 1984), as can workings in north Wales. Again, there had been many suggestions over the years that some of the working of the chalcopyrites at Great Orme's Head might be of an early date, but confirmation of a Bronze Age date via mid-second millennium BC radiocarbon dates for charcoal from areas of the mines (Timberlake and Switsur 1988) is one of the most exciting developments in the study of early metallurgy in Great Britain. All the information for Bronze Age copper ore mines in Europe so far has come from a detailed investigation of areas with known workings. It is extremely difficult to date such working via cursory examination because techniques and tools of mining changed little over time, and the methods used were controlled more by the nature of the deposit than the date of working. Similar evidence of early working is also seen at some Scottish ore deposits, but so far only those at Leadhills have even been partially explored, and nothing that could be attributed to a prehistoric date was found. There are, therefore, no Bronze Age mines or working areas yet known in Scotland, and no evidence for Bronze Age smelting, and much more basic work needs to be done.

All we have at present in Scotland for the early Bronze Age are some artifacts and some moulds, the latter showing that at least the final stages of artifact manufacture (or remelting and recasting) did take place here regardless of the original source of the metal. Since the 1950s the early Bronze Age artifactual material has been continually reassessed as typological systems have been modified and developed (eg Coles 1969; Schmidt and Burgess 1981). One thing that prompted Coles's re-examination was the publication in 1960 of analytical data on some of the metalwork, data produced as part of a European-wide programme of metal analysis undertaken by the Arbeitsgemeinschaft für Metallurgie at Stuttgart. Various compositional groupings were proposed by the Stuttgart group, but Coles reclassified the data, suggested that five main metal types could be identified within the Scottish material and tentatively ascribed the native coppers and smelted coppers that these groupings might represent to Irish and Scottish sources. Much has changed since the 1960s in the approach to analytical data from metal artifacts, and much needs to be considered as the final composition of the sample analysed depends on the composition of the original native metal or ore, the effects of any smelting process, any effects of melting, working or use on composition, burial conditions, the area of metal analysed and the analytical technique used. It is still tempting to consider Irish or Scottish sources for early Bronze Age coppers but it would be very unwise to speculate further until more fundamental work has been done. The minimum requirement to give a framework for provenance work in this area is a full-scale, detailed survey of native metal and ore deposits.

Gold

Exactly the same comments apply to gold. Examination of many archaeological aspects of the Bronze Age goldwork recovered from Scotland — form, basic typology, decoration, context (Taylor 1980) — point towards a link with Ireland, but there are also some local, indigenous elements. There is also analytical data available for some of this goldwork, again originating from the Stuttgart programmes. This needs to be reassessed, but only after more information has been obtained on native gold deposits in Scotland and Ireland.

This section on metal resources has been deliberately kept brief to emphasise the paucity of positive information we now have on the utilisation of metalliferous resources in Scotland during the late Neolithic and early parts of the Bronze Age. There may not have been any utilisation, but prompted by work elsewhere this is certainly an area that merits investigation as we move forward. The situation has progressed since Scott's paper was produced in 1951; we may be less certain, but we are probably far closer to a realistic assessment of the past. We certainly have no shortage of work to do.

Bibliography

Affleck, T. , Edwards, K. J. and Clarke, A. 1988 Archaeological and palynological studies at the Mesolithic pitchstone and flint site of Auchareoch, Isle of Arran, *Proc. Soc. Antiq. Scotland* 118, 37–59.

Aspinall, A. and Feather, S. W. 1972 Neutron activation analysis of prehistoric flint mine products, *Archaeometry* 14, 41–54.

Bradley, R. and Edmonds, M. 1988 Fieldwork at Great Langdale Cumbria 1985–87: preliminary report, *Antiq. J.* 68, 181–209.

Clarke, A. and Griffiths, D. 1990 The use of bloodstone as a raw material for flaked stone tools in the west of Scotland, in Wickham-Jones 1990, 149–56.

Clough, T. H. and Cummins, W. A. 1979 *Stone axe studies*, London.

Clough, T. H. and Cummins, W. A. 1988 *Stone axe studies. vol II*, London.

Coles, J. M. 1969 Scottish Early Bronze Age metalwork, *Proc. Soc. Antiq. Scotland* 101, 1–110.

Craddock, P. T. and Hughes, M. J. 1985 *Furnaces and smelting technology in antiquity*, London.

Craddock, P. T., Cowell, M. R., Lease, M. N. and Hughes, M. J. 1983 The trace element composition of polished flint axes as an indicator of source, *Archaeometry* 25, 135–63.

Cummins, W. A. 1983 Petrology of stone axes and tools, in Kempe and Harvey 1983, 171–226.

Fenton, M. B. 1984 The nature of the source and manufacture of Scottish battle-axes and axe-hammers, *Proc. Prehist. Soc.* 50, 217–48.

Jackson, J. S. 1984 The age of primitive copper mines on Mt. Gabriel, Co. Cork, *J. Irish Archaeol.* 2, 41–50.

Kempe, D. R. C. 1983 Raw materials and miscellaneous uses of stone, in Kempe and Harvey 1983, 53–79.

Kempe, D. R. C. and Harvey, A. P. 1983 *The petrology of archaeological artifacts*, Oxford.

Mann, L. 1918 The prehistoric and early use of pitchstone and obsidian, *Proc. Soc. Antiq. Scotland* 4, 140–9.

Moffat, D. and Buttler, S. J. 1986 Rare earth element distribution patterns in Shetland steatite — consequences for artifact provenancing studies, *Archaeometry* 28, 101–15.

Pittioni, R. 1951 Prehistoric copper-mining in Austria: problems and facts, *Ann. Report Instit. Archaeol. London* 7, 16–43.

Renfrew, C. 1973 *Before civilisation*, London.

Ritchie, P. R. 1968 The stone implement trade in third-millennium Scotland, in Coles J. M. and Simpson D. D. A. (eds) *Studies in ancient Europe: essays presented to Stuart Piggott*, Leicester, 117–36.

Schmidt, P. K. and Burgess, C. B. 1981 *The axes of Scotland and northern England*, Munich.

Scott, L. 1951 The colonisation of Scotland in the second millennium BC, *Proc. Prehist. Soc.* 17, 16–82.

Sherratt, A. 1976 Resources, technology and trade: an essay on European metallurgy, in Sieveking, G. de G., Longworth, I. H. and Wilson K. E. (eds) *Problems in economic and social archaeology*, London, 557–81.

Taylor, J. J. 1980 *Bronze age goldwork of the British Isles*, Cambridge.

Timberlake, S. and Switsur, R. 1988 Early mineworking on Capa Hill Cwmystwyth, *Proc. Prehist. Soc.* 54, 329–34.

van der Leeuw, S. E. and Torrence, R. (ed) 1989 *What's new? A closer look at the process of innovation*, London.

Wickham-Jones, C. R. 1986 The procurement and use of stone for flaked tools in prehistoric Scotland, *Proc. Soc. Antiq. Scotland* 116, 1–10.

Wickham-Jones, C. R. 1990 *Rhum — Mesolithic and later sites at Kinloch, excavations 1984–6*, Edinburgh.

Wickham-Jones, C. R. and Collins, G. H. 1978 The sources of flint and chert in northern Britain, *Proc. Soc. Antiq. Scotland* 109, 7–21.

Williams Thorpe, O. and Thorpe, R. S. 1984 The distribution and sources of archaeological pitchstone in Britain, *J. Archaeol. Sci.* 11, 1–34.

Woolley, A. R. 1983 Jade axes and other artifacts, in Kempe and Harvey 1983, 256–76.

2

SKARA BRAE: REVISITING A NEOLITHIC VILLAGE IN ORKNEY

Colin Richards

Introduction

In the winter of 1850 a violent storm severely eroded the sand dunes in Skail Bay, western Mainland, Orkney. Thus was revealed one of the most spectacular archaeological discoveries in Scotland: the Neolithic settlement of Skara Brae. The removal of sand exposed the upper levels of walls and house structures which, due to their construction in the local Caithness flagstone, remained virtually intact with only the roofing lost. Furthermore, the internal furniture of the houses was constructed in the same flagstone, thus providing a unique record of late Neolithic habitations. Such an occurrence is surely an archaeologist's dream. Although perhaps not quite of the nature of Pompeii, Skara Brae certainly offers a level of evidence of tremendous potential to a discipline concerned with the reproduction and change of past societies. However, this potential has not been fully realised; studies concerned with Neolithic social organisation and its transformation have focused attention almost entirely on chambered tombs and henge monuments (see however, Hodder 1982). Ritchie (1985, 125–6) has warned of the frailty of such schemes, a warning which has been acknowledged but excused on the basis of a lack of records and publications of the late Neolithic settlements, particularly Skara Brae (Sharples 1985, 61).

Once revealed and visible, this extraordinary site invited the curiosity of different and variably competent antiquaries and archaeologists. By 1927–8, when Professor V. G. Childe was asked to assist in the conservation and restoration of the site, hut 3 had been virtually swept away by the sea, and huts 1, 2, 4, and 5 had been 'excavated' by earlier investigators. Of these, Petrie (1868) alone communicated a detailed account of the partial clearing of huts 1, 3, and 4. Although Childe (1930, 1931; Childe and Paterson 1929) left fairly detailed accounts of his work, his excavations were apparently restricted by the main purpose of the exercise which was the conservation and presentation of the site by the Ministry of Works (cf Clarke 1976b, 233–5). Thus there is frequent reference to 'clearing out passages and huts' in his reports.

Any remaining hope concerning the possibility of conducting a contextual analysis of the material evidence sustains a further blow when it is realised that very little was kept of the huge quantities of pottery, stone artifacts and animal bone discovered by Childe. For instance, the surviving ceramic collection is extremely small, comprising merely rim and base sherds and decorated wall sherds.

However, whilst it is disappointing that a detailed analysis is not feasible, there still remains an outstanding late Neolithic settlement with all its stone furniture intact. In addition, a series of site notebooks written by Childe throughout his excavations, and preserved at the Institute of Archaeology, London, enables a reasonably detailed picture to be drawn of the site, because they include numbered lists and the provenance of artifacts within the excavated houses (Childe unpublished).

The history of the village

As seen today the settlement is essentially a combination of houses of different dates. Earlier houses, such as huts 9 and 10 (Fig. 2.1), are only revealed where they are not overlain by subsequent construction, and consequently they are only visible in peripheral areas of the settlement. Trial pits undertaken by Childe revealed substantial deposits underlying the visible buildings, including structural remains, to a depth of almost two metres in particular areas of the settlement. These deposits demonstrate numerous rebuilding episodes and an apparently lengthy history of habitation on the site. Clarke (1976a) located a similar sequence of rebuilding and accumulation of deposits within a small trench located adjacent to passage A and house 7.

Childe identified four main phases of construction at Skara Brae (1931, 61–95), which were subsequently compressed into two by Clarke (1976a, 17). However, to write in terms of entire phases of rebuilding to describe the structural history of the settlement is misleading because it is quite improbable that the entire village was simultaneously demolished, levelled and rebuilt. Indeed, the available evidence for reconstruction at Skara Brae is consistent with that from the nearby Barnhouse settlement (Richards in preparation), where individual houses were refurbished and regularly demolished and reconstructed. The interesting feature of this process of rebuilding is that a new house is frequently sited on the demolished remains of the earlier house. Childe notes:

> The flimsy huts of Skara Brae 2 need not have been inhabited for any great length of time. They would be progressively replaced by larger and solider edifices, beginning perhaps with hut 7. The dwellings of period 2 would accordingly be allowed to fall into disrepair one after another. Eventually the materials from their walls would be appropriated to the more modernized huts, and the sites of the old ones levelled up. (1931, 93)

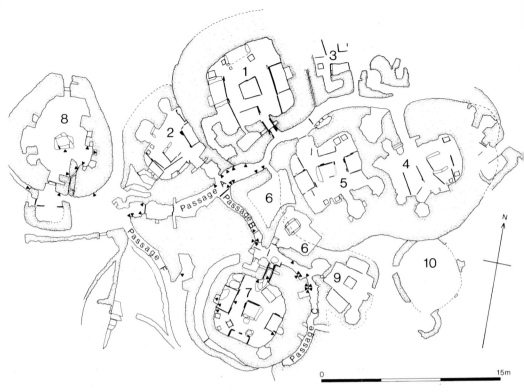

Fig. 2.1 Plan of Skara Brae showing the position of decorated stones (after Shee Twohig and Childe)

Similarly, at the Barnhouse settlement house 5 is rebuilt on at least four occasions. However, the newly built houses are always slightly offset from the foundations of previous habitations.

The combined evidence is consistent with a general pattern of houses being constructed, inhabited and eventually abandoned, following the lives and fortunes of the inhabitants. This may correspond to what is known as the developmental cycle of a domestic group (Moore 1986, 91–7), where domestic space alters in use throughout the life span or cycle of the occupying family. Differing patterns of use will inevitably create the conditions where spatial meaning is constantly altering (Richards forthcoming a) and, depending on the appropriate social rules, dwellings may be demolished and replaced for reasons other than structural failure. That this rebuilding is frequently undertaken on the site of the earlier house, as opposed to an adjacent area of the settlement, is of special interest since it involves demolishing the partially standing walls, levelling the area, and building a new house in a slightly offset position. Whilst the availability of a desirable plot of land within the settlement may have influenced this practice, it is worth considering the important role kinship and inheritance rules play in governing residence patterns.

The practice of replacement also emphasises the notion of continuity (Chapman forthcoming; Bailey forthcoming). To reside physically on the space formerly occupied by the deceased or even mythical members of a person's family, creates a number of links with the past, including those involving seniority and authority. The relationship with the ancestors, as shown in the tendency to isolate chambered tombs in peripheral areas of the landscape (Sharples 1985), appears to be ambiguous and problematic. It may be this element of danger and concern for the dead which accounts for the construction and repositioning of new dwellings as opposed to merely refurbishing older houses.

A comparison of earlier and later houses constructed within the period of settlement at Skara Brae shows marked differences in design which have tended to be played down in the archaeological literature. Certainly, the four main components of the house interior — the entrance, left- and right-hand 'beds', and rear 'dresser' situated around the central fireplace — do maintain their overall layout through time. However, the later houses have almost double the internal floor area of the earlier houses. Paradoxically, when this enlargement occurs the stone box 'beds' and rear 'dresser' are made to project from the outside wall, thereby minimising the available space for household movement and activities (Fig. 2.2). This remodelling of the interior does, however, maintain the same spatial relationship between the four main components of the house.

The clearest example of an early house at Skara Brae is hut 9. Houses of similar design are present at two other late Neolithic settlements: Barnhouse, Mainland and Rinyo, Rousay. Frequently, these houses are orientated on a north-west/south-east alignment with the internal cruciform arrangement of stone furniture corresponding with midsummer sunrise and midwinter sunset (Richards forthcoming a).

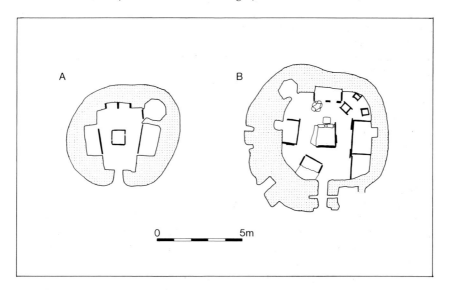

Fig. 2.2   The early (a) and late (b) style of house construction (after Clarke)

The widely held image of Skara Brae being constructed in a midden-filled hollow in the sand dunes is untenable for the original settlement. In examining the earliest period of habitation Childe (1931, 78–80) broached the question of whether the 'phase 2' houses were freestanding or inter-connected by covered passages. The presence of sand accumulation against the outer wall of hut 10 indicated the existence of open areas between the houses, consequently it was later stated that 'the village was not originally subterranean; it began in an agglomeration of free-standing huts which became embedded by successive steps in heaped up refuse — and that only partially' (Childe 1931, 95). The more recent excavations tend to support this conclusion, 'since there was very little addition to the midden outside the house before it was demolished, it must be supposed that it was conceived as an essentially free-standing structure, not buried as the later houses were' (Clarke 1976a, 13).

On the basis of this evidence it is clear that the initial 'village' at Skara Brae was quite different in appearance from that seen today. In this initial phase a number of freestanding houses were probably wrapped in a turf jacket, as occurs at the contemporary settlement at Barnhouse (see French forthcoming). With the demolition and decay of the buildings any turf surround would collapse creating widespread organic loamy deposits, and this may account for the extensive so-called 'midden' deposits at Skara Brae.

In examining the spatial organisation of Skara Brae there still remain suggestions of undifferentiated architecture (Clarke and Sharples 1985, 70), echoing Childe's claims of primitive communism (1946, 33). Differential status may not necessarily be expressed by the size of dwelling (Clarke and Sharples 1985, 33). However, the construction of social space is inevitably linked to cosmology, order and social control.

Decoration and division

At Skara Brae a number of different strategies are employed to delineate and differentiate various areas of the settlement. A combination of architecture and decoration effectively orders paths of movement into the area of human habitation, along and into the houses.

The decoration employed within the settlement is of particular signifi-cance since there is an apparent distinction made between the type of decoration, the context in which decoration is used, and the material in which it is inscribed. Within the contemporary and related Maes Howe type of chambered tombs the form of decoration employed is of typical 'passage grave' curvilinear style (Shee Twohig 1981, 227–8; Sharples 1984, Figs. 27, 28, 29), with the interesting exception of Maes Howe itself (see Ashmore 1986, 57–62). The position of such art within the Orcadian passage graves, as within the Irish examples, is considered to mark and thus define areas of importance and concern, such as the entrance to the tomb and internal thresholds (Sharples 1984, 116–7).

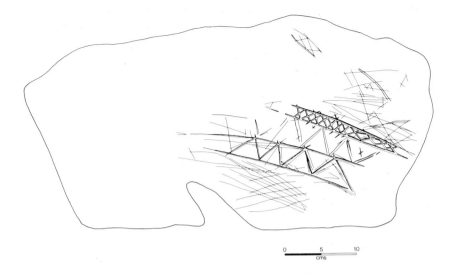

Fig. 2.3 The decorated stone from Barnhouse

In direct contrast, within the confines of the settlement at Skara Brae the decoration or art present on the walls and stone furniture is restricted to linear patterns, typically incised lines, crosses, chevrons and lozenges (Shee Twohig 1981, Figs. 287–90; Childe unpublished 1930; Clarke 1976a, Fig. 9). That this form of decoration is not peculiar to Skara Brae is demonstrated by the decorated stones recovered from two other late Neolithic Orcadian settlements at Pool, Sanday and Barnhouse, Mainland (Fig. 2.3). Hence, although decoration is deployed in a similar manner within both passage graves and settlements, different designs are appropriate to different contexts.

Within the settlements, linear decoration extends to individual stone artifacts such as skail knives (Childe 1931, Plate 52 (2); A. Clarke pers. comm.). Intriguingly, curvilinear art is also present at Skara Brae, but used solely on ceramics in the form of Grooved Ware decoration (Childe 1931, Plate 45; Clarke 1976a, Fig. 7). A similar use of circles and dots is present within the Barnhouse ceramic assemblage. Conversely, decoration on the Grooved Ware from the passage grave at Quanterness, Mainland, is linear (Henshall 1979, 77–9). Thus, here we appear to be seeing both the specificity of different styles of decoration to different contexts and also the interchangeability of these rules on different media.

The cosmological significance of spatial representation within the late Neolithic house is discussed elsewhere (Richards forthcoming a), but it is worth re-emphasising the importance of architecture as both cosmological referent and an instrument of control (Guidino 1975, 9). As cosmological referent, architecture may be mobilised through social practices to give everyday activities ontological status and thus bring legitimacy to particular actions. The creation of a socially or cosmologically derived sense of order to organise a chaotic world will inevitably make architecture an instrument of manipulation and control. The ability of architecture to cause the subject to move in certain directions, be restricted from some places at particular times, to witness some events and be excluded from others, forms one of the bases of power and authority through the control of knowledge.

A feature of late Neolithic architecture in Orkney is the continual emphasis on boundaries and clearly defined spaces (see Richards forthcoming b). Within Skara Brae some boundaries may at times take the form of physical barriers to movement, for example, doors complete with holding bars. Alternatively, more subtle devices are employed to convey the impression of moving across boundaries and through delineated space. These take the form of upright threshold slabs, restrictions in passage width by upright stones projecting from the side walls, and wall decoration. In conjunction with such boundaries, differently 'weighted' spaces are created by areas of paving, variation in roof height, and inclining or declining floor levels. It is in this area of analysis, particularly the ability to follow paths of movement throughout the settlement, that the full potential of the standing structures at Skara Brae is realised.

As it is the final period of buildings which remain intact, any architectural examination is necessarily restricted to movement within the settlement during its latter period of habitation. Unfortunately, the eastern end of passage A is completely eroded, together with most of hut 3 (Fig. 2.1). However, the western end section is intact and it will be assumed that entry into this passage could have been from either direction.

When approaching the settlement from the west an open area of pavement, known as the 'market place' (Childe 1931, 22), lies between the isolated hut 8 and the main entrance into passage A (Fig. 2.1). The outer section of this corridor is paved but unroofed. On entry a series of decorated stones on the right-hand (south) wall are passed before the primary entrance is reached. An upright sill slab and two buttresses of dry masonry projecting from the walls on either side (both decorated with incised lines) combine to create a narrowed entrance, 53 cm wide and 98 cm high. This outer threshold marks the division between the inside and outside of the main area of settlement.

Crouching into the low and narrow passageway, the subject moves forward approximately two metres before being confronted with a substantial doorway. Two monolithic slabs built into the passage walls constitute the jambs set 53 cm apart. A slab on edge forms the sill or threshold. Bar holes to secure a door are set into the inner passage.

Passing through this second division, entry into the main passage and settlement area is achieved. Moving in an easterly direction towards the main area of settlement, passage A begins to widen before the narrow passage B is passed leading off to the right. From this intersection both side walls become heavily decorated for a two and half metre length before the passage narrows and turns to the left, continuing its journey to the main area of houses.

SKARA BRAE: REVISITING A NEOLITHIC VILLAGE

Although architecture and decoration combine to create effective spatial definition when moving in an easterly direction, a more dramatic impression is gained when entering this area from the east; the main area of habitation. After turning the corner and passing the entrance to hut 6 (which is a later addition), the passageway suddenly expands and becomes highly decorated. Where hut 2 leads into this area of passage A, two features serve to separate it from this apparently important area. First, an elaborate porch-like addition to the entrance separates the house doorway from the main passage. Second, both sides of the porch area are decorated. It is clear that this portion of passage A constitutes a space of special concern, or even risk. Interestingly, it also marks the beginning of passage B and the journey to hut 7.

Passage B is entered by stepping over an upright sill slab which also acts as a step down 45 cm onto the lower floor level. After moving along and gradually down the narrow passage for approximately four metres it begins to curve around to the right (south). At this point it is traversed by an upright sill slab which forms a further step down:

> Just beyond this step one sees on either side upright slabs, set edgewise into the walls. These slabs, now broken and displaced, seem once to have projected into the passage like jambs. Between them and the sill already mentioned the walls seem to have been faced with two slabs on end, now partly shattered. Moreover, two beam-like lintel stones, projecting radially from the west wall, help to support the roof-slabs. The whole construction looks like the remains of a gate. (Childe 1931, 45)

It is exactly at this point that further incised decoration is seen on the wall. Continuing along the passage a second upright sill slab marks another step down which coincides with more elaborate decoration on the right-hand wall face. The final step down places the subject in a substantially broader and higher area known as passage C. Directly ahead is the entrance to a small cell within which the door bar of hut 7 can be controlled.

On entering passage C a further upright sill slab is stepped over, and to the left the entrance to hut 7 becomes visible. A flagstone path now leads directly along the passage and into the entrance passage to hut 7 (Fig. 2.4). Proceeding along this pathway involves a gradual descent and the crossing of another upright sill slab, before reaching the doorway of hut 7. This area was also decorated by a carved stone set high up in the passage wall (Childe and Paterson 1929, 247). In reaching this point from passage A, a descent of almost one and a half metres has been undertaken, and no less than five sill slabs and four areas of decoration have been negotiated.

The difficulties and spatial transitions incurred in reaching hut 7 via passages A and B would still have been considerable if access were possible from the south along passage C. The entrance and original route of this passage are far from clear, but if the subject was able to gain entry from the eastern side entrance into passage C, a doorway would be encountered approximately two metres inside. An upright sill

slab crosses the passage, and 'a beam-like slab spans the passage' (Childe
and Paterson 1929) and reduces the ceiling height. This boundary is once
again elaborated by six areas of incised art positioned adjacent to the
threshold. Passing through the doorway, the subject moves along the
passage, experiencing the gradual downward slope of the floor until a
second sill stone and narrowing of the walls is reached. This slab faces
a step down to a lower level. Stepping down, a decorated slab is passed
in the left-hand wall and a side cell lies to the right; the passage curves
around slightly to the left and runs towards the entrance to hut 7 which
is now visible. This approach passes three further areas of decoration in
the left-hand wall.

Clearly, whichever route is taken to gain access to hut 7 involves
passing through a number of architectural divisions of space, frequently
accompanied and embellished by decoration. Far more spatial discontinuity
has to be negotiated in reaching hut 7 than any other house in Skara Brae.
Here architecture and art frequently fuse to create greater symbolic and
spatial depth. These boundaries, however, do more than order space;
since they are only encountered through the movement of people within
the settlement they also embody temporality. In examining the spatial
organisation of Skara Brae it is clear that different forms of division and
boundary operate to segregate the settlement, mark and identify key areas
of importance, and create spatial and temporal depth to potential paths of
movement.

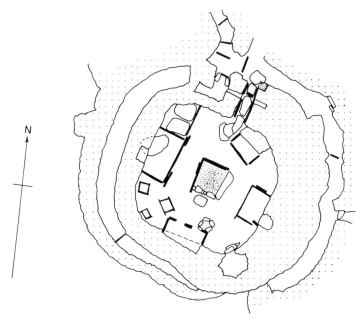

N

2.4 *House 7 at Skara Brae showing the direction of entrance paving and the
position of the hearth at the threshold (after Childe)*

The houses

The late Neolithic houses in Orkney all tend to conform to a consistent internal layout. The organisation of space is based on the cruciform arrangement of the entrance, right- and left-hand stone box 'beds' and the rear 'dresser', all positioned around a central fireplace. A distinction was noted earlier between the design of earlier and later houses, with the later examples being larger constructions with increased floor area (Fig. 2.2), although this enlargement is effectively minimised by the projecting stone furniture. This regularity in distances between furniture over a substantial period of time suggests the existence of complex rules of house layout which may have formed part of a sequence of constructional rituals and ceremonies surrounding the successful erection and bringing to life of a house (Blier 1987, 27–31; Howe 1983, 144–55). Elsewhere it is suggested that the position and alignment of the hearth stones may have constituted a primary and important part of late Neolithic house construction (Richards forthcoming a).

Once built, the house provides a place to live and undertake many activities, and in this it embodies many symbolic meanings. Architecture and its spatial representation are continually drawn upon in various social situations, as is more portable material culture. Ceramic and stone vessels, woven curtains and many other different materials will participate in the definition of space. There is always a correct place for someone and something at any time of the day or year. Consequently, the numerous activities making up the rhythms of daily life continually alter the spatial definition of the dwelling.

As the main thoroughfare winding the entire length of the settlement, passage A provides access from the outside world to all the later houses with the exception of isolated hut 8. Five dwellings are directly situated to the north west and south east of passage A, not including hut 6 which is a slightly later construction and difficult to interpret as a house. Apart from the doorways and divisional sill slabs separating the settlement from the outside world, passage A runs unimpeded through the main residential area of huts 1, 2, 3, 4 and 5, with only a single upright sill slab dividing the corridor to the north east of the entrances to huts 1 and 5. Each of the huts overlies earlier houses, and it is interesting to note that the earlier hut 4 (Fig. 2.1), with a south-east entrance orientation, faced the opposite direction to its successor. A porch arrangement protected the doorway, paralleling the porch in front of the doorway into hut 8.

Of the houses lying to the south of the passage, hut 5 pre-dates hut 4 (Childe 1931, 93–4), while the northerly houses are clearly sequentially constructed beginning with hut 1. This house has the largest internal area and, other than having its northern wall partially remodelled during the last century (including a window providing pleasant views of the bay), maintains its original construction. A typical internal layout is slightly altered by the presence of two masonry piers forming the ends of the left-hand 'bed'.

Beneath the rearmost pier a complete Grooved Ware vessel was set into the floor (Petrie 1868, 206).

Entry to hut 1 is gained through a doorway which admits the subject into the right-hand area of the house. This is a consistent feature of house architecture and recalls Hodder's (1982, 221–3) discussion of the apparent symmetry of the house belying a subtle asymmetry. The right of centre position of the doorway, together with the presence of a stone box enclosure inside the house situated to the left of the doorway, ensure access is into the right-hand area of the dwelling. This route is traced in stone paving within hut 7 (Fig. 2.4). By moving into the right side of the house the apparently equal balance of spatial depth between the right and left sides is completely altered. Hence, in some social situations, the rear dresser and the cell immediately behind it may constitute the deepest space. Alternatively, in other situations, the left-hand area will assume greater depth. It is worth emphasising that the realisation of these qualities of spatial meaning are totally dependent on people moving through space and undertaking activities at appropriate places.

In examining the rather sparse collection of material culture from huts 1 and 2 (Fig. 2.5), it becomes rather difficult to accept Childe's scheme for the abandonment of Skara Brae, which appears to be based primarily on accounting for the contents of hut 7. The tragic end to the settlement came when it:

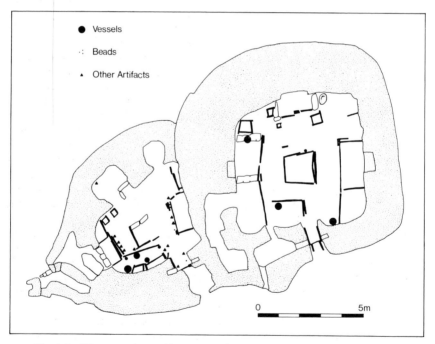

Fig. 2.5   Huts 1 and 2 at Skara Brae showing the distribution of artifacts

was eventually overwhelmed by a sudden catastrophe. The inhabitants of the huts were forced to flee from their homes, abandoning in the store rooms and on the floor many treasured possessions, fashioned with great labour and ingenuity. One woman in her haste to squeeze through the narrow door of her home (hut 7) broke her necklace and left a stream of beads behind as she scampered up the passage (C). (Childe 1950, 5)

Indeed, the distribution, type and number of artifacts recognised on the floors of huts 1 and 2 during the excavations of 1865 and 1927, indicate that they were cleared out and the normal contents removed elsewhere. With the exception of the stone cups, bowls and vessels left within the stone box enclosures to the left side of the entrance, the other finds tend to be situated adjacent to internal stone divisions with the rest of the floor area mainly free of finds (Fig. 2.5). This concurs with the floors being kept reasonably clean and stray articles becoming lost or trapped against internal furniture and the outer walls, but contrasts with both the interpretation offered by Childe, and the remains encountered within hut 7.

Hut 7

During his first season of excavation and conservation in 1928 at Skara Brae, Childe located and 'cleared out' hut 7 (Childe and Paterson 1929, 247). Being virtually intact apart from the roof, this house received extensive attention, resulting in a comparatively detailed description of its architecture and deposits (Childe and Paterson 1929, 246–60; Childe 1931, 37–41; unpublished 1928, 20–4). The hut contained the usual internal organisation of stone furniture complete with an elaborately constructed rear 'dresser'. The floor area is almost five metres square and the walls survive to the remarkable height of three metres. This preservation is partially due to the lower level of hut 7. It stands on natural sand as opposed to the other huts which overlay the levelled remains of previous houses. Given this primary position, it was considered either to have had its foundation dug through earlier deposits or to be contemporary with the earlier houses. Childe, on the basis of the layout of the interior resembling the houses of later design, preferred the former as the more likely proposition. Interestingly, neither of the two interpretations occur elsewhere within late Neolithic Orcadian settlements. Perhaps another explanation is that hut 7 was simply remodelled, as Clarke suggested after encountering circular outer walling running around hut 7 during the 1972 excavations (1976a, 14). A similar remodelling occurs within the larger house 2 at Barnhouse, which also assumes a primary position in the history of the settlement (Richards in preparation). However, only comprehensive excavation around hut 7 will provide an answer, though it is worth noting that this would have been the oldest standing house within the settlement to remain in use.

As already mentioned, the path to hut 7 involves passing numerous boundaries besides being physically quite difficult to negotiate. On eventually arriving at passage C, a line of paving leads into the entrance, suggesting this to have been the intended line of approach. A hearth is positioned in the outer doorway adjacent to the left-hand door jamb (Fig. 2.4) (Childe unpublished 1928, 20). The presence of a hearth at the threshold to this house is extremely significant since a similar use of fire to demarcate the entrance occurs in both structure 8 at Barnhouse and at the Stones of Stenness henge monument (Richards forthcoming b).

The narrow paved entrance passage into hut 7 leads past the fireplace, over an upright sill slab and through into the interior. The wall of this passage is faced on both sides with thin upright slabs through which bar holes have been cut. Holes and small recesses for door bars are present in all the well preserved huts. In all but one case the door bar is controlled, as may be expected, from within the house allowing the door to be barred once the occupants are inside. However, the situation in hut 7 is different; here the door bar is controlled from the outside. Thus, the house may be sealed from the exterior, keeping the interior safely closed off and out of view or, alternatively, preventing anyone from being able to leave. Hut 7 is, therefore, a structure of separation; a place which can be shut up and kept apart.

The paved entrance leads into the right side of the building and, when moving into the interior, the subject crosses the threshold and passes decorated stones set either side of the inner entrance. The narrow low passage opens into a wide, open expansive interior at least three metres in height. The internal area maintains similar organisation to that within other houses. However, the upper surface of the divisional slab of the right-hand 'bed' is heavily decorated with incised lines. Three further areas of decoration are positioned directly above this 'bed', as opposed to a single decorated slab within the left-hand 'bed'.

The concentration of decoration around the right-hand 'bed' assumes greater significance when it is noted that a covered burial cist lies directly below it. The capstone is, in fact, a visible part of the paved floor of the 'bed'. It also lies partially under the side wall and is, therefore, primary to the house construction. Contained within the cist were the remains of two mature females interred in a crouched position. Although the exact position of one of the burials is difficult to determine because of the method of excavation, the other burial definitely lay on its left side. Since this is the only Neolithic cist burial at Skara Brae, the presence of the dead within hut 7 throws considerable light on the many sanctions imposed on entry and exit.

The material contents of hut 7 caused Childe some anguish because, unlike the other huts, this context appeared as an archaeological 'Marie Celeste'. However, the vivid scene created to explain the apparently *in situ* contents of hut 7 fits uneasily with the evidence. Some objects may have been in their original position, but other evidence hardly suggested normal occupation: 'bits of bone, ashes, fragments of pottery, and, mingled therewith, stray implements and ornaments, were littered about everywhere. The pens D and Y (left- and right-hand 'beds') were no cleaner than the rest of the floor — a fact which militates against the view that they served as beds' (Childe and Paterson 1929, 259). It was suggested that the stone paving leading through the entrance was 'laid down to serve as stepping-stones through the morass of filth that covered the floor, or to mask deposits of bone and refuse that the inhabitants were to lazy too remove' (Childe and Paterson 1929, 259). However, it is rather more difficult to explain away the presence of the complete skull of a short horned bull, found in the left-hand 'bed', as the result of the lazy inhabitants taking 'bones to bed with them to gnaw for supper' (Childe 1931, 15).

It is clear, however, that a large number of objects, easily transportable, were left within hut 7. A number of ceramic, bone, and stone containers were positioned around the interior, particularly in the right-hand stone box enclosure (Fig. 2.6). Some appear to have contained bones, which unfortunately were not identified. A bone dish containing red pigment was set into the floor in the front left-hand corner. Moreover, large numbers of objects of adornment were distributed mainly on the left-hand side including a cache of beads and pendants in the rear cell. While the position of these items is of interest, the principal question remains why they were never removed.

Hut 8

The ruinous hut 8 was discovered by Childe in 1929 (1930, 173). It stands to the west of the main area of settlement separated by the area of paving known as the 'market place'. This paving actually surrounds the outer wall, forming a narrow platform area. This isolation is not a product of collapsed passages nor structural difficulties of incorporation. It constitutes purposeful exclusion from the other houses, even hut 7. Moreover, hut 8 has a different orientation from the normal north-west/south-east alignment of other houses, maintaining a south-south-west/north-north-east direction.

Direct access into the interior of hut 8 from the open paved area is prevented by a porch structure built around the doorway (Fig. 2.7). This construction also serves to restrict visibility into the hut. To gain admission the subject enters the porch from the east, although Childe (1931, 53) states that originally there were two entrances, one on each side. It seems unlikely that a door stood at this point, but a threshold slab marks a small 5 cm step up into the porch which is floored with a single large slab. Once within the confines of the porch a recess is seen to the left (south), flanked on either side by two upright slabs resembling door jambs. In this recess stood two large pots (Childe 1930, 174).

The main entrance to hut 8 is situated to the right and on turning to gain entry, incised decoration becomes visible on the right-hand wall. The doorway is 67 cm wide and only 9 cm high, making it an extremely small entrance. Passing through into the interior the threshold slab is crossed and 'the bar holes come as usual on the inside' (Childe 1930, 175). Internally, hut 8 maintains the same basic spatial organisation seen in the houses, but different elements are substituted for the usual furniture. For instance, the

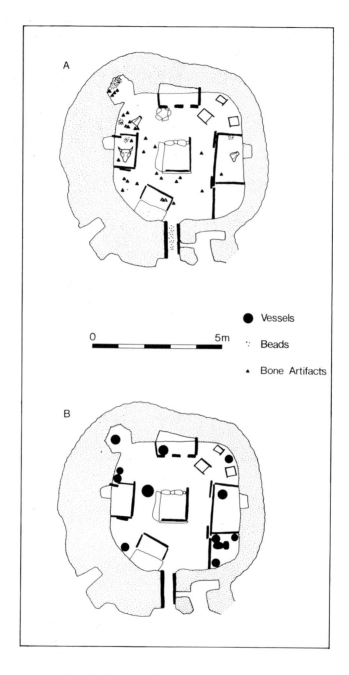

Fig. 2.6 House 7: the distribution of bone artifacts (a) and stone, bone and ceramic
containers (b)

projecting 'beds' are replaced by recesses which are obviously not used as beds. This process of architectural substitution leads Clarke and Sharples (1985, 66–8) to separate hut 8 from the other houses as not conforming in plan or in arrangement of internal fittings.

Of interest is the alignment of the fireplace which is offset from the house alignment, bringing it around to the more conventional south-east/north-west orientation. The western wall and recess were severely truncated; therefore it is difficult to establish whether the left-hand side of the house was as profusely decorated as the right. Nevertheless, the art contained in hut 8 is both superior to and more prolific than that in any other building at Skara Brae (Shee Twohig 1981, 238).

The material contents of hut 8 serve to emphasise its difference: 'The most distinctive traces of human occupation found on the floor of this hut were, however, chert and flint scrapers, cores, and chips. No less than 390 pieces were collected on the floor, 57 from the eastern alcove alone' (Childe 1930, 178). At the rear of the hut, in place of the dresser, was a partitioned area which was interpreted as a kiln (Childe 1930, 176–7). Whatever occurred within this area 'two great slabs paved the areas on either side of the gap between the north wall and the partition to the south. Upon them lay a packing of burnt stones' (Childe 1930, 177). Thus, fire seems to have played a major part in some of the activities undertaken in hut 8. Whether

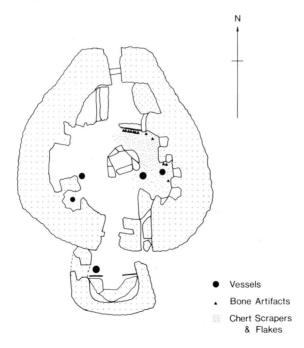

N

● Vessels

▲ Bone Artifacts

 Chert Scrapers
 & Flakes

Fig. 2.7 House 8 at Skara Brae showing the distribution of artifacts

such activity was primary to the construction is unknown, but virtually all commentators have followed Childe (1931, 49) in assuming this area to be a workshop and not a dwelling (eg MacKie 1977, 191; Clarke and Sharples 1985, 67).

In fact, there is no evidence to suggest that hut 8 was not a dwelling. But what is important about this structure is that it was deemed necessary to build it away from the main settlement complex and to decorate it profusely. From the materials located within the hut we know that some of the activities, such as chert preparation, involved fire treatment, and pottery may also have been decorated and fired there. Perhaps an answer to the question of segregation lies in the use of fire since, in this context, it primarily involves transformation from the natural to the cultural which frequently requires spatial separation and sanction (Leach 1977).

Conclusion

Skara Brae is, beyond doubt, the finest and most well preserved late Neolithic settlement in western Europe. This preservation allows thousands of visitors every year to crawl along the narrow passages and peer into the dwellings of long dead Neolithic families. Even their furniture is left standing in its original positions. Yet because of a history of poorly recorded excavations and the unsystematic collection of very few artifacts, the archaeological value of this site appears to be extremely limited. This is clearly demonstrated in the notable absence of any form of analysis of Skara Brae in the numerous studies of Neolithic Orkney. This omission may well be a product of the application of inadequate theoretical perspectives (cf Hodder 1982, 218–19). However, there still remains an intangible feeling that Skara Brae is somehow 'lost' to any critical archaeological evaluation. Most of the artifactual evidence from the site is, indeed, lost and no amount of mourning will facilitate its return. Nevertheless, Skara Brae is itself an artifact, remaining in virtually perfect condition.

In this re-examination of Skara Brae the emphasis has tended to be placed on architecture and art, and how they combine to create spatial representations as invoked and experienced by people as they moved through the settlement's narrow restrictive passages and into the impressively lofty houses. It is, however, important to stress that space and time are not independent variables in which people live out their lives, but are intrinsic to human experience and understanding of the world. In this way questions concerning the differences between houses at Skara Brae must necessarily take into account the movement and paths taken to reach the individual structures and the way in which these spaces are delineated and ordered.

The results of the enquiry show that a number of identifiably different methods are employed in the architecture of the passages to break up space. Each of these embodies different symbolic meanings and values. For instance, every boundary confronted on the way to hut 7 symbolises conceptual discontinuity along a passage from everyday areas through progressively 'weighted' sacred space to a particular goal. The undertaking of such a journey would probably have been restricted to certain times and specific events, and may have involved people being exposed to the dangers of symbolic impurity and close proximity to the dead.

On close scrutiny the Skara Brae huts, which appear very regular, are found to be extremely variable. It was also suggested that the spatial content or symbolic meaning of a particular spatial configuration is contingent on a particular social situation. Hence, houses displaying similar architecture may assume quite different meanings at any given time. Other differences between the houses at Skara Brae involve age and contents.

Hut 7 stands apart, and can no longer be identified as a normal dwelling. It is built in a primary position and despite having been remodelled is portrayed as the oldest standing house in the settlement. An identifiable distinction between the contents of this hut and the others is virtually impossible since little evidence is preserved for examination. However, a difference is noticeable in the treatment of the contents and interior of the house. Hut 7 apparently has a large proportion of its material contents left *in situ* after abandonment and, as Childe's graphic accounts tell us, was not kept in the expected clean state of a civilised family's dwelling. This situation contrasts with the position of the contents recorded in huts 1, 2, and 3, where the floors appear to have been kept moderately clean and most of the contents removed on abandonment; an occurrence consistent with the maintainance of a living space. Thus, although lacking the majority of finds from these contexts and, therefore, being unable to identify any detailed form of material patterning or conduct spatial analysis, it is possible to make a distinction between hut 7 and the other houses: a distinction which, when coupled with the other evidence, suggests that the objects in hut 7 were not available or intended for removal.

Hut 8 poses a different problem for, like hut 7, it is separated from the main area of settlement, although in a different manner. From the position and nature of its material contents it appears not to have been regularly cleaned as were huts 1, 2, and 3. However, as far as may be determined, the majority of contents were removed before abandonment.

It is to be hoped that this re-examination of Skara Brae has dispelled any remaining belief that it represents a small cluster of undifferentiated houses situated in a scoop in the sand. It is a settlement of great complexity and, through examining its architecture, it is possible to begin to understand the way socially constructed space influenced the relationships between people, families and their houses.

Bibliography

Ashmore, P. J. 1986 Neolithic carvings in Maes Howe, *Proc. Soc. Antiq. Scotland* 116, 57–62.

Bailey, D. W. forthcoming The living house: continuity and signification, in Samson forthcoming.

Blier, S. P. 1987 *The anatomy of architecture: ontology and metaphor in Matammaliba architectural expression*, Cambridge.

Chapman, J. forthcoming Social inequality on Bulgarian tells and the Varna problem, in Samson forthcoming.

Childe, V. G. 1930 Operations at Skara Brae during 1929, *Proc. Soc. Antiq. Scotland* 64 (1929–30), 158–90.

Childe, V. G. 1931 *Skara Brae: a Pictish village in Orkney*, London.

Childe, V. G. 1946 *Scotland before the Scots*, London.

Childe, V. G. 1950 *Skara Brae*, Edinburgh.

Childe, V. G. unpublished *Skara Brae excavation notebooks 1928–30*.

Childe, V. G. and Paterson, J. W. 1929 Provisional report on the excavations at Skara Brae, and on the finds from the 1927 and 1928 campaigns, *Proc. Soc. Antiq. Scotland* 63 (1928–29), 225–80.

Clarke, D. V. 1976a *The Neolithic village at Skara Brae, Orkney: 1972–3 excavations: an interim report*, Edinburgh.

Clarke, D. V. 1976b Excavations at Skara Brae: a summary account, in Burgess, C. and Miket, R. (eds) *Settlement and economy in the third and second millennia BC*, Oxford, 233–50.

Clarke, D. V. and Sharples, N. 1985 Settlements and subsistence in the third millennium BC, in Renfrew 1985, 54–82.

French, C. forthcoming Soil micromorphological analysis, in Richards in preparation.

Guidino, E. 1975 *Primitive architecture*, Milan.

Henshall, A. S. 1979 The small finds, in Renfrew, C. *Investigations in Orkney*, London, 75–93.

Hodder, I. R 1982 *Symbols in action*, Cambridge.

Howe, L. E. A 1983 An introduction to the cultural study of Balinese architecture, *Archipel* 25, 137–158.

Leach, E. 1977 A view from the bridge, in Spriggs, M. (ed) *Archaeology and anthropology*, Oxford, 161–76.

Mackie, E. W. 1977 *Science and society in prehistoric Britain*, London.

Moore, H. L. 1986 *Space, text and gender*, Cambridge.

Petrie, G. 1868 Notice of ruins of ancient dwellings at Skara, Bay of Skaill, in the parish of Sandwich, Orkney, recently excavated, *Proc. Soc. Antiq. Scotland* 7 (1866–68), 201–19.

Renfrew, C. 1985 *The prehistory of Orkney*, Edinburgh.

Richards, C. forthcoming a, The Neolithic house in Orkney, in Samson forthcoming.

Richards, C. forthcoming b Monumental choreography: architecture and spatial representation in late Neolithic Orkney, in Shanks, M. and Tilley, C. (eds) *Interpretative archaeology*, London.

Richards, C. in preparation *The late Neolithic settlement complex at Barnhouse Farm Stenness, Orkney*.

Ritchie, J. N. G. 1985 Ritual monuments, in Renfrew 1985, 118–30.

Samson, R. (ed) forthcoming *The social archaeology of houses*, Oxford.

Sharples, N. 1984 Excavations at Pierowall Quarry, Westray, Orkney, *Proc. Soc. Antiq. Scotland* 114, 75–125.

Sharples, N. 1985 Individual and community: the changing role of megaliths in the Orcadian Neolithic, *Proc. Prehist. Soc.* 51, 59–74.

Shee Twohig, E. 1981 *The megalithic art of western Europe*, Oxford.

Acknowledgements

Without the help and support of Leslie Alcock I would not be in a position to write this paper. I would like to thank Patrick Ashmore, John Barrett and Jane Downes for their comments on an earlier draft, with additional thanks to Jane Downes who also drew the illustrations.

3

PASSING THE TIME IN IRON AGE SCOTLAND

John C. Barrett and Sally M. Foster.

Archaeologists are always concerned with the spatial patterning of the material residues they hope to interpret. The role played by distribution maps in 'cultural archaeology' with its emphasis upon the diffusion of cultural influences through time and space is well known, as is the role of locational analysis in economic archaeology. The twin axes of time and space appear as the easily recognisable referents in our descriptive language. It is through those descriptions that we define sequences of monumental and artifactual remains, and recognise that those remains are the patterned residues of human activities which were once distributed over a range of landscape resources. Time and space appear as the seemingly uncontentious frame into which can be set the description of our material 'facts'.

We wish here to extend the archaeological perception of time and space, moving away from the axis by which we describe and thus order our material remains, towards a structure of understanding human history as the strategic deployment of time-space in social practice. We assume that archaeology is attempting to write history, although we accept that a great deal of modern archaeological publication would, on the face of it, refute such an optimistic assumption. As such, archaeology must recognise that time and space cannot remain as mere descriptive absolutes when it comes to the interpretation of archaeological residues. Time-space is embedded in, and constituted through, historically specific social strategies. The issue can be considered in terms of a contrast between time and space as: (1) the referents by which we may describe patterns of static archaeological residues (those residues are often referred to as 'the archaeological record'); and (2) the resources through which the past was actually lived and which brought those static residues into being. The languages of description and of interpretation necessarily employ different concepts of time and space.

Clarification of the issue may be sought with reference to one recent, and particularly influential, line of reasoning. In his important paper 'Space, time and polity', Renfrew set about establishing the fundamental premises upon which he believed a social archaeology could be built. He argued that when archaeologists become involved in the historical study of social formations they are, in fact, studying the emergence of organisational inhomogeneity within the social system (Renfrew 1982). That inhomogeneity is, it would seem, created from processes of specialisation, hierarchical differentiation and administrative authority. These terms describe the structure of the social system as formed by distinctions between persons and their differential control over specific resources. That differentiation is mapped spatially; differences between people and their access to resources emerge at different locations within the landscape. For example, a market centre and a production site involved in the specialist procurement of a specific resource are likely to emerge at different places within the landscape. Each serves a different function within the settlement system and we may expect, according to the model, the regular distribution of either market or 'redistribution' centres across a landscape containing more widely scattered production sites. Production occurs at one of a number of locations and, at an early stage in the proposed evolutionary sequence, exchange may occur between these various production sites. However, emergent inhomogeneity is marked, according to the model, by the rise of a number of higher-order redistribution or market 'centres'. This emergent inhomogeneity of settlement functions is indicative of a new level of social organisation. In the same way, Renfrew argues, the political integration of a 'polity' may involve the administrative function emerging at another specialist location. Each step in the evolutionary sequence indicates yet another level of specialist functions which are archaeologically recognisable on our distribution maps.

The attractiveness of the approach is obvious. The identification and description of spatial inhomogeneity appears to be directly translatable into statements about degrees of social inhomogeneity or, to state it another way, social structural complexity. The spatial parameters are, therefore, used to describe both the physical remains and the level of social differentiation. Time is marginalised, being used only to describe a formal sequence of social organisation. Time defines moments of change in otherwise static organisations, it is not used in understanding the routines of social life as lived within those formations.

We would argue that such analytical approaches fail to grasp the very thing they claim to have discovered, namely the historical conditions of social reproduction. The spatial patterns of artifacts and monuments, which are recovered and described by archaeologists, were created out of the routine practices by which people occupied regions of both time and space. It is those routines which also created the social system. It is, therefore, mistaken to take the patterning of that material debris as the direct record of a form of social organisation. Such social systems were consequent upon the routines of human agency, thus only when we confront the question of how such routines were sustained and transformed do we gain an understanding of the structuring of both the social system and its material residues. To describe a pattern of material residues in terms of a pattern of social institutions is simply a tautology.

Cherry has recently argued that 'a theme of importance to all social scientists is the effective modelling of the spatial operation of power and dominance' (1987, 147). This assertion embodies many of the problems we hope to identify. Certainly we can accept that power operates spatially because forms of authority do call upon people and resources over distance. However, power also operates temporally and there are both moments and places where an authority, which some may use to characterise an entire social system (eg chiefdoms), is absent. We would contend that the histories of various sources of social authority can only be understood in terms of both their presence and absence within the time-space systems through which they operated. To model the spatial distribution of power centres, such as city states, and their surrounding territories of influence, such as the 'polity', tells us nothing about the time-space strategies through which the forms of authority resident in the centres were 'presenced' amongst the population of that polity. How did people know of their obligations to some distant authority? When and in what contexts did they recognise that authority? If we are unable to answer these questions, then we will also be unable to specify the regions of social practice within which alternative forms of authority may have arisen. It is this which, in our view, explains the failure of 'systems thinking' as a means of conceptualising social conditions; the dynamic and strategic engagements between people cannot be discussed, and thus the opportunity for understanding the processes of social transformation never arises.

Archaeologists may describe their material with reference to spatial distributions and chronological sequences, descriptions which are of contemporary and static conditions (Binford 1981). However, to write history with reference to that material requires embedding these material conditions within the possible time-space engagements of social practice. It was through these engagements that people once created the material conditions of their own existence (Barrett 1988).

Let us now turn to comment upon two aspects of Iron Age archaeology in northern Britain. The first concerns the issue of the Roman Iron Age in the frontier regions of the empire, the second the rise of the early historic 'proto-state' in Caithness and Orkney.

The Roman Iron Age of northern Britain is normally discussed as if we are presented with a dichotomy — that between a 'Roman' and a 'native' archaeology. These different assemblages are taken as indicative of two separate and internally coherent systems which came into contact during the first four centuries AD. The extent and nature of that contact is regarded as one problem requiring an archaeological solution, whilst more traditional studies have tended to focus upon one or other of these archaeological assemblages. Thus Roman military dispositions are described with reference to their location and terrain, and the inferences which may be drawn from the distribution of forts. The native presence emerges only as a background. Similarly, Iron Age settlement sequences can be described as if they represented coherent social and economic systems with only passing reference being made to a phase of Roman contact. The division between the Roman and native populations is taken for granted, as a matter of fact requiring no explanation. The most recent work on the Roman Iron Age has been directed towards a consideration of contact and exchange between these systems, with particular emphasis being placed upon the changes which may have been instigated in the native system by the Roman military presence. Consequently, attention is drawn to the relationship between these two near autonomous social systems, and not towards the conditions under which such a historical dichotomy may have been created.

The difference of approach indicated here is important. The current consensus, for example, creates an image of the Roman army as a relatively stable institution, similar wherever it is encountered within the empire. It becomes possible to offer empire-wide generalisations about such issues as the supply of the army, as if strategies of supply in Egypt and northern Britain were comparable (Breeze 1984). That may have been the case, but it requires demonstrating and explaining, not assuming as the first step in analysis. Confronted by a system such as the Roman empire we are perhaps prone to seek too great a level of order. Similarly, whilst the 'Roman' and 'native' archaeologies may be mapped as two separate systems, it is misleading to interpret them historically in these terms. What we should attempt to understand is not the interface between such relatively autonomous systems (Roman/native relations, acculturation etc), but the means by which the institutional practices which created those complex human societies were reproduced. Thus, instead of starting from such accepted and seemingly unproblematic categories as 'Roman' and 'native' by which to investigate the historical conditions of the period, we must recognise the formation of these categories as a product of history, and as such it is this which demands investigation.

By this route we are guided towards a consideration of the routine, day-to-day lives of the people we are attempting to study. It was out of those people's expectations about their world, employed and monitored through their actions upon that world, that the institutions of the social system were maintained. Those expectations were structured by understanding the forms of authority upon which people drew and to which they submitted in their actions, and the range of material resources which were similarly understood and available for their use. All discourse between people is situated within a 'region' of time-space, and in pre-modern societies that region was one of face-to-face 'co-presence'. We should consider the frequency with which these time-space fields of discourse were likely to have been occupied, and the range of resources which were employed to structure them.

The emphasis upon localised, face-to-face exchanges is important. It highlights the contrast between the approaches advocated here and the stress placed by writers such as Renfrew and Cherry upon the modelling of large scale political systems. The example of the Roman Empire as one such political system will suffice. To map the empire as indicating the Roman 'polity' extending from Scotland to Syria and from the Rhineland to North Africa tells us nothing about the means by which a cluster of authorities, which we continue to personify as 'Rome', were presenced in the enormously diverse range of social expectations and assumptions by which these peoples lived their lives (Barrett 1989). The usual mistake is to assume that the emergence of such a large scale and relatively stable political system must of necessity imply similarly large scale and coherent strategies of creation. Certainly far-flung strategies of political control were instigated; the deployment of the army itself is the obvious example, but we must always recognise the reality of those strategies, practised as they were in situations of local and historical contingency. Such localised strategies of social reproduction will have drawn upon and transformed some of the image of a 'Roman' authority; the Roman empire was ultimately a discontinuous and localised invention.

We will conclude this part of the discussion with two final points about the structuring of the military and indigenous lives of the 'Roman' and the 'native'. As implied above, a consideration of the routine of military life (cf Davies 1989) must distinguish between resources which structured the passing of time according to widely understood ideas of order and authority, for example the military career structure, far-flung networks of patronage, and the various demands of state ceremony and ritual, and resources which were more specifically local, including the personal authority of commanders, the problems of supply and pay, the intervention of indigenous political structures. Indeed, it is possible to recognise here tensions between such differently operating networks of authority, those aligned towards a distant idea of Rome and those founded upon the more immediate, local and practical conditions. It is these tensions which perhaps worked towards the ultimate fragmentation of the entire system (MacMullen 1988). Local strategies included the presencing of the military within the indigenous routines of an agricultural landscape. Both Hadrian's Wall and the Antonine Wall may have fragmented the assumptions of an agricultural community dependent upon seasonal movement, whilst at the same time providing moments when an indigenous population could have been subjected to the intense scrutiny of a military authority. However, the extent to which that level of dislocation was felt amongst the agricultural community obviously depended upon the frequency with which that particular landscape was traversed. These barriers acted upon people, not to define territory. It is peculiar, given the range of archaeological survey techniques now available, that we can still say so little about the nature of agricultural land-use in the vicinity of both walls. Immediately beyond them their existence will have meant little, failing as they surely did to intervene in the more parochial routines of ploughing, herding, ditching, building, eating and sleeping. Here an intervening presence by the military will only have been effective through the extensive deployment of troops, represented not so much by the archaeological distribution of the forts and temporary camps as by the regular movement of men in the countryside between and beyond them.

Far-flung systems of political authority are effective in those moments when their demands are recognised and accepted by at least a portion of the local community. The 'landscapes of power' are created out of techniques which presence these various political demands in the day-to-day experiences of the population. They are landscapes defined by the presence of people who recognise at those moments the nature and extent of their obligations. Local strategies may create nodal points in networks of such obligations, and these in turn may be captured by, and aligned towards, a more distant political image. At other times local strategies may subvert these broader hegemonic claims.

The Iron Age of Orkney and Caithness, that is the period from about 600 BC to AD 800, can be described in terms of a four-fold chronological division, the Early Iron Age, Middle Iron Age, Late Iron Age I and Late Iron Age II (henceforth EIA, MIA, LIA I and LIA II respectively), which corresponds with recognisable changes in the architectural record; the emergence of 'nucleated' settlements by the MIA to, by the end of the LIA, discrete individual domestic units (Foster 1989a; 1989b; 1990). The sequence is summarised in Fig. 3.1 and may be set against the various literary indications that forms of political integration had emerged by the end of the period which were seemingly able to extend their authority amongst a widely distributed population. Bede, for example, made a distinction between the northern Picts who 'are separated from those of the southern Picts by a range of steep and desolate mountains' (HE III, 4), but the southern province was dominant by the late seventh century, and both areas were subsumed into a single kingdom by the late eighth century. In a late eighth- or ninth-century version, Bede's *Ecclesiastical History* records a political landscape in which Orkney was considered to be a part of the Pictish kingdom. By the time the Norse arrived Orkney and Caithness are both assumed to be Pictish.

The aim of archaeology is not to illustrate such narratives by reference to the spread of a 'Pictish' cultural repertoire. Instead archaeology should seek to investigate the material conditions of life within which such 'proto-states' may have emerged. How was a 'Pictland' constructed? On the face of it there would seem to be a correlation between the emergence of these LIA political systems and the changes in the local forms of settlement. We would interpret this as indicating the penetration of localised systems of political authority by more generalised and extensive sources of political power. In the nucleated settlements of the MIA, with their hierarchical use of space, any occupant would have experienced and would have been required to negotiate on a regular, indeed daily, basis a series of relatively rigid spatial distinctions between people and activities. By the end of the LIA, the use of discrete domestic units amounted to a change in emphasis, from internal to external space, and a trend towards more egalitarian, less-spatially prescribed on-site relations. It is suggested that this shift correlates with a move towards more extensive and generalised controls on access to agricultural resources and people, rather than the operation of localised ranking between people at the intra-site level. In terms of the typologies of social evolution this would correspond to a shift from a ranked society to the emergent state, from local power bases to, in relation to Orkney and Caithness, more distant and perhaps mysterious sources of authority. In the terminology of Mann (1986), this transformation amounts to an operational change in localised practices, including agriculture, from the ability to organise tightly and command a high level of mobilisation or commitment from participants (intensive power), to the ability to organise large numbers of people over far-flung territories in order to engage in minimally stable co-operation

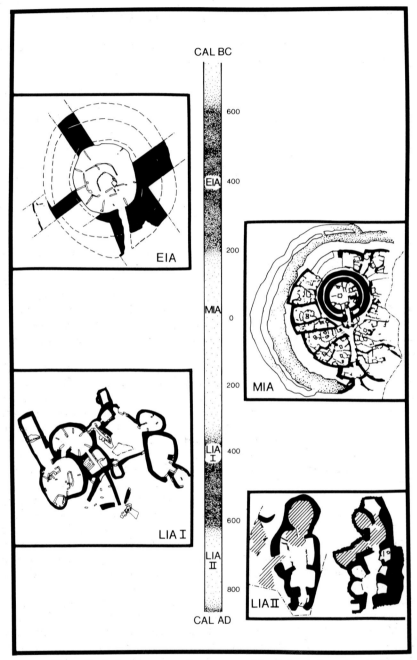

Fig. 3.1   Chronological and structural summary of the Atlantic Iron Age in Orkney
and Caithness (plans not to scale)

(extensive power) (Foster 1989a and b). This change sets the foundations for the development of a 'proto-state', the distinguishing characteristics and necessary preconditions for which Driscoll (1988, 218–22) has described. It is now necessary to identify the resources through which this new authority was exercised; the means by which the change in emphasis from local and intensive to distant and extensive power was achieved.

Mann (1986) recognises four principal sources of social power, namely the control of economic, ideological, military and political resources. These are envisaged as being drawn upon in overlapping fields of social interaction, thus structuring the institutional means of attaining human goals. The recognition of the principal sources of power is a means of understanding how large-scale social and historical processes were structured, which is our aim here. A suggested scheme for the structuring of the social system for the period from about the seventh century AD onwards is summarised in Fig. 3.2. There are three principles underlying this model: firstly that literacy was the fundamental technology for the maintenance of political and administrative resources deeply embedded in time-space; secondly that the dispersed activities of the agricultural population were orientated by obligations arising from the granting of land rights by authorities who were increasingly identified with a dominant ideological system through the church; and finally that the control of this population amounted to the control of economic and military resources. The distinction between secular (political) and ecclesiastical (ideological) power merges within the elite as the upper echelons of secular society become the hierarchy of the church.

The changes in settlement form are, it is suggested, to be correlated with changes in the organisation of agricultural production. In the MIA the practice of agriculture was also the practical re-working of the local obligations of kinship and rank. The settlement was one place where these categories of obligation could be realised in the spatial and temporal experiences of the occupants. Driscoll (1987), in his study of the Early Historic landscape of southern Pictland, argues that the traditional obligations of kinship were extended but also eroded by the institution of clientship, a process which he correlates with the growth of state-like polities in the east. The changes from the MIA to the LIA could have resulted from the emergence of expanding ties of clientship which cut across the ultimate power of more local leaders. However, it would still be the locally-based elite who administered the regions and in whose hands the effective authority lay; the growth of clientship would extend both geographically and socially the limits within which such relations of authority could operate. A major change could have come into effect as the result of the introduction of proprietary rights over the land, whether to the church or to individuals. Gifts of land went in one direction only, resulting in a permanent obligation to the giver, and could only be answered by counter-gifts in moveable wealth and services, but never discharged (Charles-Edwards 1979, 104). The territorial extent of an authority can only expand if it assumes and ultimately acquires the right to make grants of land outside its own territories. The local units could

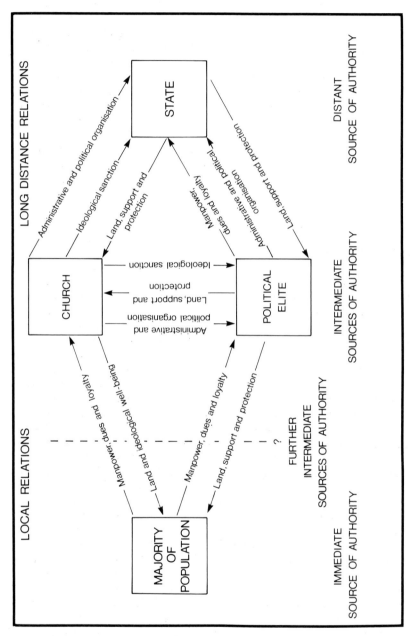

Fig. 3.2 Suggested scheme for the systemic relationship between resources and the structuring of social authority through time-space

thus become subsumed within the central authority by new administrative means independent of territoriality (cf Biddick 1984, 111). In Pictland this administrative process was probably realised through the officials recorded in later times as the *mormaer*, literally a 'great officer, High Steward' and the *toiseach* (cf Jackson 1972, 102–110). Such officials would have moved widely though the territory, being the personal representative of the king. Steinnes (1959) has suggested a similar arrangement for Norse Orkney; in return for their loyalty, the locally-based elite and church would derive benefit from the grant of land and dues, whilst striving to uphold the system from which their source of wealth derived, and which it was in their interest to succour.

The written word has the ability to produce an image of statements which are secure, near permanent and thus extend in time-space beyond the face-to-face moments of the spoken word. As such, writing is a technology which we might expect to be drawn into property transactions (Goody 1977; Giddens 1984, 258–9). However, as Clanchy has demonstrated, the word of honour may count for more than the written word and we need not expect the immediate adoption of writing for the production of property charters (Clanchy 1979). Indeed there are no surviving charters from Orkney and Caithness. Elsewhere Driscoll (1988, 228) suggests that through the erection of Class I symbol stones, which seem to have been burial markers, the heirs combined different sources of legitimacy in a permanent testimonial: their right to inheritance through descent; ideological sanction of this represented by their control of the symbols; and a *de facto* right represented by their rights to the land. These stones may, in their permanency, have been acting in the way we expect charters to operate. Although symbol stones are rare in Orkney and Caithness, a number of them are loosely associated with earlier broch sites, an association which would suggest that some of these were still recognised as a place of reference with which to identify a community.

The main evidence for the form of LIA land organization in Orkney is derived from the place-names which provide a picture of the Norse administrative system. This is unlike the system known in the Norwegian homeland, and it may be that the LIA arrangement was simply incorporated. To summarise this argument (detailed in Foster 1990, 248–9), it seems that these were divisions of land which may have been of the nominal area necessary for subsistence, and that these were related to a system of taxation. Some places are seemingly of greater importance and we might suggest a LIA land organisation on the basis of estates. A system of levy related to this could have been administered at the local level by secular and/or ecclesiastical representatives of the southerly Pictish kings. It is thus possible that such a distant authority was extended into Caithness and Orkney by assuming its right to grant property. These new transactions may have been recorded in stone and/or writing which secured their transmission through time. As the political elite granted land, the relationships and attendant ties of clientship were extended to all, and all were thus to some extent under the influence of an ultimate authority. However, that authority simply operating in this way would have appeared distant and generalised.

Certainly, that ultimate authority will have delegated responsibility for the management of the regions to its local representatives. Their reward was a share of the tribute from the land, but their duty was to administer these areas effectively, providing such loyalty, manpower and other services as their superiors might at any time demand. There are arguments to support the notion that the Brough of Birsay in Orkney was the location of one such representative, and further such locations may have been established on some of the earlier broch sites. The places associated with this administrative elite were isolated from the other settlements and tended to be very wealthy; this is a further indicator of the dialectic between the centralising powers of the state and the decentralising forces of its agents (Mann 1986). This trend might also be apparent in changing agricultural practice as local attempts were made to increase the wealth from the land and reduce dependency on external sources of authority. Unfortunately there is as yet little evidence for the agricultural changes which one might have expected to accompany major transformations in the pattern of land-holding, whether in terms of productivity or structuring of the landscape.

If a secular, administrative authority was locally present in the form of various state officials, then a second means by which a dominant authority could be presenced amongst a local community was through the Roman church. There is little evidence for believing that the earlier Columban church in Orkney and Caithness was well established. But whilst there were undoubtedly some Christian communities in seventh century Pictland, the first evidence that Christianity was being established as a dominant religious authority comes in the early eighth century with the activities of the southern Pictish king Nechtan and the appearance of Class II symbol stones (Hughes 1970, 15). Recent unpublished work by Dr Raymond Lamb suggests a network of St Peter dedications in Orkney dating to this period, always associated with former broch sites. It is important to recognise that the dedications were fixed upon monuments perhaps recognised and assigned to the traditional landscape. Lamb suggests that the dedications reflect the introduction of a Roman-style pastoral church to this area from southern Pictland, that is, of clerics who placed a heavy emphasis on administering and preaching amongst the people. A possible bishopric has also been identified. It is suggested, after Lamb, that the church was therefore not only being granted land in Orkney and Caithness by the southern king, but in return the clerics effectively acted as secular lords. The secular authority of the king was thus extended into the agricultural routines of the local community through the presence of his own secular agents and by, at least in part, its reappearance in the word of the church. Thus both these agencies operated with reference to places which were known, probably named and presumably recognised as sites of a more ancient order. The appearance of Class II symbol stones, ie those with symbols and a cross, mark, in the words of Driscoll: 'the point at which the royal administrative system has been established and the church has become a political arena where power disputes are contested through the patronage of royal establishments' (1988, 230). The juxtaposition of royal and ecclesiastical authority was partly expressed in the physical proximity of some of their establishments, but will have been created, in practice, out of a temporal juxtaposition, through the cycles of church ritual, lordly presence and seasonal movement of the agricultural year. As ever, political authority occupies not only places but also time.

Bibliography

Barrett, J. C. 1988 Fields of discourse: reconstituting a social archaeology, *Critique of Anthropology* 7.3, 5–16.

Barrett, J. C. 1989 Afterword: render unto Caesar . . . , in Barrett, J. C. , Fitzpatrick, A. P. and Macinnes, L. (eds), *Barbarians and Romans in north-west europe: from the later Republic to late antiquity*, Oxford, 235–41.

Biddick, K. 1984 Early medieval social change and resource allocation, in Biddick, K. (ed), *Archaeological approaches to medieval Europe*, Kalamazoo, 105–18.

Binford, L. R. 1981 *Bones: ancient men and modern myths*, London.

Breeze, D. J. 1984 Demand and supply on the northern frontier, in Miket, R. and Burgess, C. (eds), *Between and beyond the Walls: essays on the prehistory and history of north Britain in honour of George Jobey*, Edinburgh, 264–86.

Charles-Edwards, T. 1979 The distinction between land and moveable wealth in Anglo-Saxon England, in Sawyer, P. (ed), *English medieval settlement*, London, 97–104.

Cherry, J. F. 1987 Power in space: archaeological and geographical studies, in Wagstaff, J. M. (ed), *Landscape and culture: geographical and archaeological perspectives*, Oxford, 146–72.

Clanchy, M. T. 1979 *From memory to written record: England 1066–1307*, London.

Davies, R. W. 1989 *Service in the Roman army*, Breeze, D. J. and Maxfield, V. A. (eds), Edinburgh.

Driscoll, S. T. 1987 *The Early Historic landscape of Strathearn: the archaeology of a Pictish kingdom*, unpublished PhD thesis, University of Glasgow.

Driscoll, S. T. 1988 Power and authority in Early Historic Scotland: Pictish symbol stones and other documents, in Gledhill, J. , Bender, B. and Larsen, M. (eds), *State and society. The emergence and development of social hierarchy and political centralisation*, London, 215–36.

Foster, S. M. 1989a Analysis of spatial patterns in buildings (gamma analysis) as an insight into social structure: examples from the Scottish Atlantic Iron Age, *Antiquity* 63, 40–50.

Foster, S. M. 1989b Transformations in social space: Iron Age Orkney and Caithness, *Scottish Archaeol. Rev.* 6, 34–55.

Foster, S. M. 1990 *Aspects of the Atlantic Iron Age*, unpublished PhD thesis, University of Glasgow.

Giddens, A. 1984 *The constitution of society*, Cambridge.

Goody, J. 1977 *The domestication of the savage mind*, Cambridge.

HE *Historia Ecclesiastica Gentis Anglorum*, Harmondsworth (1968).

Hughes. K. 1970 *Early Christianity in Pictland*, Newcastle.

Jackson, K. H. 1972 *The Gaelic notes in the Book of Deer*, Cambridge.

Mann, M. 1986 *The sources of social power I. A history of power from the beginning to AD 1760*, Cambridge.

MacMullen, R. 1988 *Corruption and the decline of Rome*, London.

Renfrew, C. 1982 Space, time and polity, in Friedman, J. and Rowlands, M. J. (eds), *The Evolution of Social Systems*, London, 89–112.

Steinnes, A. 1959 The Huseby system in Orkney, *Scottish. Hist. Rev.* 38, 36–46.

4

THE FUTURE OF ROMAN SCOTLAND

W. S. Hanson and D. J. Breeze

This paper is divided into three sections: a consideration of the nature and limitations of the database; an examination of the gaps in our present knowledge; and suggestions for some possible directions for future work. Roman Scotland is throughout taken to mean Britain north of the Tyne-Solway isthmus since this is a more sensible geographical unit.

The nature of the data base

The documentary sources for Roman Scotland are very patchy. Tacitus' *Agricola*, the biography of his father-in-law, is the fullest single account and provides valuable evidence relating to the years of the conquest up to the battle of Mons Graupius in AD 83. Thereafter there is nothing until the Antonine advance of AD 139–143, which is only briefly mentioned three times in different literary sources and one of those is probably garbled (*SHA* Antoninus Pius 5; *Pan. Lat. Vet.* 8 (5) 14; Pausanias 8, 43). The northern tribes, and possibly the Antonine Wall, are referred to in connection with the invasion of the mid-180s (Dio 72, 8); the Caledonians and Maeatae in AD 197 (Dio 75, 5); while the Severan campaigns of AD 208–211 merit more detailed attention because of the direct involvement of the emperor (Dio 76, 11–77, 1 *passim*; Herodian 3, 7–15 *passim*). Thereafter relations with the Picts attracted comment intermittently throughout the fourth century, culminating in the lengthier account of the unrest of the 360s (Ammianus Marcellinus 20, 1; 26, 4; 27, 8).

Not all of these documentary sources are of equal value or validity. The *Scriptores Historiae Augustae*, the source for the Antonine advance and the construction of the Wall, as well as other snippets of information concerning the northern frontier, is notoriously unreliable. It was written in the fourth century, probably using an early third-century source which was itself over sixty years later than the events described. It is, for example, one of several sources which credit Severus with the building of what we now know as Hadrian's Wall (*SHA* 18, 2). But all literary sources must be subject to careful scrutiny. Even the *Agricola* must be treated with caution (Mann and Penman 1978, 64; Hanson 1987, 4–23; 1991, 1,742–8). It is well larded with stock phrases, light on detailed geographical information and, so far as the achievements of Agricola are concerned, largely unsubstantiated by any other source, an important qualification considering the biased nature of the work. Nor is it always factually correct, as for example when referring to the involvement of the Brigantes in the Boudican uprising (*Agricola* 31).

Inscriptions, as contemporary public records of specific events, might be thought to provide a source of unbiased factual information. Indeed they furnish useful evidence on the builders of the Antonine Wall and the date of its construction; details of the troops based in Scotland; information on aspects of religion; and data concerning both civilian as well as military personnel (Collingwood and Wright 1965; Keppie 1983). But inscriptions too are not without their problems. The material is biased both chronologically and socially. The majority of the inscriptions known from Scotland date to the Antonine period and are weighted towards official inscriptions and dedications by members of the higher social strata, thus providing relatively little evidence for the bulk of the population. Some inscriptions are incomplete and can offer difficulties of restoration: many are difficult to date. Evidence from elsewhere in the empire can be of assistance, though sometimes with unexpected results, as with the altar from Castlecary on the Antonine Wall erected by Italian and Norican citizens and thought to date at least twenty years after that frontier had been abandoned (Jarrett and Mann 1970, 194). Similarly the altar of *cohors I Baetasiorum* from Old Kilpatrick has been dated on stylistic grounds to the Severan period and quoted in support of a Severan reoccupation of the Antonine Wall (Birley 1983, 76), though this dating is disputed (Breeze and Dobson 1970, 120; Keppie 1983, 401–2). It should also be noted that practically no inscriptions are found in relevant archaeological contexts: even today most are chance discoveries.

Numismatic evidence from Scotland is also important and has been well catalogued (eg Robertson 1975; 1983). Coins from archaeological sites provide useful dates, though essentially only *termini post quem*. However, study of circulation patterns and refinements related to the amount of wear on coins can offer an indication of the time lapse between date of issue and loss, as the recent discussion of the date of the abandonment of the more northerly Agricolan conquests demonstrates (Hobley 1989). But individual sites rarely provide sufficient coins to allow statistical analysis. Problems also remain in other areas: the significance of coin hoards is disputed (eg Hanson and Maxwell 1986, 141–2 *contra* Robertson 1983, 424–5) and the distribution pattern of individual coins of fourth-century date is misleading, as those from eastern mints have been interpreted as modern losses (Casey 1984).

Scotland possesses a rich resource of well preserved Roman military works, many of which survive as visible earthworks. These include the remains of at least two frontiers (the Agricolan dispositions across the Forth-Clyde isthmus and the Antonine Wall), the legionary fortress at Inchtuthil together with its labour camps and ancillary structures (though some of the latter are visible only as crop marks), the auxiliary forts at

Ardoch and Birrens, the fortlets at Castle Greg, Durisdeer, Kaims Castle and Redshaw Burn, watch towers on the Gask Ridge, camps at Pennymuir, Ardoch, Kirkbuddo, Raedykes and elsewhere, the putative training area at Burnswark, and stretches of roads across the Borders, some still lined by quarry pits (Breeze 1979; Keppie 1986). This visible resource is supported by many other military sites surviving beneath the turf, often known only through aerial photography which continues to add to the picture (Maxwell and Wilson 1987). Many of these sites have been examined by excavation, though to varying degrees of intensity.

The very longevity and intensity of research into military affairs in the north of Britain is also important. Observation and comment on Roman remains commenced at the end of the sixteenth century; detailed survey in the eighteenth; and excavation in the nineteenth (Maxwell 1989, 1–25). There has been continuity in action, planning, thought and communication of ideas. This is coupled with a large archive of published material, not just excavation reports, but also syntheses (eg Breeze 1982; Breeze and Dobson 1987; Hanson 1987; Hanson and Maxwell 1986; Keppie 1986; Maxwell 1989; Robertson 1990).

The position of Roman Scotland within a world empire allows evidence from other parts of the empire to be brought to bear upon local studies. Indeed this is particularly relevant to the interpretation of the Roman army. Much evidence on the structure and organisation of the army, and on the arrangements made for civilians in the frontier zone, is derived by analogy from other frontiers.

The Roman military remains are complemented by numerous upstanding settlements of the Roman Iron Age. These range from small enclosures containing one or two houses to the great hill-fort at Traprain Law; from slight earthworks to massively constructed drystone brochs, such as Torwood. Sometimes the probable longevity of their occupation is emphasised by structural changes as at Edin's Hall, where a broch-like structure and stone houses overlie a small defended enclosure (Plate 4.1), or Castle Law, where a souterrain has been placed within one of the ditches of the hill-fort. Again this visible resource is greatly supplemented by aerial reconnaissance so that the data base continues to expand. Longevity of occupation of these sites is sometimes hinted at by the complexity of their defences, as was confirmed by excavation at Broxmouth. The hill-fort went through several phases before its abandonment, though occupation of the site continued thereafter well into the Roman period (Hill 1982b).

But these archaeological data are no less subject to problems of interpretation than other forms of evidence. In particular, not only is the database incomplete, but we have only a general idea of the nature of its partiality, especially in respect of native sites. More specifically the latter are exceedingly difficult to date even to the Roman period, let alone more closely within that range. While there has been considerable study of, and excavation on, Roman Iron Age sites, allowing the settlement types and their development to be understood (eg Jobey 1974a; 1982a), there has been only limited general synthesis of this material in its wider social and economic context (eg Ralston 1979; Macinnes 1983; 1984b).

Nevertheless, the study of Roman Scotland, like that of Roman Britain generally, offers a particular challenge to its practitioner through the complex interplay of these various strands of evidence, literary and epigraphic sources, numismatic and archaeological material, and evidence by analogy from other parts of the empire, allowing the history of the period to be written. But in this process there has been a tendency to assume the primacy of the literary sources (eg Jarrett and Mann 1970; Mann 1988). Moreover, archaeology and history are often assumed to coincide. Imprecisely dated archaeological events tend to be linked to more closely dated historical events. Thus the dating of temporary camps north of the Forth-Clyde isthmus starts from the premise that there were only two occasions when

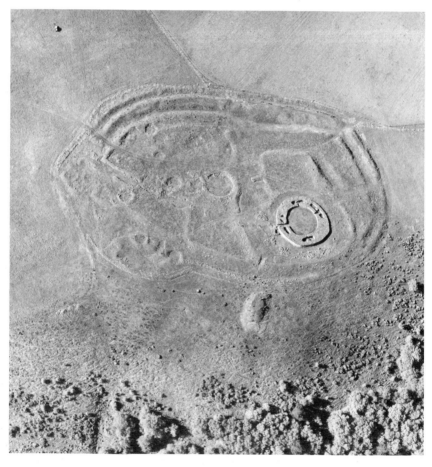

Pl. 4.1   Edin's Hall from the air. The broch-like structure sits within a defended enclosure which is overlain by stone-built houses (HBM)

Roman arms penetrated the area: the campaigns of Agricola and Severus, even though there are a number of other possibilities (Hanson 1978, 140–1). Similarly, interpretations of the significance of archaeological phenomena tend to be tied to preconceived historical models. Thus burnt deposits have generally been interpreted as evidence for hostile action; evidence of rebuilding seen as restoration following destruction by the enemy (Breeze and Dobson 1972, 200–6). Attempts to relate the different types of evidence are now treated with more caution and each is given its due weight. Even more fundamental has been the tendency to concentrate on historical and military aspects of the period at the expense of wider considerations of contemporary native society, a position which is only now beginning to change.

The present state of knowledge

The political history of Roman Scotland is reasonably understood and provides a vital framework for more detailed study. Literary sources record that there were three invasions by the Roman army which led to the occupation of some territory north of the Tyne-Solway isthmus, though there were also a number of other military contacts with less tangible results. The first invasion took place under the command of Agricola in AD 79/80 (Tacitus *Agricola* 18–40); the second, led by Lollius Urbicus, in the early 140s (*SHA* Antoninus Pius 5, 4), the date refined by an inscription from Corbridge (Collingwood and Wright 1965, no. 1147) and the subsequent triumph confirmed by coin issues of AD 142/3; the third in AD 208/9 under the direct command of the emperor Septimius Severus (Dio 76, 11–77, 1; Herodian 3, 14–15), the completion of the conquest confirmed by a coin issue of AD 211.

A single reference by Tacitus refers to fort building under Agricola (*Agricola* 22), while Dio refers to forts abandoned by Caracalla and therefore presumably built by his father (Dio 77, 1, 1). All other evidence concerning the campaigning or the nature and extent of the conquest is provided by archaeology. The nature of the first- and second-century occupations is reasonably clear (eg Fig. 4.1), less so in the case of the third. In all three periods, however, the terminal date of the occupation has been a matter of debate.

The best evidence until recently for the date of the end of the Flavian period in Scotland has been provided by pottery. Nearly twenty years ago Hartley suggested, on the basis of his study of the samian evidence, that the forts north of the Forth were abandoned by about AD 90 (1972). This date has now been refined to AD 87 or 88 on the basis of the numismatic evidence (Hobley 1989). Archaeological excavation has demonstrated that several of the forts in southern Scotland have two structural phases in the late first century and pottery evidence supports the occupation of these sites continuing longer than their northern counterparts, confirming that the withdrawal from Scotland as a whole was phased. The terminal date for the

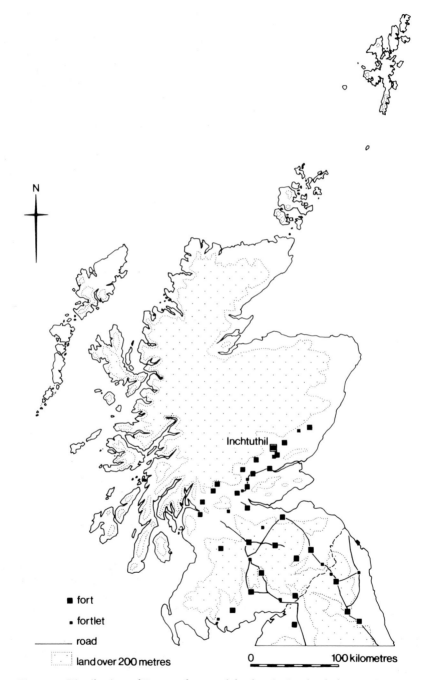

N

Inchtuthil

■ fort
▪ fortlet
—— road
land over 200 metres

0   100 kilometres

Fig. 4.1   Distribution of Roman forts and fortlets in Scotland about AD 86/7.

final stage, however, still rests upon a coin of AD 103 found in a construction trench of the second period fort at Corbridge (Gillam 1977, 60).

Suggestions for the date of abandonment of the Antonine system have ranged from the 160s (Haverfield 1899; Hartley 1972; Gillam 1975), through the 180s (Macdonald 1934), 195 (Mann 1988), 197 (Birley 1963) to 207 (Jarrett and Mann 1970, 203). It is now generally accepted that the ceramic and numismatic evidence support abandonment of the Antonine occupation of Scotland as early as the mid 160s, which coincides with the building activities of the governor Calpurnius Agricola in northern England (Hartley 1972; Breeze 1975; Shotter 1976). Nonetheless, the reliability of such dating methods continues to be challenged, based on a reassertion of the primacy — indeed almost exclusive primacy — of the literary evidence (Mann 1988).

The precise date of abandonment of Severus' conquests remains problematic. Dio states that Caracalla abandoned his father's conquests and returned to Rome (Dio 77, 1, 1), but an inscription from Carpow points to Caracalla building there after his father's death (Wright 1974), which suggests that Dio may have conflated events.

The nature of Roman involvement north of the Tyne-Solway frontier after the collapse of the Severan initiative remains vague. Two literary references may suggest some continuing Roman presence. The Ravenna Cosmography refers to *diversa loca* located north of Hadrian's Wall as far as the Tay. Richmond suggested that these were designated meeting places in the territory of friendly tribes supervised by Roman officers (1940, 97). This interpretation has been seriously challenged by Rivet and Smith, in their critical reassessment of the text, who suggest that they are simply a list of miscellaneous places which the Cosmographer had omitted to mention earlier (1979, 212). In discussing the events of AD 367/8 Ammianus Marcellinus refers to the disbanding of the *areani*, people who patrolled over long distances north of Hadrian's Wall on behalf of Rome (28, 3, 7). Archaeological evidence confirms the existence of outpost forts well to the north of the Wall, though the date of their abandonment appears to be somewhat earlier (Casey and Savage 1980). Other brief military expeditions into Scotland referred to in various sources lack confirmed archaeological manifestations.

Our understanding of the extent of the invasions of Scotland is almost entirely dependent upon archaeology. Roman marching camps in Scotland were surveyed as early as the eighteenth century (Roy 1793), though since 1945 our knowledge of them has increased dramatically through aerial photography. Nevertheless, the most northerly camp known to Roy — Glenmailen (Ythan Wells) — is still only the third most northerly camp known today. However, our knowledge of the size and shape of camps has increased to the extent that they have been classified into groups (St Joseph 1969, 113–19; 1973, 228–33). These groups seem to have some validity when based on individual characteristics, such as the Stracathro-type with their distinctive form of entrance, or on consistent size and morphology, such as the 63-, 115-, 130- and 165-acre series.

But the classifications have changed as evidence has grown and groups have been redefined, notably the 120–acre series which it is now suggested should be divided into two series of 110 and 130 acres respectively (St Joseph 1973, 231–3; 1977, 143–5). It would thus be sensible to remain cautious about any particular classification (Hanson 1978; Maxwell 1980). Though, through selective excavation, it has been possible to offer a relative chronology for some of the groups, difficulties are encountered when absolute dates are assigned. Only one member of one group, the 115–acre camps, has furnished datable archaeological material, a sherd of first-century pottery from Abernethy (St Joseph 1973, 220). Attempts to estimate the length of time which had elapsed between the construction of members of different series of camps has been inconsistent. At Ythan Wells the gap between the two overlapping camps was at first regarded by the excavator as brief, but was subsequently extended to over 100 years when this better fitted a new theory (St Joseph 1973, 232). Further discussion is hampered by the lack of a complete catalogue of known camps and constrained by the tendency, noted above, to restrict the chronological parameters. In addition to the two well attested campaigns of Agricola and Severus, Lollius Urbicus certainly campaigned in Lowland Scotland and possibly beyond the Forth-Clyde isthmus. Other historically attested Roman military activities in, for example, the 160s, early 180s, 297, 305, 342/3, 367/8, 382 or circa 400 could have led to the construction of camps in north Britain, and there were no doubt other occasions when Roman troops operated north of Hadrian's Wall which have not been recorded in any literary source (eg Collingwood and Wright 1965, no. 2034).

One fundamental difficulty is likely to remain. Lack of knowledge of marching camps in an area cannot be taken as proof that none existed, especially given their ephemeral nature and the usual method of their discovery through aerial photography. It is thus dangerous to argue that Dio (76, 13, 3) is incorrect in stating that Severus reached the end of the island on the basis of our failure to discover marching camps in the far north, or that the 144–acre camp at Durno was unique (contra St Joseph 1973, 23 and 1977, 143–4).

The nature of the occupation of north Britain is well understood. Inscriptions, literary sources and other documents provide considerable evidence on the number and location of the regiments of the Roman army in Britain, its organisation and supply, and the means it used to exercise control, and this material is supported and amplified by evidence from the rest of the empire. Excavation over the last hundred years and more has provided detailed information on Roman frontiers, fortresses, forts, fortlets, towers and roads throughout north Britain. Thus has been built up a clear picture of the pattern of occupation in the late first century (Fig. 4.1) and in the middle second century, though the early third century is less clear primarily because of a relative paucity of evidence. Forts and fortlets on the main roads north-south, each apparently about a day's march apart, housed the troops charged with the task of defending the province from attack and controlling the provincials in the frontier zone.

Tacitus records that Agricola placed a line of garrisons across the Forth-Clyde isthmus (*Agricola* 23). The identification of these sites has, however, proved illusive. Coins, pottery and glass found in Antonine Wall forts has long been taken to indicate their earlier occupation (Robertson 1979, 20–2), but the discovery of a small fort of late first-century date at Mollins immediately to the south of the Wall opened up the discussion (Hanson 1980; Hanson and Maxwell 1980). The new chronology for this period has raised the possibility that the watch towers on the road from the Teith to the Tay (the so-called Gask frontier) relate to Agricola's dispositions rather than a later episode of withdrawal (Hobley 1989; Hanson 1991, 1,765–7).

Information about the Antonine Wall has been built up steadily over the centuries. Nonetheless, there is still doubt about the location of its eastern terminus (Bailey and Devereux 1987). Distance slabs indicate both who were the builders, the soldiers of the three legions in Britain, and how they divided up the work, while sections across the Wall have provided important evidence about the nature of the rampart, ditch, upcast mound and military way, which in turn may be tentatively related to the work of particular legions (Keppie 1974). Such evidence will no doubt continue to be supplemented by the discovery of temporary camps along the Wall, which suggest that the legions were divided into smaller groups for the construction work (Hanson and Maxwell 1986, 117–21).

Forts have long been known to exist along the Antonine Wall, though there is still some uncertainty about whether we know the full sequence (Breeze 1980, 52). Until 1945, however, only one fortlet was known, though by 1975 the number had increased to four. Following the general scheme proposed by John Gillam, who advanced the view that the plan of the Antonine Wall was based on that of Hadrian's Wall in its developed form (1975), investigative survey and excavation have increased the number to nine or ten and provided some confirmation of his basic hypothesis (Keppie and Walker 1981). Gillam also suggested that towers may have been built on the Antonine Wall, as they occur both on Hadrian's Wall and on the later German frontier, but none has yet been found. The discovery in 1976 of a hitherto unknown type of small enclosure attached to the Antonine Wall raised hopes, but subsequent excavation of one example failed to reveal its purpose (Hanson and Maxwell 1983). No more have yet come to light so that both the function and distribution of these small enclosures also remains unknown.

The relationship between the occupying Roman forces and the indigenous population is relatively poorly understood. Literary references concentrate primarily upon the military relationship between Roman and native. It is recorded almost in passing that Rome had treaty relations with both the Maeatae and the Caledones at the end of the second century (Dio 75, 5, 4) and evidence by analogy indicates that such treaties between Rome and her northern neighbours would have existed throughout the period. The apparent maintenance of the defences around the large hill-fort of Traprain Law and the continuous flow of Roman goods to the site, combined with an absence of Roman forts in the area, has led to the suggestion that the tribe in whose territory it lay, the Votadini, were in treaty relationship with Rome, perhaps even a client state (eg Breeze 1982, 57; Hanson 1987, 91–2). But alternative interpretations are possible. Hill has argued that the site was abandoned as a defended town before the arrival of the Romans and used as a ceremonial centre until, in the disruption of the late Roman or post-Roman period, it was refortified (1987). This view is not widely accepted (eg Close-Brooks 1987), for it is difficult to argue from negative evidence for a site where investigations are of early date and small scale, but does serve to highlight a problem. Even on a site like Traprain Law, which has produced relatively large quantities of datable artifactual material, there is insufficient evidence to be certain that occupation was continuous through the later second into the third century, a situation exacerbated on most other settlements which have been examined by the paucity of Roman artifacts recovered (Hill 1982a, 10; Burgess 1984, 171–2).

The *pax Romana* has frequently been cited as the occasion for changes in settlement patterns in north Britain. Thus, for example, hill-forts were considered to have been abandoned at the behest of the Romans. The appearance of stone-built settlements is associated with this process, since in many cases houses overlie the defences of an abandoned hill-fort (Jobey 1966, 1–13). Now, however, it seems possible that many of the hill-forts went out of use before the Romans arrived in the area (Hill 1982a, 9). The noted increase in the size of the stone-built settlements over time has been considered as a possible indication of population increase in the Roman period, though other factors might also have led to such changes, including the abandonment of hill-forts (Jobey 1974b). At present the imprecision of the dating evidence will not allow such causal relationships to be confirmed (Jobey 1982b).

Similarly, any estimate of the impact of the Roman arrival on agriculture and the environment has to be set against a long time-scale. Our view of the environment at this period is based on a limited number of pollen diagrams, most of which are undated, and samples from a small number of specific military and native sites of the Roman period (cf Hanson and Macinnes 1980; Boyd 1984). There is, at present, relatively little evidence from Iron Age sites to indicate the extent of exploitation of the pre-Roman environment. Further, there is for Iron Age and Roman Scotland no general background picture based upon regional pollen analyses against which the site-specific work can be judged. The distribution of available samples is weighted towards west-central Scotland and Northumberland. Nonetheless, the pattern which is beginning to emerge suggests that the effect of the Roman army's presence was minimal. A phase of woodland clearance is now seen to last from the pre-Roman Iron Age to the post-Roman period in northern Britain (Turner 1979). Thus when the Romans arrived towards the end of the first century at Elginhaugh, the area was already largely cleared of woodland and the site itself in pasture (Dickson forthcoming), while at Mollins the pollen analysis indicated a moderately cleared landscape with grassland (Boyd 1985). Similar indications were obtained from samples taken from the second-century forts at Bearsden and Bar Hill (Dickson 1989,

136; Boyd 1984). However, the question of the area from which the pollen derives, and thus the extent to which wider extrapolation may be made, remains a problem for site-derived samples.

It is usually assumed that forest clearance is associated with increased agricultural activity, but the archaeological evidence confirms that this process too had a long history. Improvements in agricultural tools are now seen as a pre-Roman phenomenon (Rees 1979, 472), while field systems of pre-Roman date are being increasingly attested (Gates 1982, 38; Halliday 1982, 84–7).

Manning has argued that much of the food requirements of the Roman army would have been supplied locally, and that this would have had an expansionist effect upon agriculture (1975), but the hypothesis remains difficult to demonstrate in the north either for cereals or meat. Consideration of the supply of non-perishable goods, however, particularly pottery, has progressed considerably, challenging the suggestion that supplies were dependent on large military contracts (Breeze 1977 *contra* Gillam 1973). Indeed, it is now clear that much more Roman pottery was made in Scotland than hitherto believed, though probably not by local native potters (Hartley 1976; Breeze 1986).

Archaeological investigation coupled with generations of recording and publication have provided a record of the distribution of Roman artifacts found on non-military sites, which are seen as providing an indication of Roman-native contacts (Curle 1932; Robertson 1970) (Fig. 4.2). However, the nature of that contact remains unclear. Macinnes has drawn attention to the distribution of Roman artifacts of the late first century on higher status native sites, especially brochs, probably reflecting primary contacts with local elites (1984a). In the second century, on the other hand, Roman objects reached a wider range of settlements, presumably reaching further down the social scale, possibly because of the longer period of contact. The paucity of Roman finds in Scotland after the second century emphasises the army's role in the exchange system, though the mode of exchange remains elusive (Macinnes 1989, 112–24). Coin hoards in Scotland, whose dates of deposition do not equate directly with periods of Roman occupation, are generally seen as reflecting one level of contact, the encouragement of local leaders to become or remain pro-Roman (Robertson 1970, 210), although the reasons for their deposition have been little considered (Aitchison 1988).

Possible directions for future work

It would be easy to suggest that simply by further excavation we could expect to increase the level of our knowledge about Roman Scotland. To an extent this is true, but such excavation has to be focused on particular goals and, given the inevitable limitation on resources and the continuing spiralling cost of excavation, biased towards carefully specified aims.

The examination of large areas within Roman forts, in order to understand their layout, has now been achieved at a number of sites. Thus there seems

Fig. 4.2   The distribution of Roman material from native sites in Scotland

little value in further large scale excavation within auxiliary forts which aims only at determining sequence and establishing the nature of the garrison (eg Frere and Wilkes 1989, 1–2). All the more so as recent work at Elginhaugh has indicated that even with a complete plan the latter cannot be established with confidence (Hanson *et al.* forthcoming) and, along with work at Bearsden and Strageath (Breeze 1984; Frere and Wilkes 1989), suggested that each fort is unique.

It would be worthwhile, however, to take any opportunities that arise for further large scale examination of fort annexes. Many forts and a number of fortlets were provided with an annexe or annexes, sometimes covering an area greater in size than the installation to which they were attached, as is graphically illustrated at Oxton (Plate 4.2). The few examples which have been examined indicate that occupation was both varied and fluid (McCord

Pl. 4.2 The Roman fortlet with multiple annexes at Oxton from the north (RCAHMS)

and Tait 1978; Breeze 1984, 47–58; Hanson *et al.* forthcoming) and would, therefore, require large scale work in order to be understood. But more importantly, further investigation of annexes is more likely to provide information relating to the important questions of logistics and supply, and in particular the extent of local involvement in those processes, than the examination of any number of fort interiors.

By way of contrast our knowledge of some of the smaller permanent installations of the Roman army is sufficiently limited to justify further excavation merely on the grounds of improving our reference base. There has, for example, been only one large scale modern excavation of a fortlet, the single period second-century site at Barburgh Mill (Breeze 1974). Examination of a first-century example should be a high priority so that we may determine morphological features which might aid the broad dating of other sites without recourse to excavation, as well as furthering our understanding of the role of such sites.

Scotland is particularly rich in the remains of temporary camps and has long been in the forefront of research into this monument type (St Joseph 1973, 228–33; 1977, 131–45; Hanson 1978; Maxwell 1980). Though there is still value in small scale work to confirm the outline and size of such camps (eg Keppie 1988), since it is largely on this basis that they have been analysed, recent experience at Inveresk (DES 1985, 30–1) and Kirkpatrick Fleming (DES 1990) suggests that there is little value in large scale examination of their interiors. This should not preclude investigation of examples, such as those at Inchtuthil and Glenlochar, where internal features are visible on aerial photographs, or of some of the smaller camps where a function other than overnight protection on campaign is suspected, or of sites where the post-Roman agricultural regime offers the chance of the survival of slight features, as for example at Ardoch. In general, however, it is through aerial photography filling out and extending distribution patterns, and more rigorous morphological analysis, supported by excavation at sites where camps overlap, that we will enhance our knowledge of these sites and broaden our understanding of their significance. The starting point, however, must be the production of a comprehensive corpus of known examples.

Indeed, the role that aerial photography has to play in the discovery of new sites generally, as for example in the recent expansion of the extent of the Gask frontier (Maxwell 1989, 118–21), and facilitating more detailed morphological analysis of all classes of Roman military monuments, is considerable. Here the ready identification of Roman military sites by their distinctive morphology is important and should not lightly be ignored. The morphology of the enclosure at Easter Galcantray alone would suggest that the site is not a Roman fort (*contra* Jones 1986), even without the negative evidence provided by the failure to recover any Roman pottery over several seasons of excavation (Frere 1987, 309).

Unless Roman permanent sites are identified in the Highlands or in the far north of Scotland, there being currently no strong grounds for either possibility (*contra* Jones 1986), our understanding of the broad pattern of the Roman military occupation is unlikely to see radical change, though explanation of that pattern and how it evolved and developed, particularly through comparison with other frontier areas, requires some further work. Similarly, considerations of chronology are likely to involve refinement rather than major reassessment (*contra* Mann 1988). There is, however, much that can still be learnt in detail about Roman frontiers in Scotland to fill in the gaps outlined above, particularly in relation to the watch towers between Forth and Tay, the so-called Gask frontier, and fortlets and other minor structures on the Antonine Wall.

However, the main directions of future research lie in assessing the impact of the Roman presence on the indigenous population and more generally on the Scottish landscape. To this end a variety of approaches is possible ranging from excavation via environmental studies and regional analysis to the erection and testing of theoretical models.

Various areas of concern can be readily identified. The most obvious is the presence of civilian settlements outside Roman forts. The opportunity provided by the Scottish examples, where the periods of Roman occupation are both well defined and relatively brief, to further our understanding of the early development of this phenomenon is considerable. However, few are known and even less have been subject to investigation, though this is not for want of trying and has been a research priority of HS for over 12 years. Particular attention is drawn to the potential of Inveresk for further detailed study. The combination of Roman stray finds from a widespread area around the fort (Thomas 1988, 141–4), the attested presence of the provincial procurator (Maxwell 1983, 385–9) and the excellent aerial photographic cover, including a field system whose Roman date has recently been confirmed by excavation (DES 1990), points to a thriving and extensive settlement. This was probably linked to the role of Inveresk as a port of supply for the Antonine Wall, but is also of potential major significance for our understanding of the political relationship between Roman and native in the area (Hanson and Maxwell 1986, 190–1).

This question does, however, serve to highlight the need to consider Roman forts as merely a focus of activity and be aware of the potential of the immediately surrounding area, even if no archaeological traces are attested. Roman military sites with their precise dating can, for example, provide valuable chronological horizons for environmental samples. Pollen sealed beneath ramparts or roads can be usefully compared with that from ditch or pit fills to indicate something of the impact of the Roman presence on the environment, or samples contrasted with those from sites of different periods in the same area (eg Boyd 1985). Recent such analyses from various Roman forts (see above) suggested that such impact was minimal because the area was already heavily cultivated and cleared of forest cover before the Roman arrival. But given the localised nature of pollen rain, further such studies are necessary to help build up a regional picture.

Indeed we remain surprisingly ignorant of the extent of pre-Roman Iron age deforestation, woodland management and the nature and wealth of the agricultural base. Though possible indications of Roman Iron Age hedges have been identified at Bar Hill (Boyd 1984), no certainly attested evidence of coppicing is yet available despite recent analyses of wattle samples from Elginhaugh and Bearsden (Crone forthcoming; Dickson 1989, 137). We need to obtain more dated pollen cores for Scotland, comparable to the extensive cover available for north-east England (Turner 1979) to extend regional coverage and provide a context into which local site-based samples may be fitted. In addition, to facilitate comparisons between sites and between areas, we need to instigate a systematic and consistent environmental sampling policy during excavation, whether of a Roman military site or a native settlement. The recovery of both good macroplant and pollen evidence is essential if we are to improve our understanding of the economic base and, accordingly, priority should be given to the excavation of sites with good organic survival.

Relatively little work has been done on bone evidence from sites in Scotland because of its poor survival. The basic work on the supply of animals to the military is based on early excavations at Newstead and Mumrills. At Newstead cattle were seen to predominate, with sheep and pigs being scantily represented in the bone assemblage, and both the presence of improved breeds and of many young animals was indicated (Ewart 1911). At Mumrills, however, a contrasting picture was revealed, with no improved breeds and all adult animals, leading Ritchie to suggest that the soldiers did not have herds of their own but were dependent on acquiring animals from local tribesmen (1929, 572). The examination of further large bone assemblages from both Roman and native sites, when and if they become available, is a priority and must be a potentially fruitful source of enquiry for improving our understanding of the general economic background of the Iron Age as well as the logistics of supply to, and diet of, the Roman troops. All the more so in the latter case when work on the botanical remains from the second-century fort at Bearsden has demonstrated that the balance of the diet there was mainly vegetarian (Dickson 1989; Knights et al. 1983).

But perhaps the most valuable general approach to future research is that which moves away from the individual site focus to a regional perspective and attempts to consider contemporary landscapes. One of the factors which has militated against such a development in the past is the compartmentalisation of archaeology and archaeologists. Too few Roman military archaeologists have concerned themselves with later prehistory, other than as 'background', or with the immediate post-Roman archaeology; too many prehistorians seem to feel that the arrival of the Romans marks the end of their particular area of concern; and few working in the early medieval period are inclined to consider their inheritance from Roman Britain. There is as yet no one doing for Scotland what Jobey has done for north-eastern England (eg 1966) or Higham is doing for northern or, more specifically, north-western England (eg 1982; 1986). There is considerable scope for further regional studies of the sort undertaken by Macinnes of prehistoric and Roman settlement patterns in three relatively limited areas of lowland Scotland (1983) or by Driscoll attempting to identify the Pictish settlement pattern of the kingdom of Strathearn (1987), both based primarily on the plotting and assessment of the abundant aerial photographic data. Such studies provide the best evidence for the development of the landscape, as well as a framework within which excavated sites can be set and priorities for fieldwork and further excavation assessed. In this context it is encouraging to note the work currently being undertaken at Newstead, where Jones is investigating not only the annexes of the Roman fort, but a series of native sites in the vicinity using aerial photography, geophysical survey and limited excavation (Jones 1990). Similar investigations around Traprain Law, where the potential significance of rectilinear sites identified from the air was recognised many years ago (Maxwell 1970), would offer the opportunity for valuable contrasts and comparisions to be made. A combination of arable fieldwalking and sample excavation, ideally linked with examination of a limited area within Traprain Law itself, could reap considerable rewards.

Less obvious, but potentially just as informative, is the detailed study of a particular area, such as the Esk valley, where over a long time-span both Roman and native sites are being examined under the rescue aegis as they come under threat, though an up-to-date and detailed plot of the known archaeological features in the valley is still lacking (Fig. 4.3). To date sites excavated have included the first-century Roman auxiliary fort and annexe at Elginhaugh (Hanson *et al.* forthcoming), the mid-second-century Roman auxiliary fort and *vicus* at Inveresk (Thomas 1988; DES 1990), the Roman temporary camp and unenclosed Iron Age settlement at Monktonhall (DES 1985, 30–1) and the probable Iron Age enclosure at Melville Nurseries (DES 1989, 52–3). This should result in a gradual accumulation of knowledge about fort, *vicus* and countryside within a coherent framework. Nonetheless, there is still a need for further investigation of native Iron Age sites in the area, and elsewhere, particularly those with good organic preservation in order to maximise environmental data recovery.

One major problem is the lack of precise dating evidence for rural sites. In most cases the only indication of a Roman date has been the presence of Roman artifacts (but see Alcock 1963, 225 for a cautionary note). But this introduces a bias towards sites in receipt of Roman material, which may not find its way to all contemporary occupation sites. Indeed, there is a strong probability that Roman goods had a limited distribution, being confined mainly to the elite within native society (Macinnes 1984a). There is also a possibility that the distribution may be biased towards sites with ritual or religious associations (Hill 1987). There is no simple solution to this dilemma, but the closer study and detailed future recording of the context of such material is essential if our understanding of it is to improve. Independent scientific dating methods provide some hope of identifying rural sites occupied in the Roman period. Dendrochronology may be of value for crannogs and sites where waterlogged structural remains survive, provided the timber involved is oak and not alder, as proved to be the case at Elginhaugh fort, Erskine crannog and predominantly at Bearsden (Crone forthcoming; Dickson 1989, 137). Thermoluminescence may provide useful dates for native pottery, for there is still scope for improvement in dating precision through sample replication (Dr. D. Sanderson pers. comm.).

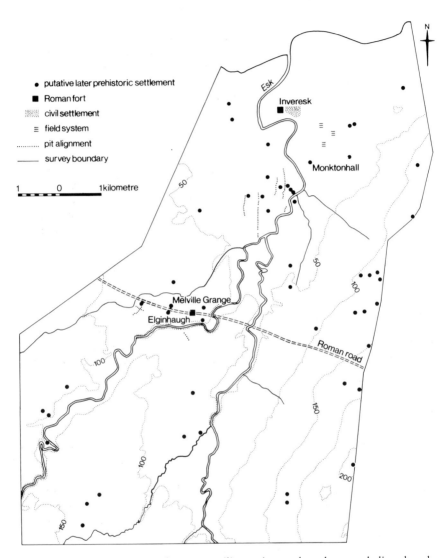

- • putative later prehistoric settlement
- ■ Roman fort
- ▦ civil settlement
- ≡ field system
- ·········· pit alignment
- ———— survey boundary

Fig. 4.3 The distribution of Roman military sites and settlements believed to be of Iron Age or Romano-British date in the lower Esk valley

There are, however, other directions for artifact studies. Though there has been a good deal of work identifying Roman material on native sites (Curle 1932; Robertson 1970), with attempts to explain its significance (Fulford 1985; Hill 1987; Macinnes 1989), there has been little attempt to trace the opposite trend. No one has yet attempted to catalogue the occurrence of native pottery on Roman military sites. Also in this context, possible candidates for further detailed consideration are the glass bangles which are so common on both Roman military and native sites, but have a distribution largely restricted to the northern military zone (Stevenson 1974), and button-and-loop fasteners which have a similar distribution and were certainly manufactured on at least one native site in Scotland (Gillam 1958, 79–85; Wild 1970). Indeed, both types of artifact raise the question of what exactly constitutes Roman material culture in the north. In all cases the emphasis of study should be on the archaeological context of the material.

This sort of approach naturally leads on to more statistical analysis of the data. There is great scope for quantification and subsequent consideration of the comparative distributions of various forms of artifacts, ecofacts and structural forms at different levels. Firstly between different areas within Britain, such as within and beyond a frontier zone, as in the case of Wales and Scotland (Hanson and Macinnes 1990), or on either side of a boundary. Secondly between Britain and other frontier zones (eg Fulford 1985; 1989). Further refinement can be then introduced, where the data will allow, by consideration of such variations through time, including the immediately pre- and post-Roman situation. Until such basic work has been undertaken we will not be in a position to attempt to apply some of the various theoretical approaches, such as core/periphery models which have proved valuable in improving our understanding of relations between Roman and native both within and beyond the frontiers of the empire (eg Haselgrove 1982; Hedeager 1987), or to test hypotheses concerning the relationship between native social structure and the extent of romanisation (Macinnes 1989; Millett 1990, 99–101).

Bibliography

Aitchison, N. 1988 Roman wealth, native ritual: coin hoards within and beyond Roman Britain, *World Archaeol.* 20.2, 270–84.

Alcock, L. 1963 *Dinas Powys*, Cardiff.

Bailey, G. B. and Devereux, D. F. 1987 The eastern terminus of the Antonine Wall: a review, *Proc. Soc. Antiq. Scotland* 117, 93–104.

Barrett, J. C. , Fitzpatrick, A. P. and Macinnes, L. (eds) 1989 *Barbarians and Romans in north-west Europe*, Oxford.

Birley, A. R. 1963 *Hadrian's Wall*, London.

Birley, E. 1983 A Roman altar from Old Kilpatrick and interim commanders of auxiliary forts, *Latomus* 42, 73–83.

Boyd, W. E. 1984 Environmental change and Iron Age land management in the area of the Antonine Wall, central Scotland: a summary, *Glasgow Archaeol. J.* 11, 75–81.

Boyd, W. E. 1985 Palaeobotanical evidence from Mollins, *Britannia* 15, 37–48.

Breeze, D. J. 1974 The Roman fortlet at Barburgh Mill, Dumfriesshire, *Britannia* 5, 130–62.

Breeze, D. J. 1975 The abandonment of the Antonine Wall: its date and implications, *Scottish Archaeol. Forum* 7, 67–80.

Breeze, D. J. 1977 The fort at Bearsden and the supply of pottery to the Roman army, in Dore, J. and Greene, K. (eds) *Roman pottery studies in Britain and beyond*, Oxford, 133–45.

Breeze, D. J. 1979 *Roman Scotland: the visible remains*, Newcastle upon Tyne.

Breeze, D. J. 1980 Roman Scotland during the reign of Antoninus Pius, in Hanson, W. S. and Keppie, L. J. F. (eds) *Roman frontier studies 1979*, Oxford, 45–60.

Breeze, D. J. 1982 *The northern frontiers of Roman Britain*, London.

Breeze, D. J. 1984 The Roman fort on the Antonine Wall at Bearsden, in Breeze, D. J. (ed) *Studies in Scottish Antiquity*, Edinburgh, 32–68.

Breeze, D. J. 1986 The manufacture of pottery in Roman Scotland, *Proc. Soc. Antiq. Scotland* 116, 185–9.

Breeze, D. J. and Dobson, B. 1970 The development of the mural frontier in Britain from Hadrian to Caracalla, *Proc. Soc. Antiq. Scotland* 102 (1969–70), 109–21.

Breeze, D. J. and Dobson, B. 1972 Hadrian's Wall: some problems, *Britannia* 3, 182–208.

Breeze, D. J. and Dobson, B. 1987 *Hadrian's Wall*, (3rd edn) Harmondsworth.

Burgess, C. 1984 The prehistoric settlement of Northumberland: a speculative survey, in Miket and Burgess 1984, 126–75.

Casey, P. J. 1984 Roman coinage of the fourth century in Scotland, in Miket and Burgess 1984, 295–304.

Casey, P. J. and Savage, M. 1980 The coins from the excavations at High Rochester in 1852 and 1855, *Archaeol. Aeliana* 5.8, 75–87.

Clack, P. and Haselgrove, S. (eds) 1982 *Rural settlement in the Roman north*, Durham.

Close-Brooks, J. 1987 Comment on Traprain Law, *Scottish Archaeol. Rev.* 4.2, 92–4.

Collingwood, R. G. and Wright, R. P. 1965 *Roman inscriptions of Britain* vol 1, Oxford.

Crone, A. forthcoming The waterlogged wood, in Hanson *et al.* forthcoming.

Curle, J. 1932 An inventory of objects of Roman and provincial Roman origin found on sites in Scotland not definitely associated with Roman constructions, *Proc. Soc. Antiq. Scotland* 66, 277–397.

DES *Discovery and excavation in Scotland*, Edinburgh.

Dickson, C. A. 1989 The Roman army diet in Britain and Germany, *Archaeobotanik. Dissertationes Botanicae* 133, 135–54.

Dickson, C. A. forthcoming Pollen analysis, in Hanson *et al.* forthcoming.

Driscoll, S. T. 1987 *The Early Historic landscape of Strathearn: the archaeology of a Pictish kingdom*, unpublished PhD thesis, University of Glasgow.

Ewart, J. C. 1911 The animal remains, in Curle, J. *A Roman frontier post and its people: the fort at Newstead in the parish of Melrose*, Glasgow, 362–77.

Frere, S. S. 1987 Roman Britain in 1986, *Britannia* 8, 301–77.

Frere, S. S. and Wilkes, J. J. 1989 *Strageath: excavations within the Roman fort 1973–86*, London.

Fulford, M. 1985 Roman material in barbarian society c. 200 BC-400 AD, in Champion, T. C. and Megaw, J. V. S. (eds) *Settlement and society: aspects of west European prehistory in the first millennium BC*, Leicester, 91–108.

Fulford, M. 1989 Roman and barbarian: the economy of Roman frontier systems, in Barrett *et al.*, 81–95.

Gates, T. 1982 Farming on the frontier: Romano-British fields in Northumberland, in Clack and Haselgrove 1982, 21–42.

Gillam, J. P. 1958 Roman and native, AD 122–197, in Richmond, I. A. (ed) *Roman and native in north Britain*, Edinburgh, 60–90.

Gillam, J. P. 1973 Sources of pottery found on northern military sites, in Detsicas, A. (ed) *Current research in Romano-British coarse pottery*, London, 53–62.

Gillam, J. P. 1975 Possible changes in plan in the course of the construction of the Antonine Wall, *Scottish Archaeol. Forum* 7, 51–6.

Gillam, J. P. 1977 The Roman forts at Corbridge, *Archaeol. Aeliana* 5.5, 47–74.

Halliday, S. P. 1982 Later prehistoric farming in south-east Scotland, in Harding 1982, 84–7.

Hanson, W. S. 1978 Roman campaigns north of the Forth-Clyde isthmus: the evidence of the temporary camps, *Proc. Soc. Antiq. Scotland* 109 (1977–78), 140–50.

Hanson, W. S. 1980 Agricola on the Forth-Clyde isthmus, *Scottish Archaeol. Forum* 12, 55–68.

Hanson, W. S. 1987 *Agricola and the conquest of the north*, London.

Hanson, W. S. 1991 Tacitus' 'Agricola': an archaeological and historical study, in Haase, W. (ed) *Aufstieg und Niedergang der römischen Welt* II 33.2, 1741–84.

Hanson, W. S. and Macinnes, L. 1980 Forests, forts and fields: a discussion, *Scottish Archaeol. Forum* 12, 98–113.

Hanson, W. S. and Macinnes, L. 1990 Soldiers and settlement in Wales and Scotland, in Collis, J. (ed) *Britain in the Roman Empire*, Sheffield, forthcoming.

Hanson, W. S. and Maxwell, G. S. 1980 An Agricolan praesidium on the Forth-Clyde isthmus (Mollins, Strathclyde), *Britannia* 11, 43–9.

Hanson, W. S. and Maxwell, G. S. 1983 Minor enclosures on the Antonine Wall at Wilderness Plantation, *Britannia* 14, 227–43.

Hanson, W. S. and Maxwell, G. S. 1986 *Rome's north-west frontier: the Antonine Wall*, Edinburgh.

Hanson, W. S, Yeoman, P. A. and Terry, J. forthcoming *Elginhaugh: a Flavian fort and its annexe*, Edinburgh.

Harding, D. W. 1982 *Later prehistoric settlement in south-east Scotland*, Edinburgh.

Hartley, B. R. 1972 The Roman occupation of Scotland: the evidence of the samian ware, *Britannia* 3, 1–42.

Hartley, K. 1976 Were mortaria made in Scotland?, *Glasgow Archaeol. J.* 4, 81–9.

Haselgrove, C. C. 1982 Wealth, prestige and power: the dynamics of political centralisation in south-east England, in Renfrew, C. and Shennan, S. (eds) *Ranking, resource and exchange*, Cambridge, 79–88.

Haverfield, F. 1899 On a Roman altar to Silvanus found near Barr Hill and on the Roman occupation of Scotland, in Glasgow Archaeological Society (eds) *The Antonine Wall report*, Glasgow, 153–68.

Hedeager, L. 1987 Empire, frontier and barbarian hinterland: Rome and northern Europe from AD 1–400, in Rowlands, M. , Larsen, M. and Kristiansen, K. (eds) *Centre and periphery in the ancient world*, Cambridge, 124–40.

Higham, N. J. 1982 The Roman impact upon rural settlement in Cumbria, in Clack and Haselgrove 1982, 105–22.

Higham, N. J. 1986 *The northern counties to AD 1000*, Harlow.

Hill, P. 1982a Settlement and chronology, in Harding 1982, 4–43.

Hill, P. 1982b Broxmouth hill-fort excavations, 1977–78, in Harding 1982, 141–88.

Hill, P. 1987 Traprain Law: the Votadini and the Romans, *Scottish Archaeol. Rev.* 4.2, 86–91.

Hobley, A. S. 1989 The numismatic evidence for the post-Agricolan abandonment of the Roman frontier in northern Scotland, *Britannia* 20, 69–74.

Jarrett, M. G. and Mann, J. C. 1970 Britain from Agricola to Gallienus, *Bonner Jahrbücher* 170, 178–210.

Jobey, G. 1966 Homesteads and settlements of the frontier area, in Thomas, C. (ed) *Rural settlement in Roman Britain*, London.

Jobey, G. 1974a Excavations at Boonies, Westerkirk, and the nature of Romano-British settlement in eastern Dumfriesshire, *Proc. Soc. Antiq. Scotland* 105 (1972–4), 119–40.

Jobey, G. 1974b Notes on some population problems in the area between the two Roman Walls, *Archaeol. Aeliana* 5.2. 17–26.

Jobey, G. 1982a The settlement at Doubstead and Romano-British settlement on the coastal plain between Tyne and Forth, *Archaeol. Aeliana* 5.10, 1–23.

Jobey, G. 1982b Between Tyne and Forth: some problems, in Clack and Haselgrove 1982, 7–20.

Jones, G. D. B. 1986 Roman military site at Cawdor, *Popular Archaeology* 7.3, 13–16.

Jones, R. F. J. 1990 The Newstead project: the archaeological search for acculturation, *Scottish Archaeol. Rev.* 7, 104–113.

Keppie, L. J. F. 1974 The building of the Antonine Wall: archaeological and epigraphic evidence, *Proc. Soc. Antiq. Scotland* 105 (1972–4), 151–65.

Keppie, L. J. F. 1983 Roman inscriptions from Scotland: some additions and corrections to RIB I, *Proc. Soc. Antiq. Scotland* 113, 391–404.

Keppie, L. J. F. 1986 *Scotland's Roman remains*, Edinburgh.

Keppie, L. J. F. 1988 Excavation of a Roman temporary camp at Annan Hill, Dumfriesshire 1985–86, *Trans. Dumfriesshire Galloway Nat. Hist. Antiq. Soc.* 63, 13–21.

Keppie, L. J. F. and Walker, J. J. 1981 Fortlets on the Antonine Wall at Seabegs Wood, Kinneil and Cleddans, *Britannia* 12, 143–62.

Knights, B. A, Dickson, C. A. , Dickson, J. H. and Breeze, D. J. 1983 Evidence concerning the Roman military diet at Bearsden, Scotland, in the second century AD, *J. Archaeol. Sci.* 10, 139–52.

McCord, N. and Tait, J. 1978 Excavations in the northern annexe of the Roman fort at Camelon, near Falkirk, 1961–3, *Proc. Soc. Antiq. Scotland* 109 (1977–78), 151–65.

Macdonald, G. 1934 *The Roman Wall in Scotland*, Oxford.

Macinnes, L. 1983 *Later prehistoric and Romano-British settlement north and south of the Forth: a comparative survey*, unpublished PhD thesis, University of Newcastle.

Macinnes, L. 1984a Brochs and the Roman occupation of Lowland Scotland, *Proc. Soc. Antiq. Scotland* 114, 235–49.

Macinnes, L. 1984b Settlement and economy: East Lothian and the Tyne-Forth province, in Miket and Burgess 1984, 176–98.

Macinnes, L. 1989 Baubles, bangles and beads: trade and exchange in Roman Scotland, in Barrett *et al.* 1989, 108–116.

Mann, J. C. 1988 The history of the Antonine Wall: a reappraisal, *Proc. Soc. Antiq. Scotland* 118, 131–7.

Mann, J. C. and Penman, R. G. (eds) 1978 *Literary sources for Roman Britain*, London.

Manning, W. H. 1975 Economic influences on land use in the military areas of the Highland zone during the Roman period, in Evans, J. G. , Limbrey, S. and Cleere, H. (eds), *The effect of man on the landscape of the Highland zone*, London, 112–16.

Maxwell, G. S. 1970 Early rectilinear enclosures in the Lothians, *Scottish Archaeol. Forum* 2, 85–90.

Maxwell, G. S. 1980 Agricola's campaigns: the evidence of the temporary camps, *Scottish Archaeol. Forum* 12, 25–54.

Maxwell, G. S. 1983 Two inscribed Roman stones and architectural fragments from Scotland, *Proc. Soc. Antiq. Scotland* 113, 379–90.

Maxwell, G. S. 1989 *The Romans in Scotland*, Edinburgh.

Maxwell, G. S. and Wilson, D. R. 1987 Air reconnaissance in Roman Britain 1975–84, *Britannia* 18, 1–48.

Miket, R. and Burgess, C. (eds) 1984 *Between and beyond the Walls: essays on the prehistory and history of north Britain in honour of George Jobey*, Edinburgh.

Millett, M. 1990 *The Romanization of Britain; an essay in archaeological interpretation*, Cambridge.

Ralston, I. 1979 The Iron age (c. 600 BC-AD 200): northern Britain, in Megaw, J. V. S. and Simpson, D. D. A. (eds) *Introduction to British prehistory*, Leicester, 446–79.

Rees, S. 1979 *Agricultural implements in prehistoric and Roman Britain*, Oxford.

Richmond, I. A. 1940 The Romans in Redesdale, in Dodds, M. H. (ed) *A history of Northumberland*, vol 15, Newcastle upon Tyne, 63–159.

Ritchie, J. 1929 The animal remains, in Macdonald, G. and Curle, A. O., The Roman fort at Mumrills, near Falkirk, *Proc. Soc. Antiq. Scotland* 63 (1928–29), 568–73.

Rivet, A. L. F. and Smith, C. 1979 *The place-names of Roman Britain*, London.

Robertson, A. S. 1970 Roman finds from non-Roman sites in Scotland, *Britannia* 1, 198–226.

Robertson, A. S. 1975 The Romans in north Britain: the coin evidence, in Temporini, H. (ed) *Aufstieg und Niedergang der römischen Welt* II. 3, Berlin, 364–426.

Robertson, A. S. 1979 *The Antonine Wall* (3rd edn), Glasgow.

Robertson, A. S. 1983 Roman coins found in Scotland, 1971–1982, *Proc. Soc. Antiq. Scotland* 113, 405–48.

Robertson, A. S. 1990 *The Antonine Wall* (4th edn) revised by L. J. F. Keppie, Glasgow.

Roy, W. 1793 *Military antiquities of the Romans in north Britain*, London.

St Joseph, J. K. S. 1969 Air reconnaissance in Britain, 1965–68, *J. Roman Stud.* 59, 104–28.

St Joseph, J. K. S. 1973 Air reconnaissance in Roman Britain, 1969–72, *J. Roman Stud.* 63, 214–46.

St Joseph, J. K. S. 1977 Air reconnaissance in Roman Britain, 1973–76, *J. Roman Stud.* 67, 125–61.

Shotter, D. C. A. 1976 Coin evidence and the northern frontier in the second century AD, *Proc. Soc. Antiq. Scotland* 107 (1975–76), 81–91.

Stevenson, R. B. K. 1974 Romano-British glass bangles, *Glasgow Archaeol. J.* 4, 45–56.

Thomas, G. 1988 Excavations at the Roman civil settlement at Inveresk, 1976–77, *Proc. Soc. Antiq. Scotland* 118, 139–76.

Turner, J. 1979 The environment of north-east England during Roman times as shown by pollen analysis, *J. Archaeol. Sci.* 6.3, 285–90.

Wild, J. P. 1970 Button-and-loop fasteners in the Roman provinces, *Britannia* 1, 137–55.

Wright, R. P. 1974 Carpow and Caracalla, *Britannia* 5, 289–92.

Acknowledgements

We would like to thank Dr. Lesley Macinnes for her comments on an earlier draft of this paper and Chris Unwin for producing the line illustrations.

5

THE ARCHAEOLOGY OF STATE FORMATION IN SCOTLAND

Stephen T. Driscoll

The kings of Scotia and Scotland stamped unity upon four or five disparate peoples north of the Tweed and Solway; yet the precosity of a single kingdom of Scotia or Alba in the mid-ninth century . . . seems to excite little comment . . . The only Celtic realm with well formed and independent political institutions at the beginning of the 'high middle ages' was that with apparently the smallest cultural heritage, Scotland'. (Duncan 1975, 110)

'thanages . . . were all situated in those eastern districts which formed originally the seat of Pictish Tribes, and afterwards fell under the dynasty of the Scottish race'. (Skene 1890, 277)

Historical explanation and archaeological initiative

Perhaps the biggest issue yet to be directly addressed by Scottish archaeologists is the formation of their state. Although Duncan's comment refers to contemporary silence, it is equally apt for today. What passes for historical debate on the topic serves to make plain that as far as text-bound historians are concerned, the process of Scottish state formation remains a paradox if not a mystery. And yet Skene had a century ago identified the key to the mystery, a key which he was unable to employ due to the limitations of the documentary resources.

In this paper I would like to outline some of the ways in which archaeology can take the initiative in this endeavour. It is a way which requires considerable integration of historical and archaeological scholarship. Its strength is that it provides a freedom from the constraints which are inherent in the approaches confined to documentary sources or to artifact studies. Although this paper is not intended as a critique of historical methods and attitudes, its brevity inevitably introduces a polemical tone to the discussion on the value of integrated historical and archaeological endeavour (see Driscoll 1988a for fuller discussion of the problem). Therefore, it is worth stressing at the outset that this is a constructive attempt to build upon the framework provided by Scottish historians and to suggest how the archaeological evidence can be deployed to explore the crucial questions surrounding the formation of the Scottish state.

A key methodological problem has been to rely too much on political texts for evidence of institutional development. Leaving aside the ideological questions of elitist history, strict documentary history is limiting as an approach because it places too little priority on the structural developments in society which gave rise to the insitutions of the state. These are not to be seen primarily in the King Lists (Anderson 1980, 80), nor are they to be discovered by charting the ebb and flow of military fortunes as noted in the Annals (Anderson 1922; Smyth 1984). Rather they are to be discovered in social and economic arrangements as revealed in the patterns of landholding and agricultural exploitation, as illuminated by comparison with how states elsewhere have evolved, and by asking questions of the archaeology which texts cannot address.

There are significant reasons for discussing the political and ideological process of state formation in archaeological terms. Firstly, it provides a materialist perspective which is missing from the text-based histories. The study of early medieval Scotland gains a reciprocal advantage from considering state formation, because the 'big process' provides a framework for otherwise poorly connected groups of facts about brooch type, interlace styles, fortification techniques, quern types and so on. Moreover, without placing the archaeological evidence within such a framework it is deprived of political resonance and provides no connection with contemporary Scotland.

Areas of institutional development

Three areas of social and political activity stand out as crucial for the study of the growth of the Scottish state. The first two have long been recognised: centres of royal authority such as Forteviot or Scone, or centres of religious authority, such as Abernethy or St Andrews. But little attention has been devoted to the third, the structure of settlement and the pattern of land control. These are, of course, not exclusive categories, because places of secular authority included religious elements (pagan and christian), abbeys were great landlords, and local centres of production could develop into centres of regional importance. In fact to divide the early medieval world into three estates may be convenient, but is a distortion. There were intimate connections between the three areas I have isolated, the most prevalent of which was the way in which social relations were forged to maintain control over agricultural production. There are three contemporary historians who can be identified with these particular areas: Leslie Alcock with centres of secular authority, Gordon Donaldson with the Church, and Geoffrey Barrow with the organisation and control of land.

As indicated above the major methodological problem surrounding Scottish state formation is to integrate two academically divided bodies of knowledge: texts and material culture. My starting assumption is that power in medieval Scotland flowed from the land. Consequently the basis for understanding state institutions is an understanding of how land was controlled and how agricultural production was managed. At this most fundamental level it is the patterns of landscape organisation that we must seek to understand, that is we must seek to produce a coherent image of the early medieval landscape with its attendant social practices and political institutions.

In studying the settlement evidence I have followed two paths in an attempt to develop the latent historical meanings. One has been to combine the archaeological sites with the known historical geography derived from the contemporary sources, medieval texts and place-name studies. The other approach has been to use the historical texts to generate a systematic model with which we can interpret the historical evidence for settlement.

The first method has a credible track record. It has been used by anti-quarians and modern historical scholars to locate sites of interest and to enhance their documentary findings. It is certainly the appropriate method to begin the study of major centres of the religious and secular authority. Alcock's campaign to uncover the early historic fortifications of Scotland may be taken as a model of how to proceed (1981; 1988), since he considers sites which are mentioned explicitly in annalistic sources as well as more oblique references embedded in hagiographic narratives. The method has even proved useful for providing cropmark sites with historical contexts; see for instance Alcock (1982) and Anderson (1980, 203–4) on Forteviot. The obvious limitation here is that there is no way to compensate for lacunae in the survival of historically recorded names: sites like Restenneth, Clatchard Craig and Burghead, although important Pictish centres, are consigned to an historic limbo.

It is the second approach which I wish to concentrate upon because it attempts to account for all settlement, not simply those sites prominent (or lucky) enough to have entered the documentary record. By drawing on what evidence there is for pre-feudal administrative systems and social relations, it is possible to propose a model which accounts for the social hierarchy and settlement correlates. The sources of our knowledge about Pictish society and administration are late and difficult to use, but not impossible. It is this second path, marked out by Skene and improved by Barrow, that appears the most promising because it allows us to use one of the most important archaeological assets: aerial photography.

There is a neat coincidence of the newest and least exploited archaeo-logical resource and the location of the key economic resources for the early medieval period. The great number of cropmark sites to have been recorded since the early 1970s provides an opportunity for the first time to obtain geographically and socially representative information about past settlement systems in eastern Scotland. The importance of this resource can be simply illustrated by comparing the settlements recorded as upstanding monuments, which in Strathearn are all hill-forts, to those recorded as aerial photographs up to 1984 (Figs 5.1 and 5.2) (Driscoll 1987, 204–54). Similarly striking patterns have been revealed by Macinnes' comparative

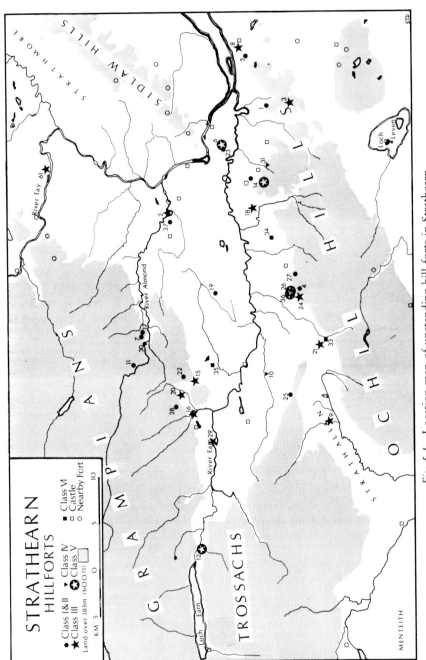

Fig. 5.1   Location map of upstanding hill-forts in Strathearn

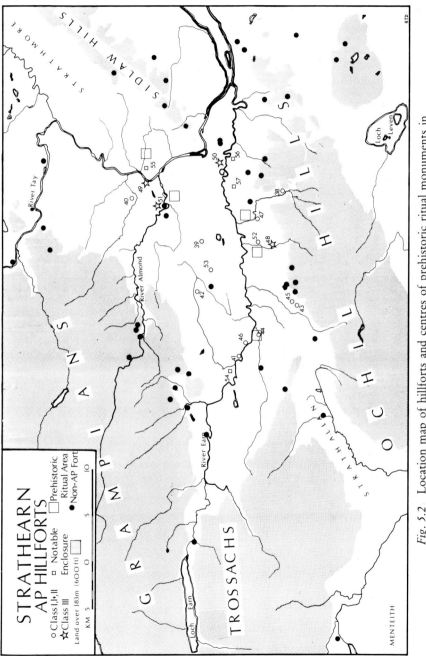

Fig. 5.2   Location map of hillforts and centres of prehistoric ritual monuments in Strathearn recorded by aerial photography (up to 1984)

studies of the other major cropmark producing areas, the East Lothian plain and north-east Fife and Angus (1982; 1983). The new evidence of aerial photographs has radically altered our perception of prehistoric and medieval settlement and these recent studies are the first comprehensive attempts at analysing and synthesising the evidence on a regional basis.

Because of the eastern bias in the distribution of cropmark sites and the need to make the best use of the existing documentary evidence, most of the discussion which follows relates to Pictland and, in particular, to Strathearn. The importance of Strathearn was in recent years identified by Leslie Alcock, who recognised in the valley a unique combination of well preserved upstanding monuments, good cropmark coverage and good documentation (1982; Alcock *et al.* 1989). As a study area for investigating the origins of the Scottish state, it had the additional attraction of being located where that state first took clearest shape: at the heart of the pre-eminent kingdom of Southern Pictland, Fortriu (Wainwright 1955). It is also an attractive area on which to base generalisations, because its physical geography and archaeological resources make it representative of eastern Pictland from Fife to Aberdeen.

Points of departure: social institutions and landscape models

The first task is to seek out ways of making sense of the separate settlement sites, many of which are best represented in the aerial photographic record. Interpreting aerial photographs remains a topic of vigorous debate too complex to discuss here, other than to say that a great deal of chrono-logical uncertainty surrounds most unexcavated aerial photographic sites (see Driscoll 1987 for further discussion). Rather than focus on cropmark typology, facinating though that is (see, for example, Whimster 1989), the best way to construct an interpretative model of the landscape is to begin with the structure as revealed in the evidence for the organisation of Pictish and early Scottish society.

To produce something resembling an integrated model of the social landscape, we can begin by examining the institutions which helped to define that landscape. There are at least two ways of viewing these social institutions. The perspective commonly adopted is from the top down or, more accurately, the top alone, isolated from the rest of the population. The nature of the documentary record has encouraged the major historians of the period, including Duncan, Donaldson, M. O. Anderson and Smyth, to focus on the top levels of society. The reverse, a bottom-up perspective, Hill's 'worm's eye view' (1972, 14)) has not really been attempted. Barrow (1973) is to some extent an exception because, having devoted so much attention to the problems of land tenure, he has revealed aspects of lordship from the client's perspective. However, at the end of the day his concern is essentially to explain how these institutions help us to understand the activities of the aristocracy. By focusing attention on the archaeological evidence for settlement we may remedy this bias. This exercise should help us to recognise better the expressions which are encoded within the architectural forms and site locations. To do so demands that we in return consider architectural practice as a means of discourse, and read in the building of houses, laying out of fields and construction of fortifications statements about the social conditions which the people of Fortriu created for themselves.

Historical scholarship on the early development of the great national institutions, the monarchy and church, is not without its value, even for studies which aspire to adopt the bottom-up approach. Donaldson's efforts at elucidating the development of the diocesan structure of Scotland include many points of relevance for us (1953; 1985). In addition to demonstrating the early, largely Pictish, origins of the bishop's sees at Abernethy, Dunblane, Dunkeld, Brechin and St Andrew's, his study makes it clear that the church organisation in the east was fundamentally different from that in Dal Riada and Ireland. In the east before the accession of Kenneth mac Alpin, the church appears to have been far less monastic in character than in the west and more orthodox in its division into bishoprics and parishes. Its development as an administrative organisation seems to be bound up with related administrative developments within the Pictish kingdoms. This is echoed by Anderson who suggests that the presence in eleventh- and twelfth-century Scotland of 'regional bishoprics, and of a high status accorded to bishops . . . may have their roots in the eighth-century reforms introduced into Pictavia from Northumbria' (1982, 128–9). Whether it was due to the Northumbrian influence or the earlier practices introduced at the time of conversion, it seems clear that 'the Picts had grown used to something more like an orthodox 'Roman' organisation' (Anderson 1982, 130). This was all changed with the introduction of an Irish-type monastic church organisation. The erection of a church by Kenneth in AD 848–9 at Dunkeld to house the relics of St. Columba is a sign of this transformation and seems to mark a significant break in Pictish/Scottish cultural history.

One result of the introduction of an Irish-style church and the replacement of Pictish-speaking clerics with Gaelic speakers was to enhance claims that Columba was an important influence in the conversion of the Picts, claims which have been repeated from Skene's day to our own (Hughes 1980). Donaldson and Anderson have shown that, although monasticism was not unknown, a strong Columban influence is not apparent in the early organisation of the Pictish church. This is especially true for southern Pictland. In this respect the Pictish church can be said to have been shaped along orthodox lines by local political concerns, rather than Irish missionary monasticism. These observations have important implications for the study of statehood, because they suggest that the church will have followed local practices in the administration of its estates and that the evidence regarding the organisation of the church's estates may provide a sound basis for generalisation about Pictish estate management. The key text here is, of course, the Gaelic notes in the *The Book of Deer* (Jackson 1972).

Similarly, the history of the Pictish monarchy suggests that stable, if antagonistic, political entities emerged at the same time as king lists, perhaps as early as the middle of the sixth century (Anderson 1980, 139–45; Miller 1979, 11). If we are to accept Smyth's (1984) interpretations of the king lists and annals, then it appears that from the sixth century onwards several highly competitive dynastic groups from different areas of southern Pictland were grappling for the paramount kingship, which was usually based in Fortriu. Moreover, as Davies has pointed out, the reference to the death of several royal officials, described in the Annals of Ulster as *exactatores*, presumably a corruption of *exactores*, 'collectors of dues' or 'agents', suggests that by the early eighth century the 'Pictish kings were developing some real machinery of government' (1984, 70; Anderson 1980, 178).

Collectively these scattered details attest to the formation of the administrative apparatus of the medieval state. We cannot doubt that the development of these institutions had a strong impact on the organisation of society. But at the same time there exists compelling evidence that these administrative techniques grew out of pre-existing social practices. We will come to the details of this evidence shortly, but there are also theoretical arguments supporting this notion of pre-feudal administrative structures. In essence the argument is that cultures do not work by plucking social practices out of the air for the amusement of anthropologists; there must always be reference to what has gone before. It is this recursive property of culture that encourages us to postulate the antiquity of some of the institutions which we only begin to see clearly in the twelfth century.

The most fundamental of these institutions was the administrative structure known as a thanage, which, as its name suggests, was managed by a thane, a royal official appointed to look after the scattered royal holdings. The so-called small shire was an equivalent in terms of internal organisation to the thanage, but was not held by a royal official. The important thing, as Barrow explains (1973), is that, despite the first historical emergence of the thanage into the documentation of the twelfth century and its Anglo-Saxon terminology, its origins lie in the traditional obligations of lordship or clientage. These grew up around the small 'tribal kingdoms' and ultimately have their origins in kin-based organisations. It is here with the lord — client relationship that any attempt to write history from the bottom up must begin, and it is in these traditional obligations of clientage that we must ultimately seek our explanations of the settlement system.

Social transactions

The order and coherence evident in the twelfth century *notitiae* in the *Book of Deer* provide us with confidence in the existence of Pictish institutions of clientage and associated landholding practices (Driscoll 1987, 260–74), but it is from other less unified or systematic sources that we learn the more specific details of the Pictish social order and its reproduction. To summarise arguments drawn from anthropology and sociology which are detailed elsewhere (Driscoll 1987): the tenure of land does not in itself confer permanent rank or social position. Within any society position and status are the result of continual negotiations and interactions among its members, some of which focus on control of land. It frequently transpires that specific social transactions become institutionalised and assume an added importance beyond the immediate value of the goods or services or words exchanged. Such transactions come to symbolise the relationship itself. It is these sorts of transactions which enter into the historical record because of their implicit meanings of fealty and loyalty, or, when they were violated, of treachery. At first sight, it may seem that the rendering of food or the performance of military service are too 'practical' or too 'functional' to carry meaning beyond the self-evident. However, as Jaques Le Goff has shown us (1980), in the early middle ages it was from the repertoire of the common-place and the routine that acts of particular symbolic significance emerged, and part of their efficacy comes precisely from their simple fundamental origins.

In medieval Scotland we may identify significant social transactions in several areas. There are acts performed by dependants for their superiors and a reciprocal set of acts performed by the superiors. These acts may involve either the exchange of material goods or of services. As the law tracts from Ireland and Anglo-Saxon England make plain, the acts and the goods appropriate to a specific relationship were sharply defined and were not interchangeable.

The main material obligations of dependent participants in the social contract are the provision for their superiors of *cain* (agricultural products) and *conveth* (hospitality). Barrow was not the first to identify the similarities between early Scottish institutions and those found in Northumbria and Ireland (1973), but his reading of them is important because it appears to take the traditional Scottish obligations of food render and labour services back into the Pictish era. It should be noted that he is cautious in attributing specific developments to the Pictish period, but it is impossible to conclude that he does not believe in a strong Pictish influence in these developments.

Social relations and settlement organisation

That a connection between social relations and settlement organisation existed cannot be questioned; what is at issue are the details of the relationship. One of the underlying assumptions I have followed is that the imposition of spatial order on the landscape is a dimension of social reproduction, that is a way of maintaining and regenerating social practices. Further the principal relationships — whether kin-based or client-based — involved undertaking reciprocal obligations, many of which focused ultimately on aspects of agricultural production. The foremost forces shaping the settlement systems were, then, of an agricultural nature. We must, therefore, expect to find within the settlement patterns, systems designed to control and maintain these fundamental relations of production. Given our relative ignorance of the details of early medieval agriculture, this must be regarded as a priority area for research.

Certainly the most common figure in the landscape was the least prominent historically or archaeologically. It was the person whose labour contributed the most to the production of food and raw materials, and who may be described as the unfree 'dependant' of a lord. There is no way of telling how large a proportion of the population such individuals constituted, nor of assessing what degree of economic and social freedom they enjoyed. However, we may suppose that they constituted a substantial majority, and that throughout our period their numbers were increasing as population grew and the middle strata of society shrunk with the growth of the dynastic magnates. Whether they were tied to the land, in the sense that serfs were, is a moot point since the identification of the kindred with particular tracts of land, and the lack of a land market, will have enforced residential stability. There are, however, signs from elsewhere in Britain that, in certain circumstances, people could be bound to the land as in seventh-century Wessex (Charles-Edwards 1976, 186) and similarly in early medieval Wales (Davies 1982, 68). Such a situation may have prevailed in Pictland, and certainly by the twelfth century we hear of men who were bound to the land in Fife (Barrow 1981a, 17).

To ask where these people lived starts to return us to the archaeology, because it requires that we look at the ground. Presumably they lived upon the estates of the nobility or on something akin to later townlands, which were operated by the free commoners. The distinction between an estate and a townland arrangement is probably not one we should press too far in our period, since any tenants were likely to be of the same kin-group or lineage as their immediate lord (Driscoll 1987, 50–144). Nonetheless the joint tenancy farm may provide a good analogy to the ways in which tenurial obligations were satisfied at the farm level (Whittington 1973, 542). It may also provide a useful guide to earlier settlement location, much as the Irish and Anglo-Saxon literature show how tenurial arrangements were translated into living arrangements, whether extended families occupied a single farmstead or were scattered around the countryside. But in the Celtic world, with few exceptions, people did not cluster in large villages. It may be that they lived in the small houses which are adjacent to the complexes of enclosures and field systems observed in the aerial photographic record, or in the apparently isolated small unenclosed settlements possibly considered as part of the estate's appurtenances (see below the example of Easter Kinnear).

It was the social relations within the estate or township which determined the organisation of the fields. Although it is possible in specific instances (as in the example of Aberargie below) to argue that strip cultivation respects or overlies a settlement site, we are not in a position yet to generalise from aerial photographs about the origins and development of open fields.

Place-names and settlement

Place-names are the most enigmatic type of documentary evidence to handle, particularly when we move away from the security of identifying specific places (cf Alcock 1981) to assess the significance of the generic place-name elements. For the Picts the obvious place-names are those beginning with the element pit- (Wainwright 1955). The prefix pit-, which derives from the word *pett* probably meaning 'portion or piece of land', survives in over 300 places in north-east and, more rarely, northern Scotland. It has received the most attention because it is 'practically the only place-name element which can be said to be exclusively limited to the Picts' (Nicolaisen 1976, 151). Although there are at least six other P-Celtic place-names found in Pictland, none is as well studied as the pit- places.

Some of the most informative work has been done by geographers (Whittington and Soulsby 1968; Whittington 1975), who have closely analysed the physical geography of *pett* places. Their findings show a very strong preference for well sheltered, well drained locations with good loamy soils. Coastal situations and locations above 183 m OD are generally avoided by *pett* names. This has been interpreted by the geographers as avoidance of these settings by the Picts. In short 'the distribution of the pit-sites appears to agree with the distribution of the best soils in eastern Scotland; those which are best suited to agriculture' (Whittington 1975, 102). Probably, what this means is that the *pett* places were the most favoured and thus tended to survive intact, maintaining their name as well as their geographic identity.

The survival or continuity of land was one of the major themes considered by Barrow in his 1985 Rhind lectures. The implications of Barrow's work on place-names is that the linguistic survival in Strathearn of P-Celtic names like Comrie, Moncreiffe, Pitkeathy, Aberdalgie, Pitversie, Abernethy, Pitcuran and Carpow serve as an index of Pictish settlement and social continuity. Thus, while he recognises that the introduction of the Q-Celtic stratum of place-names between *c.* AD 800 and 1100 effected a quick and deep transformation in place-names, he places rather more weight on the P-Celtic place-names as a sign of stability. His avoidance of the traditional date of 843 suggests that he regards the process of Gaelicisation as a subtler, more complex process than the migrationists allow. In effect Barrow is echoing (without the migrationist slant) Jackson's recent view that the *pett* place-names:

> were formed as we have them sometime after the Gaelic settlements in Pictland in the middle of the ninth century, whether the original Pictish second elements of old *pett*- names were translated into Gaelic, or were replaced by Gaelic name-elements, or whether they were wholly new foundations of Gaelic date. In this last case, the Gaels must have adopted the unquestionably Pictish *pett* as a name forming element for their own new place-names, no doubt because it expressed some characteristic feature of Pictish land tenure foreign to them but adopted by them when they settled among the Picts. (Jackson 1980, 174)

It is clear from this that Jackson is arguing that the usage of the term implies an acceptance of the pre-existing system and a continuity of land-use organisation.

Petts *and thanages*

The people with this authority over the use of the land, the peers of the English ceorls and Irish free commoners, should probably be identified with the holders of the *pett-* units. If the analogy between the ceorl and the hide can be extended to Pictland, then it seems that the Pictish equivalent to Bede's 'land of one family' was the *davoch*. There is certainly an intimate relationship between the the terms *davoch* and *pett*, which Barrow (1962, 133; 1973, 59ff; 1981a, 15ff) and Jackson (1972, 118) have both commented upon. While both words are directly concerned with the division of the landscape, *davoch* is ultimately a measure of productive capacity, while *pett* is concerned with the organisation and location of settlement. The terms cannot be reconciled entirely; they do not correspond exactly. Nor should we expect them to. The term *pett* probably referred to holdings which varied considerably in extent and fertility, as we know from the Domesday Book was the case with the soke in Yorkshire (Kappelle 1979, 76). Barrow has drawn attention to instances where a *davoch* bears a pit- place-name and he takes this as an indication that the typical *pett* consisted of a *davoch*. He extends the argument and identifies the *davoch* and the *pett* as the holdings appropriate to a free commoner, bearing roughly the same social status and responsibilities as the English ceorl (Barrow 1973, 59ff; 1981a, 15). Given that the *davoch* represented an area of something of the order of 400 Scotch acres (Whittington 1973, 543) we can well imagine that a good number of tenants would have been required to operate a *pett*. For this reason the proprietor of a *pett* should probably be considered as a minor lord, at least with respect to his own estate and tenants. This would help to distance the freeman from phrases like 'prosperous farmer' or 'free peasant' which are frequently employed and which obscure the power over land and tenants he must have had, and generally make him seem less important and privileged than he was.

   The word *pett*, meaning 'portion', clearly implies it was part of a larger entity. This meaning may derive from the *pett* being a portion of the kindred's territory or part of a multiple-estate made up of discrete elements, or it may derive from being part of a larger administrative entity like the thanage. These three alternatives need not conflict and the most economical explanation would be to draw them together. When the thanage appears in the historical record in the twelfth century it is a large multiple-estate, which was managed for the the king by a member of the nobility. Thanages, or shires as they were known south of the Forth, were important instruments of royal administration. They were the units for the collection of royal cain and conveth, for the organisation of military service and for the administration of justice — in all these respects they closely resemble the Northumbrian shire. The thanage also seems to bear a structural resemblance to the 'multiple estate' as described by Glanville Jones (1976; 1984). The thanes who ruled the Scottish shires resemble their English counterparts in being royal officers who, in exchange for an estate (presumably a *pett* within the shire), carried out administrative duties varying from tribute collection and military organisation to maintaining order. However, despite the Northumbrian resemblances and the English terminology, Barrow argues that these institutions — thane and shire/thanage — are English in name only and that like *davoch* they grow out of pre-Norman roots and ultimately Pictish seeds. The strongest argument supporting a Pictish origin is that based on distribution (see Muir 1975). This is, of course, Skene's argument for a Pictish origin for the thanages (1890, 242). In *Celtic Scotland* he observed that there are no thanages in the west, so it seems unlikely, to say the least, that they were introduced by the Scots. The thanages closely resemble Northumbrian shires, but the Anglo-Saxons cannot be directly responsible for their common occurrence north of the river Forth and especially north of the Tay. Therefore, they must have grown out of local political circumstances in Pictland, but not unique circumstances since similar institutions grew up in England and Wales. The shared terminology with the English, introduced perhaps in the tenth century (Barrow 1973, 64), only serves to underscore the close cultural links extending along the north-east coast of Britain.

The ideal thanage: settlement model for the state

The thanage is the earliest recognisable organisational unit below the level of kingdom that we can now detect. It gave a physical reality to the notion of a social hierarchy based upon tribute payments, and as such provided the framework for the smaller constituents of the settlement pattern. It also provided the means by which these small units became effective elements in a larger institutional structure of the state. It is, therefore, appropriate that we propose a model of the settlement system which takes account of the preceding discussion on social relations, performs the tasks needed by a state, and accommodates the archaeological evidence. Indeed, it is hoped that the model will help to frame further questions for the field archaeologist.

The ideal thanage

There can be little question that the organisation of a thanage was hierarchical and that at its heart, or rather at its head, was the principal residence of the thane or other authority. Conventionally, this principal residence is called a *caput*. We do not, of course, know that this Latin term was used of these places in early medieval Scotland, but it will be convenient for us to use it. Although it was not necessarily a fortified stronghold, in Strathearn the best examples of a *caput*, Dundurn and Clatchard Craig, were fortified and can be recognised by the combined evidence for agricultural, military and manufacturing activities in conjunction with a noble residence. Similarly, it seems likely that several of the unexcavated forts served as the head and heart of the thanage. Indeed, the terminology can be confusing. The place-name element derived from *cather* (fort) has been used in contexts which can refer to both a secular stronghold and to a monastery (see Barrow 1973, 65–6; Jackson 1972; Driscoll 1987, 317–19). This ambiguity underscores the suggestion that the *caput* of a thanage had more in common with the great house of a large estate than with a fortified garrison, despite being frequently ensconced in ramparts.

The institution of the shire can be said to have worked on two levels. It served to define or order a territory within which were found men who owed services and tribute to a lord. At this level the shire served to integrate the interests of the primary producers and the local aristocracy (and here I am including the church as an element of the aristocracy). At another level the thanage served to articulate the interests of the local aristocracy with those of a regional or national lord. It is at this second level that the thanage has exercised the attention of most historians, and not surprisingly, since there exists ample justification for studying the thanage in terms of a proto-feudal institution. The formalisation of the social and political relations described by thanage certainly was a key step in the making of the Scottish kingdom. However, if we are interested in understanding the order behind the random scatter of settlements within the thanage, it is at the base level of local economic and social relations that the thanage must occupy our attention.

If the great residence or monastery was the head of the thanage, its body consisted of fields and farmsteads. Not only were there differences in land usage, but direct control of the land seems to have been distributed amongst various farms. The thanage was evidently made up of (or subdivided into) portions which, among other things, allowed individual farmers to pay closer attention to the farming. The portions are, of course, the *pett* places which have given us the settlements bearing pit- place-names. One conclusion to be drawn from the distribution of *pett* place-names is that this particular system of land division and management was a pervasive feature of Pictish culture, so much so that linguists should seriously consider Maxwell's suggestion that the name Pict derives from their characteristic land division the *pett* (1987, 32–3).

Whittington's arguments regarding the possible antiquity of joint tenancy farms are interesting in the context of modelling the workings of the *pett* (1973, 542). He has worked the model out in considerable detail on the Pitkellony estate in the ancient Muthill thanage in Strathearn (Whittington 1973, 552–67). His evidence is necessarily late, post-medieval in fact. But it is the clearest model of the spatial arrangement of infield, outfield and moorland, which should be applicable to the earliest two-field system and may be appropriate for our period. Whittington, however, makes no claims for the antiquity of this infield – outfield model and quotes Barrow to the effect that 'there is no indication in early documents of any system of infield and outfield cultivation, although the texts are not incompatible with the existence of such a system' (1962, 127). Essentially, Whittington's model is a concentric one, with the settlement located within or at the edge of the infield core, the intensively cultivated land. This is surrounded by out-field, portions of which were cultivated in rotation, and is in turn surrounded by permanent pasture and moorland. As a starting place for appreciating a *pett* on the ground and for visualising its internal arrangements, this work on the Pitkellony estate is invaluable. Clearly, as our knowledge of medieval agriculture grows, this model will prove a useful point of comparison.

In the aerial archaeological record the most likely settlement features which might be taken to mark the principal farmstead of the *pett* are the simple ditched enclosures of which Aberargie (Plate 5.1), with its associated strip fields, and Dalpatrick (Plate 5.2), with its possible timber hall, are reminiscent of the fortified thanage *caput*. It seems clear enough that the entire population of a *pett* did not live in a nucleated settlement about the principal farmstead. It seems most likely that they inhabited small clusters of houses which might be an early fermtoun. Perhaps the best example of this is the recently excavated settlement at Easter Kinnear, Fife (Plate 5.3) (DES 1989; 1990). But even the dense cropmarks at Easter Kinnear hardly merit the term hamlet when one allows for a degree of settlement shift and rebuilding.

We can, therefore, cautiously suggest that a *pett* consisted of scattered dwellings, some of which may have been built on so slight a scale as to be scarcely visible archaeologically, as would be the case for Easter Kinnear if it were not on such a freely draining soil. It probably included at least one relatively substantial or elaborate farmstead. Given that constructing an enclosure ditch or wall is one of the few architectural techniques for aggrandising a settlement, it seems reasonable to propose that the principal settlement of a *pett* was a ringfort or in exceptional cases a more complex enclosure. However, given that ditches are about the only architectural techniques for elaborating a site which we can observe without excavation, and then only in places favourable to the production of cropmarks, this should be accepted with caution. I am proposing a model of the *pett* that is a miniature of the shire, or rather the reverse, that the shire took its form from a pre-existing structure found in the *pett*. In fact, since even places like Dundurn yield evidence of farming activities, we could consider that the thanage *caput* was a particularly successful *pett* that managed to achieve a sort of overlordship over adjacent *petts*. These were then rationalised into shires and parishes at a later date.

We are, if anything, less capable of describing those things which are thought of conventionally as composing the landscape. For instance we are unable to say what proportion of the fields was arable and what was pasture, or how much of the valley was given over to woodland. We might imagine that woods, copses and orchards, as well as stretches of permanent pasture, acted as boundaries between *petts*, but there is no

Pl. 5.1   Aerial photograph of enclosed settlement and associated strip fields at Aberargie, near Abernethy (RCAHMS)

Pl. 5.2   Aerial photograph of an enclosure with everted entrance and possible timber hall at Dalpatrick, near Strageath (RCAHMS)

supporting evidence beyond the presence of timber, wattle and fruit on a particular site, like Dundurn (Alcock *et al.* 1989). Similarly, it is likely that some sort of infield — outfield system was used with the intensively cultivated land closer to the settlements, surrounded by pasture, woods and, beyond those, common grazing. But, aside from the early documentary notices of common grazing land, the evidence is late. For what it is worth, Whittington's infield — outfield model indicates that the usual arrangement was one portion of infield to three of outfield, but since only a quarter of the outfield was likely to be under cultivation, in effect half the arable was under crop at any one time (1973, 544 and 551). In addition to this there was considerable permanent pasture. We can go on to suggest that at higher elevations a greater portion of the land was given over to pasture. But, as with the structure of the *pett*, most of this is informed speculation. The only

Pl. 5.3 Excavation photograph of some of the scooped houses in the unenclosed settlement at Hawkhill, Easter Kinnear, which were revealed by aerial photography (RCAHMS)

comfort to take from this is that the situation will certainly improve as more palaeobotanical work is done on sites of later prehistoric to medieval date.

The third principal component of a thanage is more difficult to establish since it was not directly related to agriculture or settlement, but seems to have been a focal point for shire administration as well as being significant in the formation of the identity of the shire. I am referring to those ceremonial centres which served as meeting places, the place to hold popular courts and the sites of quasi-religious inagurations to high office. The prime example of this is, of course, Moot Hill at Scone. But there are good reasons to believe that, while this mound was pre-eminent, it was not unique. In fact, to judge from regional studies, it seems that court hills or meeting places were a common feature of the political landscape of early medieval Britain and Ireland, suggesting that every autonomous political entity possessed one. As the political scene gradually came to be dominated by fewer and fewer kingdoms, so it seems that the meeting places of particular dynasties came to prominence, like Scone, while the majority slipped into obscurity. The majority of lesser meeting places must have continued to function at a local level for some time, since they do manage to survive in oral tradition late enough to be recorded. For instance, Watson quotes the *Old Statistical Account* regarding the survival of one such meeting place: 'there is a large artificial mound of earth, where in ancient times courts were held; near to which the Duke (or rather Mormaer) of Lennox had a place of residence' (1926, 223). The residence survives as Catter (from *cathir*) near Kilmarnock, and Watson identified the meeting place with a reference in a charter to *forcas nostras de Cather*, 'our gallows of Cather' (1926, 223). This use of a meeting place as the later location of a gallows appears to be a widespread practice.

There has been no systematic survey of the evidence for these sites in Scotland, but Barrow has looked in detail at one of the place-name elements which he believes indicates the location of popular courts in early medieval Scotland (1981b). The place-name generally survives in modern usage as cuthill or a variation of this; its suggested etymology is from Gaelic *Comhdhail* (Old Irish, *comdal*), 'assembly', 'meeting', 'conference', 'tryst' (Barrow 1981b, 3). The distribution of these places complements that of the thanage, and indeed of pit- place-names, although it is less common than either. Barrow's observations about the geographical situation of these sites is of particular interest:

> That the meeting-places indicated — if, indeed, they are indicated — by the cuthill element had an antiquity comparable with the hundred, small shire and wapentake meeting places in England is strongly suggested by their geographical association, in an appreciable number of cases, with major pre-historic monuments, especially cairns, stone-circles and standing stones. Moreover, in the case of [seven examples given] the cuthill name is associated with the holding of courts and with punishment. (Barrow 1981b, 10)

There are no cuthill names in Strathearn, but this association of meeting places with prehistoric monuments is of some significance for any attempts to ascertain the significance of ancient monuments in Early Historic times. That they were actively used is hinted at by the presence of Christian graves in the North Mains of Strathallan henge monument and is implied by the intermingling of square barrows with prehistoric monuments at Forteviot. We might also cite the significant cropmark complex composed of prehistoric monuments at Blairhall near Scone. Elsewhere in Scotland the survey of Mid-Argyll by Campbell and Sandeman revealed a dozen cases which could be supported by references of varying degrees of antiquity and credibility (1962, 89–91).

This scatter of examples forms a backdrop for the arguments that Dunadd was one of the major meeting places in Dal Riada which saw royal inaugurations (Thomas 1879). The close physical association between the royal residence and such meeting places is important, but we should perhaps play down the royal aspect in favour of noting their ubiquity and local importance. Although it seems that prehistoric burial mounds were on occasion used as meeting places, they were clearly purpose-built at Catter and Clougher, Co. Tyrone (Warner 1988), and also, it would seem, by the Anglo-Saxons (Adkins and Petchley 1984). In this context, it is perhaps worth questioning the Ordnance Survey field officers' conclusions that the Moot Hill at Scone was a natural and not an artificial mound (OS record card).

In our study area, there is a conjunction between the presence of prehistoric ritual monuments, royal residences and major meeting places in two locations. Whether this should be taken as a general pattern is too soon to say, but it may prove a useful rule of thumb, since otherwise these meeting mounds would be impossible to distinguish from a burial mound without excavation. That they formed a key element of the thanage seems plain enough: the administrative duties of the lord of the shire will have demanded such a facility.

To sum up, the model thanage included: a *caput*, possibly fortified, a number of *pett* elements, and a meeting place or ceremonial centre. With this hypothetical framework in mind, we can now examine the archaeology of specific thanages in Strathearn.

The archaeology of thanages

It will be clear from the preceding discussions that the most influential recent study of the pre-feudal shires and thanes of Scotland is the long essay published by Barrow in 1973. In that essay he had frequent occasion to discuss places in Strathearn, because he made heavy use of the charters compiled in the *Inchaffray Liber* and the *Lindores Chartulary*. A notable feature of that paper was the presentation of reconstructions of 'conjectural shires', three of which are in Strathearn. These maps appear to have been intended primarily to illustrate the extent and composition of a pre-feudal thanage. Without knowing how they were compiled — Barrow does not describe his methodology — it is difficult to assess the exact historical intentions behind the maps. It looks as though Barrow has culled the place-names from the charters and other more recent sources and placed them within the modern parish boundaries with little or no modification. It is important to note that Barrow makes no claims for the historical precision of the maps and, indeed, only refers to them in passing. Nor does he use this geographical information to construct any specific arguments about the nature of the thanage. The maps provide illustrative support for the verbal argument. Nonetheless one is bound to feel that Barrow would not have bothered presenting the maps if he did not think them a valid representation of a pre-feudal shire.

A minority of the places included on the maps has contemporary medieval references, but the remainder, we must assume, have been included for good linguistic reasons. Likewise we must accept the implicit assumptions that the modern parish boundaries are in reasonable agreement with the charter evidence. Given that parishes in Scotland began to adopt their current shape by the twelfth century at the latest, this seems acceptable. There is a further assumption that, in the case of the old unchanged parishes, like Muthill, the thanage boundaries coincided. Indeed, elsewhere Barrow has pointed to the continued existence of Clackmannan and Kinross as evidence of the resilience and longevity of the thanage as an administrative unit (1981a, 16–17). For these reasons I have followed this method in producing maps to illustrate the thanages discussed below.

In my thesis (Driscoll 1987) I was able to consider seven thanages, the three intensively studied by Barrow — Abernethy, Muthill (Cather Mothel) and Catherlauenach — as well as the others in Strathearn at Forteviot, Dunning and Strowan, and across the Tay at Scone. Here space requires that we focus on three: Abernethy, Dunning, and Forteviot.

Abernethy

The archaeological elements of Abernethy (Fig.5.3) are well known; the remarkable round tower of tenth-century date with the symbol stone attached to it. The presence of several other fragments of Early Christian sculpture from the village is all that would be expected of an impor-tant monastery. The survival of one of its probable boundary crosses at Mugdrum is remarkable. In addition to these physical remains, relatively early references to the territorial extent of Abernethy survive (Anderson 1980, 95), but these are vague and, in any case, are much more restricted than Barrow's conjectural shire. The *caput* of Abernethy must have been the religious house for which there is so much archaeological and historical evidence, but if Barrow's reconstruction is correct Clatchard Craig also fell within the shire.

There is good reason to believe that the two sites were occupied contemporaneously, although Abernethy certainly lasted longer. It may be that the religious house gradually made the fort redundant, or it may be that the fort survived through to the end of our period; the dating evidence is inconclusive on this point. However that may be, it is certainly the case that

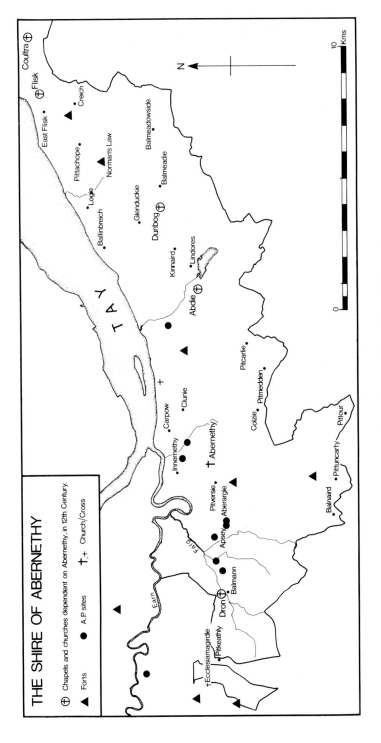

Fig. 5.3   Conjectural map of the shire of Abernethy

the fort did not survive long enough to pass on its Pictish name; Clatchard Craig is completely Gaelic (Close-Brooks 1986). The map of the shire effectively illustrates the density of P-Celtic place-names including the eight *pett* names in the immediate neighbourhood of Abernethy itself. In several cases it is possible to point to cropmarks which one might wish to identify with the settlement bearing the ancient name: Aberargie, (see Plate 5.1) Balgonie, Carpow and Clunie. It is also worth pointing out the limitations of aerial reconnaissance with respect to the place-name distribution.

There are no obvious places which might be regarded as the shire meeting place other than the church itself, which did host one of the more dramatic meetings in Scottish history, the one between William of Normandy and Malcolm Canmore in 1072 (Kappelle 1979, 139). At the moment no conspicuous clusters of prehistoric ritual monuments are known in the shire.

Forteviot

The royal associations with the village of Forteviot (Fig.5.4) are well known, as is the common lingistic root it shares with the Pictish kingdom of Fortriu (approximately the same as modern Strathearn). It is, therefore, not surprising that within the parish we can locate with confidence all the elements of the shire, although place-name evidence for the productive sites is lacking. The historical evidence (Alcock 1982) suggests that the palace site, the *caput*, was in or near the modern village. There is little place-name evidence indicative of the division of the shire into *pett* places, but the best candidates on archaeological grounds are Jackshairs fort near the eastern boundary of the parish and the cropmark site of Green of Invermay, upstream from the village.

The ceremonial aspects of the thanage are bound to be complex because of the royal attribution (Skene 1857). The Forteviot cropmarks (Plate 5.4), with their striking mix of early prehistoric ritual monuments and apparently Pictish burials in square barrows, have been sufficiently discussed by Alcock (1982). Alcock also considered at length the significance of the carved monolithic arch, which must be regarded as one of the most important of the early Christian monuments of Scotland in purely archi-tectural terms. It implies in the strongest sense the presence of a royal chapel as part of the palace complex, if not a small monastery. It is worth drawing attention to the place-name Gallows Knowe, which lies upsteam and west of the May Water from the main concentration of cropmarks. Here, too, are abundant cropmarks, mostly of an agricul-tural or domestic nature. Elsewhere the gallows place-name element has been associated with a court site or meeting place. It is interesting that it lies on the opposite side of the prehistoric ritual monuments from the village itself with its presumed royal palace. It gives the impres-sion that vast areas of the parish possessed a symbolic significance, in a way that is familiar from Irish royal sites such as Rathcrogan, Co. Roscommon.

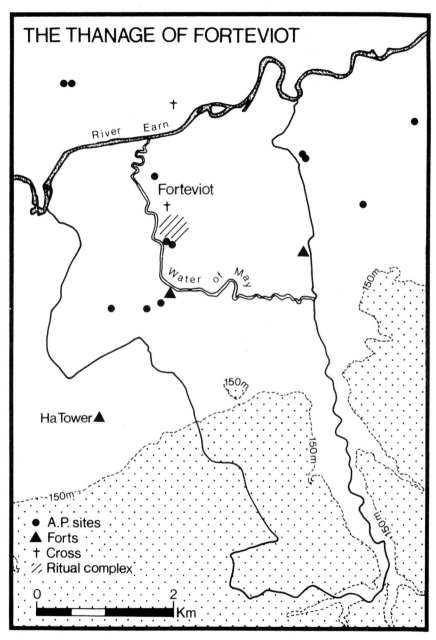

Fig. 5.4 Conjectural map of the thanage of Forteviot

Dunning

Dunning (Fig.5.5) emerges as the prime example in Strathearn of how aerial archaeology can enhance our understanding of the early historic landscape. In addition to helping to locate the *caput* of the shire on Dunknock, aerial photography revealed other elements of the thanage. This fort (Plate 5.5) stands on the slight knoll to the south of the modern village. The village itself focuses on St Serf's church which, in addition to the important dedication to an early saint, possesses a tower which belongs to the earliest group of church towers surviving in Scotland. Fernie dates them to the eleventh century (1986). An additional hint as to the significance of Dunning is that nearby Duncrub has been identified with *dorsum crup*, the site of a tenth-century battle between rivals for the Scottish kingship (Watson 1926, 56).

Pl. 5.4   Aerial photograph of prehistoric ritual monuments at Forteviot with the village and the supposed site of the palace in the background (RCAHMS)

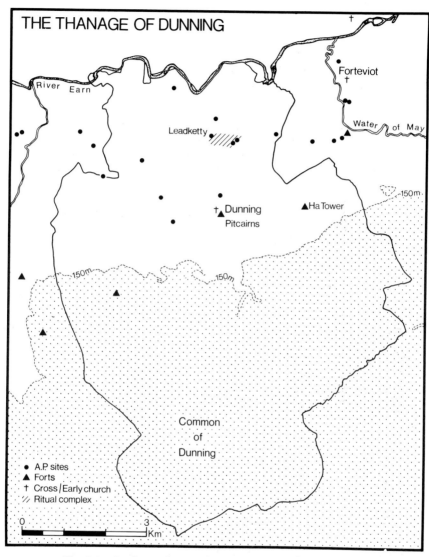

Fig. 5.5   Conjectural map of the thanage of Dunning

As at Abernethy, the *pett* places extend southwards into the hills. There are, on the other hand, only a few obvious P-Celtic names in the alluvial areas north of the village towards the river. This scant place-name evidence is, however, bolstered by the scatter of settlement sites in the aerial record. The one apparent correspondence of cropmark features and a P-Celtic place-name provides a unique insight into one aspect of past land use. At the Haugh of Aberuthven, the funnel shaped ditches suggest that the riverside meadows were used as pasture. It is a finding which should not surprise us since these same fields are liable to flooding even today. Additionally, aerial photography has revealed at Leadketty (NO 021159) a complex of Neolithic monuments, including a Meldon Bridge/Forteviot type of pit-defined enclosure, adjacent to a possible causewayed camp and henge. Such a concentration of prehistoric ritual features could point to the general location of the shire meeting place. Obviously these suppositions about the location of the *caput*, farms and ceremonial centre all require further

Pl. 5.5   Aerial photograph of the hillfort on Dunknock looking towards St. Serf's church in the centre of Dunning (RCAHMS)

investigations of an archaeological nature, since they are unsupported by any specific documentary evidence.

The model shire

In this summary I will try to draw together the particular observations made on the archaeology and history of Strathearn and add more general observations about the social relations encapsulated in the pre-feudal Scottish thanage. By so doing I hope to make explicit the social importance of specific archaeological features.

We begin with the land itself. The thanage typically stretched across several ecological zones, from riverside meadows to hilltop moorland, and included a fair proportion of good agricultural land. The main business of its inhabitants was farming crops and raising livestock. This business was carried out in farmsteads that were disbursed across the shire.

Three broad social levels of settlement may be distinguished in the archaeological record. In population terms the most common were certainly the dependent commoners; archaeologically their presence is hardest to detect. We may attribute to them the small unenclosed settlements. In many cases it is likely that their houses were too flimsy to detect archaeologically, although their handiwork in the laying out of fields and the construction of the lord's ramparts is evident enough.

The free farmer, to whom the dependent farmers probably owed food rent and services, occupied major farmsteads, some of which were termed *pett*. Archaeologically these are likely to include some of the smaller enclosed farmsteads which survive predominantly as cropmarks. The occupants of these more elaborate structures may have included minor members of the nobility or at least those who served as the heads of their kingroup.

The *caput* of the shire could assume several forms. The most common was the small hill-fort with several closely spaced ramparts. Other possibilities included religious houses and, rarely, unenclosed royal palaces. The principal authority of the shire will have assumed the type of residence appropriate to his social affiliation. Not surprisingly this last level is the best represented in the archaeological and documentary record.

The non-residential infrastructure of the thanage included, of course, fields and corrals, fences and walls, orchards and woods, but of their precise form we can say little. The most important and probably the least understood non-residential component of the thanage was the meeting place, the place where court could be held, and where the local lord may have been inaugurated. The meeting place seems to have been marked by a small mound and also seems to have been preferentially located near areas of ancient ritual activity, places where prehistoric monuments tend to cluster. This hints at a pre-Christian religious aspect of the meeting place as an important centre for focusing local group identity.

Historical implications of the model

Throughout this paper I have stressed that it is concerned with the historical development of the Scottish state as revealed primarily in Strathearn. The results presented here are hardly conclusive, yet even at this premature stage it is worth suggesting how some of the observations can be used to further research into the development of the Scottish state.

The origins of the pre-feudal shire can be seen more clearly to have Pictish roots, although it is not yet clear how coherent our putative Pictish shires were. A coordinated effort to investigate the evidence of a well-documented shire by both archaeologists and historians would probably be fruitful in helping to identify origins. The archaeological identification of a social institution like a shire presents a real challenge, but it is possible if attention is focused on agricultural evidence and indications of the local circulation of high quality craft goods, such as might be produced under the lord's patronage.

The identification of origins is of little value if it is divorced from attempts to understand the social processes involved in the development of the thanage. These focus on the subordination of kinship to clientage, or family to fealty. There can be little doubt that important social changes occurred as the political arena in which the lords of Strathearn found themselves evolved — from Fortriu, to southern Pictland, to Scotland. I have described elsewhere the construction of administrative networks with increasing disregard for kinship relations as characteristic of the development of states (Driscoll 1988b). In that paper I sought to link that social development with the Pictish symbol stones; here I have drawn attention to the shire and its attendant features. I believe the two phenomena to be related, but can only support the suggestion with the observation that both features developed in east central Scotland at roughly the same time and both would fit nicely with certain ideas about the origin of the thanage. These ideas emerged from this work, but are somewhat hypothetical and should probably be regarded as a 'working model', subject to revision and refinement.

We can start from the supposition that the thanage represents the vestiges of an archaic tribal entity comparable to the Irish *tuath* and that, like the Irish tribes, these Pictish tribes competed amongst one another for overlordship. By the time the historical curtain opens on Pictland, Strathearn is the polity of Fortriu, which we may suppose was made up of numerous tribes, a few of which were sufficiently strong to contest the kingship. Political entities the size of Fortriu are probably at the upper size limit of what may be ruled by political networks based exclusively on kinship; any bigger and new administrative techniques are required. By the time the kings of Fortriu begin participating in the overkingship of Southern Pictland, they seem to have developed some of the administrative rudiments of statehood. I have mentioned the evidence for this — the existence of royal officials and the close interrelationship between the ecclesiastical officials and royalty — at various points. One strength of this scenario is that the origins of the administrative structure of thanages need not be seen as a 'primitive' model of Mediterranean state bureaucracy. Rather, there is every indication that it was modelled on the relations of clientship which were, in turn, the outgrowth of kin dominated political structures.

I began this paper by suggesting that archaeology had a role to play in examining the origins of the Scottish medieval state. In the course of it I hope I have shown that archaeologists are in a position to participate actively in these debates which are so fundamental to Scottish History. I have endeavoured to show how archaeologists can engage in discussions of issues like the formation of the Scottish identity not only from the perspective of the texts, but through a broader examination, involving archaeology, of the construction and maintenance of the social forms which developed into the medieval state.

Bibliography

Adkins, R. A. and Petchley, M. R. 1984 Secklow Hundred mound and other meeting place mounds in England, *Archaeol. J.* 141, 243–51.

Alcock, L. 1981 Early Historic fortifications in Scotland, in Gilbert, G. (ed) *Hill-fort studies*, Leicester, 150–81.

Alcock, L. 1982 Forteviot: a Pictish and Scottish royal church and palace, in Pearce, S. M. (ed) *The early church in western Britain and Ireland*, Oxford, 211–39.

Alcock, L. 1984 A survey of Pictish settlement archaeology, in Watson and Friell 1984, 7–42.

Alcock, L. 1988 Activities of potentates in Celtic Britain, AD 500–800, a positivist view, in Driscoll and Nieke 1988, 22–46.

Alcock, L. , Alcock, E. and Driscoll, S. T. 1989 Excavations at Dundurn, St. Fillans, Perthshire, 1976 and 1977, *Proc. Soc. Antiq. Scotland* 119, 189–226.

Anderson, A. O. 1922 *Early sources of Scottish history*, Edinburgh.

Anderson, M. O. 1980 *Kings and kingship in early Scotland*, (revised edn) Edinburgh.

Anderson, M. O. 1982 Dalriada and the creation of the kingdom of the Scots, in Whitelock, D. *et al.* (eds) *Ireland in Early Medieval Europe*, Cambridge, 106–32.

Barrow, G. W. S. 1962 Rural settlement in central and eastern Scotland, *Scottish Stud.* 6, 123–44.

Barrow, G. W. S. 1973 *The Kingdom of the Scots*, London.

Barrow, G. W. S. 1981a *Kingship and unity*, London.

Barrow, G. W. S. 1981b Popular courts in early medieval Scotland: some suggested place-name evidence, *Scottish Stud.* 25, 1–24.

Campbell, M. and Sandeman, M. 1962 Mid-Argyll: an archaeological survey, *Proc. Soc. Antiq. Scotland* 95 (1961-2), 1–125.

Charles-Edwards, T. 1976 The distinction between land and moveable wealth in Anglo-Saxon England, in Sawyer, P. (ed) *Medieval settlement: continuity and change*, London, 180–7.

Close-Brooks, J. 1986 Excavations at Clatchard Craig, Fife 1953–4 and 1959–60, *Proc. Soc. Antiq. Scotland* 116, 117–84.

Davies, W. 1982 *Early Medieval Wales*, Leicester.

Davies, W. 1984 Picts, Scots and Britons, in Smith, L. M. (ed) *The making of Britain: the Dark Ages*, London, 63–76.

DES *Discovery and excavation in Scotland*, Edinburgh.

Donaldson, G. 1953 Scottish bishops' sees before the reign of David I, *Proc. Soc. Antiq. Scotland* 87 (1952–53), 106–17.

Donaldson, G. 1985 *Scottish church history*, Edinburgh.

Driscoll, S. T. 1987 *The early Historic landscape of Strathearn: the archaeology of a Pictish kingdom*, unpublished PhD thesis, University of Glasgow.

Driscoll, S. T. 1988a The relation between history and archaeology: artifacts, documents and power, in Driscoll and Nieke 1988, 162–88.

Driscoll, S. T. 1988b Power and authority in Early Historic Scotland: Pictish symbol stones and other documents, in Gledhill, J. , Bender, B. and Larson, M. (eds) *State and society: the emergence and development of social hierarchy and political centralization*, London, 215–36.

Driscoll, S. T. and Nieke, M. R. (eds) 1988 *Power and politics in Early Medieval Britain and Ireland*, Edinburgh.

Duncan, A. A. M. 1975 *Scotland, the making of the kingdom*, Edinburgh.

Fernie, E. C. 1986 Early church architecture in Scotland, *Proc. Soc. Antiq. Scotland* 116, 393–412.

Goff, J. Le 1980 The symbolic ritual of vassalage, in *Time, work and the culture of the Middle Ages*, Goldhammer, A. (trans), Chicago, 237–87.

Hill, C. 1972 *The world turned upside down*, Harmondsworth.

Hughes, K. 1980 *Celtic Britain in the Early Middle Ages*, Dumville, D. (ed), Woodbridge.

Jackson, K. 1972 *The Gaelic notes in the Book of Deer*, Cambridge.

Jackson, K. 1980 The Pictish language, in F. T. Wainwright (ed) *The problem of the Picts*, (revised edn) Perth, 129–66 and 173–6.

Jones, G. R. J. 1976 Multiple estates and early settlement, in Sawyer, P. H. (ed) *Medieval settlement*, London, 15–40.

Jones, G. R. J. 1984 The multiple estate: a model for tracing the interrelationships of society, economy and habitat, in Biddick, K. (ed) *Archaeological approaches to Medieval Europe*, Kalamazoo, 9–42.

Kappelle, W. E. 1979 *The Norman conquest of the north*, Chapel Hill.

Macinnes, L. 1982 Pattern and purpose: the settlement evidence, in Harding, D. W. (ed) *Later prehistoric settlement in south-east Scotland*, Edinburgh, 57–74.

Macinnes, L. 1983 *Later prehistoric and Romano-British settlement north and south of the Forth: a comparative survey*, unpublished PhD thesis, University of Newcastle-upon-Tyne.

Maxwell, G. S. 1987 Settlement in southern Pictland — a new overview, in Small, A. (ed) *The Picts: a new look at old problems*, Dundee, 31–44.

Miller, M. 1979 The last century of Pictish succession, *Scottish Stud.* 23, 39–67.

Muir, P. 1975 Thanages, in MacNeill, P. and Nicholson, R. (eds) *An historical atlas of Scotland, c.400–c.1600*, St. Andrews, 27–8, 126.

Nicolaisen, W. F. H. 1976 *Scottish place-names*, London.

Skene, W. F. 1857 Observations on Forteviot, the site of the ancient capitol of Scotland, *Archaeol. Scotica* 4, 271–9.

Skene, W. F. 1890 *Celtic Scotland. Vol. III: land and people*, (2nd edn) Edinburgh.

Smyth, A. 1984 *War lords and holy men*, London.

Thomas, F. W. L. 1879 Dunadd Glassery, Argyllshire; the place of inauguration of the Dalriadic kings, *Proc. Soc. Antiq. Scotland* 13 (1878–79), 28–47.

Wainwright, F. T. 1955 The Picts and the problem, in Wainwright, F. T. (ed) *The problem of the Picts*, Edinburgh, 1–53.

Warner, R. W. 1988 The archaeology of Early Historic Irish kingship, in Driscoll and Nieke 1988, 47–68.

Watson, G. and Friell, G. J. P. 1984 (eds) *Pictish studies*, Oxford.

Watson, W. J. 1926 *A history of the Celtic place names of Scotland*, Edinburgh.

Whimster, R. 1989 *The emerging past, air photography and the buried landscape*, London.

Whittington, G. 1973 Field systems of Scotland, in Baker, A. R. H. and Butlin, R. A. (eds) *Studies of field systems in the British Isles*, Cambridge, 530–79.

Whittington, G. 1975 Place-names and the settlement patterns of Dark Age Scotland, *Proc. Soc. Antiq. Scotland* 106 (1974–75), 99–110.

Whittington, G. and Soulsby, J. A. 1968 A preliminary report on an investigation into pit place-names, *Scottish Geog. Mag.* 84, 117–25.

Acknowledgements

This paper derives from a Glasgow University PhD thesis (Driscoll 1987). Here I would like to extend a particular thanks to Leslie Alcock for his guidance as my supervisor. The focus of the study and its subject matter were largely identified for me by him. I am equally indebted to my colleagues who were engaged in archaeological research for creating such a stimulating environment for early medieval studies. Finally I would thank the University Court of Glasgow for the financial support I received while originally working on this study.

6

MEDIEVAL RURAL SETTLEMENT: THE INVISIBLE CENTURIES

Peter A. Yeoman

All that is solid melts into air. (Karl Marx)

In the twenty years which have passed since the publication of Fairhurst's first review (1971) of this subject, archaeologists have made only minor advances towards furthering our understanding of man's endeavours in the countryside during the twelfth to seventeenth centuries. Geographers and historians have provided most of the insights to date, but due to the restrictions of their material have failed to illuminate the lives of the farming population. Archaeologists are uniqely qualified to do just that.

The aim of this paper is to reintroduce the subject to a new generation of archaeologists, and also to provide an updated review of fieldwork and excavation results. This will be followed by a discussion of how the questions posed by other disciplines can be pursued and answered by archaeological research. The eastern heartlands of the medieval kingdom will form the core of this study. An outline review of the evidence from field survey in Caithness and Sutherland is already available (Mercer 1980), and the recent work of the Royal Commission in Perthshire promises to result in a far better understanding of the medieval settlement of the Highlands (RCAHMS 1990).

Accidents of survival and the comparative visibility of sites within the historic landscape have ensured that archaeologists have rarely pursued the unattractive and often invisible sites of medieval rural settlements. The paradoxical situation, whereby we understand far more about the Iron Age landscape than we do the medieval landscape, has previously been discussed (Whittington 1980, 40). The reflected glory of hill-forts and stone circles has blinded us to the more subtle but all-pervading traces of our more immediate ancestors. The popular perception of the medieval historic landscape is, therefore, restricted to isolated centres of trade, power and worship — burghs, castles, churches and abbeys; those sites which protrude through the visibility barrier, wholly divorced in our minds from the agrarian society in which the vast majority of the population, up to 80 per cent, lived and laboured to create the wealth upon which the occupants of the chief places depended.

A view has been expressed that the archaeology of this period is nothing more than a 'footnote to history'. Clearly the contribution made by English medieval archaeologists to achieving a broader understanding of medieval society reveals the ignorance at the base of this view. Widely held fallacies have grown-up; namely that the sites do not survive at all, and that where they do exist they can only represent the final development of farms on the eve of improvement in the eighteenth century. Searching the NMR database for all the classifications related to the medieval countryside produces a print-out weighing 5 lb — an enormous quantity of mainly unsynthesised data relating to rig and furrow and other cultivation remains, deserted settlements, shielings, head dykes, pillow mounds, hunting reserves, mills, mottes, ringworks, moated sites, churches and chapels.

All the major questions remain to be answered:-

- What regional, social, economic, and agrarian changes can be identified?
- Can frameworks be created to date field systems and the time of settlement desertion?
- Can desertion be linked to specific historic events, eg the Black Death, climatic change, change of landlord?
- Is there continuity in the settlement pattern from the later Iron Age?
- Did feudalism change farming practices and settlement?

Factors influencing settlement

Because of the general lack of excavation and survey it is impossible to state the specific factors which governed the creation and development of individual settlements in the various regions. Thanks to the research of historians and geographers, however, the general factors at work can be defined:-

1 *The introduction of military feudalism*: new lords improving the management of agricultural production, to pay their dues, to increase their wealth, and to marshall resources in times of strife. Celtic thanes would never have been able or inclined to support and sustain prolonged military campaigns.

2 *The introduction of a reformed Roman church and European monastic orders*: likely to act as a stimulus to increase production. Teinds (tithes) had to be paid to a progressively increasing number of parish churches, and the evidence from England would strongly suggest that the monasteries brought with them a number of agricultural improvements, notably new systems of integrated agricultural management. Moreover, monks may have been responsible for the introduction of the heavy mould-board plough coupled with a wheeled forecarriage which enabled

the cultivation of more land qualities (Parry 1976, 6). They were also reponsible for large-scale landscape works, as in the case of the Cistercians of Coupar Angus who supervised the draining of much of the Carse of Gowrie between 1170 and 1230 to create a large expanse of open fields on an English scale (Duncan 1975, 321). Nor did they stop there, for they also bought out neighbouring landowners establishing their own granges and fermtouns. This would have necessitated population displacement as the Cistercians did not rely on serfs and tenants, but farmed directly using lay-brothers.

3 *Market economy*: substantial surpluses were required to feed feudal lords and their followers, and to supply the newly created urban populations.

4 *Climatic change*: the above factors would have made their greatest impact during the mid twelfth to mid thirteenth centuries, during the latter part of a period of optimum climatic conditions, when the mean temperature was 0.5 degrees centigrade higher than now. This resulted in mild wet winters and warm dry summers (Morrison 1990). This was followed by the Little Ice Age which lasted well into the nineteenth century. Although conditions were not universally bad (Grove 1988, 407), the worst times were during the fourteenth and seventeenth centuries, when temperatures were 1–1.5 degrees centigrade worse than pre-1250 (Ian Morrison pers. comm.).

5 *Political influences*: the expansion of centralised royal power, for example into Moray and Galloway in the late twelfth century, is reflected in the distribution pattern of earthwork castles (Yeoman 1988, 128). The redistribution of landholding which followed may also have resulted in significant changes which should be detectable in the archaeological record of individual settlements.

Political acts would also have brought settlement expansion, for example, the decree of Alexander II in 1214, which ordered the peasantry to take substantially more land into cereal production. By the same token, warfare, for example during the long Wars of Independence, could have caused the temporary abandonment and destruction of farms.

6 *Population pressure*: the population of Scotland at the start of this period has been estimated at 250,000, and it has been suggested that this had doubled or even trebled by the late sixteenth century (Dodgshon 1980a, 47), although the accuracy of the former figure is difficult to gauge. So even taking into account regular occurrences of crop failure and plague, there was significant pressure on land especially during periods of rapid increase in the twelfth-thirteenth centuries and the sixteenth-seventeenth centuries (Dodgshon 1980a).

All these factors worked separately and in tandem to create a very dynamic settlement pattern prone to ebb and flow. A very important factor, and certainly the least predictable, is that of human behaviour; this alone should make us very wary of imposing any simple deterministic models when attempting interpretation.

Settlement form and distribution

The physical remains of medieval rural settlement, most commonly rig and furrow, are the most consistently ignored features of the historic landscape. Rig can be observed in many parts of Edinburgh, notably along with earlier cultivation remains around Arthur's Seat. Archaeologists and historians tend to ignore it, whereas geographers have subjected it to lengthy typological (Parry 1976) and functional analyses (Whittington 1973; Dodgshon 1980b), in each case failing to include the human dimension which would bring us closer to an understanding of the lives of the farmers whose existence was dependent on the rigs.

Wherever the rigs are, the settlement will not be far away. North of the Forth individual dispersed farming units called fermtouns existed, defined by Adams as 'a small community of four to eight families of joint tenants who farmed in runrig' (1967, 60). It is difficult to avoid presenting a stereotyped image of these hamlet-clusters, and indeed Whyte has warned against doing so by defining variations of the form, but with the limited amount of site-specific data available it is difficult not to oversimplify. Copious amounts have been written about this form of settlement and the factors which created and sustained it. Although at first glance these publications appear to offer much to the medieval archaeologist, on closer examination they tend to deal primarily with the seventeenth and eighteenth centuries when good documentary evidence first appears (Fairhurst 1971; Morrison 1980; Dodgshon 1980a and 1980b; Whyte undated). Conditions are likely to have been the same or at least similar to that of the preceding centuries, but by the same token much is likely to have changed. There is no reason to believe that, as culture and society developed in the burghs, it stagnated in the countryside.

A fermtoun consisted of a core settlement surrounded by its fields. The enclosed settlement comprised a number of farmhouses, likely to be of 'longhouse' type, with associated barns, byres, stores and pens. Unfree labourers would have lived in small cottages. The constantly cultivated infield rigs, each a strip-field, may have existed alongside hay meadows, depending on the altitude of the location. In some areas the infield may have been separated by a bank or dyke from outfield rigs and pasture, which occupied poorer quality, stonier, higher ground (see Barrow 1973, 264 for a clear definition of these and other related terms). The fermtoun may have an associated but remote area of shieling (upland summer grazing) lands, a practice first recorded in the late twelfth century (Barrow 1973, 276) but likely to have originated in prehistory.

The bounds of the lands of a fermtoun were defined at the time of the creation or confirmation of an estate to the landlord by the feudal superior. These were physically marked out by a combination of topographical and man-made features, now often difficult to trace having been subsequently obscured by reorganisation, or by modern forestry or ploughing. This formal definition meant that expansion, when required, may have been difficult to achieve. Service and amenity centres such as mills, workshops, smithies, churches and castles are found amongst the fermtouns, but did not necessarily act as foci for settlement.

Nucleation is observed south of the Forth where northern English village forms existed in suitable low-lying areas. The area between the Mounth and the Forth, containing large areas of good arable land, may have supported a mixture of settlement forms and agricultural practices. It has previously been noted that 'green village plans may underlie Fife burghs such as Crail' (Whyte undated, 23).

Excavated settlements

Though two reviews of the excavated evidence have already been published, this paper is the first for twenty years. Fairhurst's work (1971) discussed the usefulness of the documentary and cartographic sources of the seventeenth and eighteenth centuries, but dealt mainly with his own pioneering excavations on two highland fermtouns, known as 'clachans', at Rosal in Sutherland and Lix in Perthshire (Fairhurst 1967 and 1968). Both sites are first mentioned in medieval land grants, and although the final form of these settlements was dated by documentary and archaeological evidence to the eighteenth and nineteenth centuries, desertion was caused by the clearances. Extensive survey combined with limited excavation revealed a number of cruck-roofed long-houses with associated enclosures containing outbuildings, barns and hay-rick bases. The buildings were originally of turf on stone foundations. Prehistoric settlement traces were found in and around both sites, but no evidence of continuity through to the medieval period was found, though seeking this would be the aim of any excavator. It is worth noting that all the excavations discussed here were small scale.

Another well-preserved eighteenth-century milltoun complex with farm buildings and corn-drying kilns was investigated more recently at Polmaddy, New Galloway (Yates 1977). The question of the relevance of excavated evidence from eighteenth-century sites as an indicator of conditions in the preceding centuries remains open and unanswered.

Laing, in his review (1969), shone some light on the problems of the re-use of prehistoric sites and the longevity of a circular building tradition so often seen as a trait of pre-medieval structures. An example of the latter is the site near Manor, Peebleshire, excavated in 1939. A walled scooped enclosure, 50 metres in diameter, was found terraced into the hillside. Within the enclosure was a cluster of semi-circular huts with stone wall-bases and roofs supported on more than one post. This form of site would, without excavation, normally be ascribed an Iron Age date, but the evidence here indicated construction and occupation in the fifteenth and sixteenth centuries (Stevenson 1940, 92).

A site with more characteristically medieval building forms was found at Knapps, Renfrewshire located within a 40 metre diameter walled enclosure which originated in the late Neolithic/early Bronze Age. This had been reused in the fourteenth-fifteenth century and laid out with cobbled yards, a main farmhouse/hall, granary, flour store, threshing floor, barns and byres (Newall 1965, 6). This form is unrelated to the lower-status eastern fermtouns and is rather more comparable to northern English manor sites.

Another contrasting example of a higher-status site reusing prehistoric fortifications is Lour, Peeblesshire where a tower house was built *circa* 1600 within an Iron Age double-ditched enclosure. In places the Iron Age defences were overlain by rig and farm buildings, the largest of which measured 16 metres by 5 metres. Examples of similar castletons are known elsewhere in south-east Scotland (Dunbar and Hay 1960).

All the excavated sites in the south and west exhibit unusual features which made them attractive to archaeologists. This has resulted in a lack of understanding of the more numerous, lower-status farming sites. Another unusual site is on the island of Clairinch, Loch Lomond, where a group of seven stone buildings enclosed by a bank form a settlement already in existence by 1225 when it was mentioned in a charter. The buildings were all sub-rectangular, with one or two rooms. One building was unusual in that it has a semi-circular cell at one end which was either a corn-drier or else a domed oven. This site produced evidence of earlier Iron Age occupation, and was located close to a crannog and to nearby medieval monastic settlements (Frend 1983).

At least two excavated sites are related to Dark Age precursors. At Kirkconnel, Dumfries a large Dark Age hall was found on the site of a deserted medieval settlement (Clough and Laing 1969). A lower enclosure of the Dark Age fort of Little Dunagoil, Bute, contained two houses attributed a medieval date. They appeared to have stone foundations with turf walls, and measured 14 metres by 7 metres. The roof of each building was supported by internal timber posts. There are problems, however, with the dating of these structures as they produced not only medieval pottery, apparently imported from France, but also Roman and Dark Age pottery (Marshall 1964).   .

Upstanding sites which survive in the east and south-east are almost all to be found in upland unimproved pasture and moorland. Recent excavations in Angus and Roxburgh have provided important new data concerning settlements in good cereal producing areas (Pollock 1985; Dixon 1988).

Only Pollock has so far attempted to untangle and investigate the medieval horizons of the cropmark record of eastern Scotland, concentrating on the Lunan Valley, Angus. The area was very well selected for study as the free-draining light soils overlying the bands of sands and gravels have made this an attractive agricultural area for many centuries. Other significant factors are: good road communications with the medieval burghs of Brechin and Montrose; and a good documentary framework for landholding provided by the charters of the rich abbey at Arbroath, the existence of which acted as an impetus for production. Area surveys and trial excavations were conducted during 1983 and 1984 at a number of sites including Chapelton where an extant burial ground was contained within a rectilinear cropmark enclosure ditch. This U-shaped, shallow ditch had been cut through an earlier cultivation soil (Pollock 1985, 362). Dating was provided by medieval pottery found in the ditch fills. Apart from a now-lost medieval chapel and burial ground, it was postulated that the ditch would also have enclosed a farming settlement, and this was proved to be correct when excavation within the enclosure revealed the site of a group of four corn drying kilns. Three of these had large oval bowls, 1.5 metres in diameter, the fourth being much smaller. They were stone-built and stoked through a short passage, the fire being set in a bowl beneath a raised, vented floor. No more than three of the kilns had been in use together, their function being to prepare cereals for milling, for storage as seed corn, or else as part of the malting process (Fenton 1978, 375). The report does record the discovery of charred wheat and weed seeds, the latter possibly being threshing waste, but sadly the nature of the project did not allow for a programme of specialist environmental and botanical sampling (Pollock 1985, 367).

Such kilns are not an unusual discovery, and indeed a number have been excavated in recent years. The three kilns excavated by this author on the motte at Strachan, Kincardineshire may have served this purpose (Yeoman 1984, 334), as was certainly the case at Capo, Kincardineshire and Abercairney, Perthshire (Gibson 1989). The latter two sites are unusual and very important in that they were scientifically dated, producing radiocarbon dates of the eleventh and thirteenth-fourteenth centuries respectively, along with useful samples of botanical remains which are discussed below (Gibson 1989, 226). These circular kilns, traditionally ascribed a post-medieval date, have now been shown to originate at the beginning of our period, if not earlier. There is considerable scope here for future experimental work, where kiln capacities and lifespan could be tested to provide information on fluctuations of harvest size and population growth within an individual settlement.

The limited excavations at Chapelton failed to reveal the site of any associated houses, although slight traces of a timber building were found. These were interpreted as a barn or granary which may have been attached to or covering one or more of the kilns (Pollock 1985, 367). Indeed no substantive building remains were found on any of the sites investigated in the Lunan Valley. Pollock does, however, postulate a number of ideas concerning recognition of medieval farmsteads from cropmark and cartographic evidence: for example, looking for anomalies within the regular layout of planned post-improvement farms, such as curvilinear boundary walls, may well identify the line of earlier fermtoun enclosures (Pollock 1985, 371). When such enclosures around existing hamlets appear as cropmarks, some dark blobs within them may well be kilns.

Regional and functional variations within the settlement record are underlined by the results of Dixon's excavations during 1985 and 1986 at Springwood Park, one kilometre to the south-east of the deserted medieval burgh of Roxburgh (Dixon 1988). The site is located in one of the richest, and potentially most reconstructable, medieval landscapes in Scotland, on the edge of rich arable land. The buildings examined formed part of a larger settlement of what appeared to be terraced cottages, laid out along a road, and exhibiting a complex developmental sequence from the twelfth to fourteenth centuries. Dating evidence was provided by quite a rich assemblage of coins and pottery (Dixon 1988, 6).

A primary phase timber building was found, measuring 7 metres by 3 metres. This was well-made, with paired posts forming three bays and supporting the principal roof timbers. This building fronted onto the road, whereas during phase two a line of three houses was built with their gables onto the road. These were spaced some 15 metres apart, with stone wall foundations containing good evidence for some of the earliest cruck-construction in Scotland (Dixon 1988, 27). At some time during the mid-thirteenth century this row was replaced by a conjoined terrace of three houses, each approximately 4 metres by 10 metres, again fronting onto the road. These were interpreted as cruck houses with thatched roofs, possibly standing 5 metres tall, containing cobbled floors with stone-lined and capped drains — suggesting a progression from the simple domestic cottages of the earlier phases to later longhouses containing a byre at the down-slope end (Dixon 1988, 30). The excavator argued that this was a purely agricultural community, with the evidence for cereal production being reinforced by the discovery of querns. The best parallels for this settlement form are to be found further south rather than elsewhere in Scotland. This site can be seen as a suburban development occupied by bonded tenants engaged in cereal production destined for the nearby royal, burghal and monastic centres of consumption. The change of axis on two separate occasions coupled with the regularity of building forms may indicate central planning at the behest of a superior (Dixon 1988, 32).

The fields

No one has ever set out to excavate medieval fields with the sole aim of retrieving information concerning their construction, development and dating, although excavation does occasionally occur by accident when the fields happen to overlie earlier sites, or when encountered beneath later sites. The term 'fields' is used rather than simply 'rig-and-furrow' as this is only one of a variety of open-field systems which existed. Spade cultivation is likely to have been important in some instances, creating a 'lazy-beds' system of cultivation.

Rigs and the runrig system developed in response to local environmental conditions which were neither universal nor stable. Rigs were clearly an advantage in areas with low quality, poorly drained soils and heavy rainfalls, where the ridging process created a greater depth of soil angled down-slope to encourage drainage into the furrow. The disadvantage was the loss of production in the area taken up by the furrows. Therefore, the earliest rigs are likely to have developed in upland areas, where some prehistoric sites have indeed been found in association with limited areas of narrow 'cord' rig with a wavelength (distance from rig top to adjacent rig top) of only 3 or 4 metres. An example is Cowden Hill, Fife, the site of an apparently

Iron Age homestead occupying a promontory at a height of 190 metres overlooking the Loch of Lindores. The space between it and the tip of the promontory is filled with 15–20 short rigs. Another question raised by isolated examples such as this is that of the dating and longevity of prehistoric settlement forms.

In the well-drained areas of eastern Scotland, prior to the late thirteenth-century climatic deterioration, the archaeological evidence points towards the existence of long, narrow, flat fields. These are observed on the gravels in Fife and Angus, where the ring-ditches and earlier enclosed fields are overlain by a pattern of widely-spaced, parallel boundary ditches. This theory is reinforced by the results of excavations. At Corbie in the Lunan Valley, Pollock revealed evidence of two phases of flat, area ploughing where rig formation had clearly been discouraged. This was finally abandoned during the medieval period due to a disastrous storm which deposited 1 metre of sand over the site — more evidence of climatic deterioration? (Pollock 1985, 389). Another excavated example, the prehistoric farm at North Straiton, Fife, was sealed by two phases of medieval fields, the earliest being flat, divided by wide, round-bottomed boundary ditches. The field system was dated by the ceramic evidence to the twelfth–thirteenth centuries. This was sealed by rigs which also produced medieval pottery (DES 1987, 15 and Driscoll pers. comm.).

The serious implication of the above for the archaeologist is that the fields on the best land dated to the earlier part of our period may not leave any trace, neither rig earthwork nor furrow cropmark, and can only be revealed by excavation. It should be noted however that rigs and unridged fields existed concurrently, as recorded in a twelfth-century charter of Malcolm IV referring to Ballebotlia in Fife (Barrow 1960, 227).

Excavation of fields on carefully selected sites is now essential. As Pollock has already stated, rigs cannot be dated by material retrieved from their sufaces or furrows, but only from beneath the rigs themselves (Pollock 1985, 386). Useful environmental data may also be retrieved from these sealed old ground surfaces, whereas information about the desertion and reoccupation of settlements may result from the discovery and investigation of layered rig systems. Such a feature may also identify significant event-horizons, for example the reordering of fields at the time of a change in landlord.

We are also lacking information concerning ploughs and ploughing, which in Denmark has been obtained by a combination of excavation and experimentation. At the Historical–Archaeological Research Centre in Lejre a reconstructed wheeled-forecarriage plough was used to investigate rig formation. They found that substantial rigs could be formed over the period of only a few years 'by ploughing the furrows of a strip inward so that in every season the furrow-slices were moved about their own breadth towards the middle of the ridge' (Lerche 1986, 136). Their plough furrows were excavated and compared with those from archaeological sites to aid interpretation. Special attention was paid to the different marks left in the soil by the various parts of the plough — the sole, mould-board, share and coulter (Lerche 1986, 147–9). The wooden sole and mould-board of their reconstructed plough was fitted with pebbles which acted to absorb some of the friction, and it is interesting to note that 'plough pebbles' of this kind are often found in fields in East Lothian and the Borders (G. Sprott pers. comm.).

Homefarm, Wardhouse: a case study

While excavating the moated site at Mains of Wardhouse in Aberdeenshire the author began to study the very well preserved fermtoun site at Homefarm (NJ 571304) about 3 kilometres to the west (see Fig. 6.1 and Plate 6.1). The site survives under permanent pasture, except to the south where modern ploughing of improved arable has destroyed rigs. A deep gulley on the north side effectively constrained the medieval ploughmen. One of the most attractive features is the longevity of occupation, whether continuous or not, indicated by the prehistoric settlement and enclosed fields located 150 metres south-east of the central area of the later fermtoun. Some of the clearance cairns to the east are likely to be associated with the earlier settlement, which at some time may have shifted or else was more extensive than appearances would suggest. This conclusion was reached from the results of both field and geophysical surveys, when two further possible hut circles were located within and under the fermtoun (Gater 1988, 4). On this granitic till the resistivity survey failed to successfully outline the structures of the fermtoun, which also showed up poorly from the air. It is also possible that the sub-circular structure at the western entrance was a house which, unlike the others, forms an integral part of the fermtoun earthworks: more evidence for medieval hut circles, or simply the opportunistic reuse of an existing stone foundation?

The field survey plan shows an area 100 metres east-west by 110 metres enclosed by an irregularly curving bank, which is presumed to be medieval, punctuated by four or more entrances. The outlines of three or four rectangular houses, on average 15 metres long by 4–8 metres wide, are visible to the west, with associated enclosures. The evidence would suggest the existence of more than one house on the same site. Other buildings of less permanent construction are likely to be present. The detail and function of all these elements are impossible to interpret without excavation, although the foundations of the main structures are clearly of stone. The use of organic building materials — timber, turf and earth — which leave little surface trace severely decreases the chances of locating fermtoun buildings on this and many other sites.

The hollow-ways to east and west show the main access routes deepened by the constant wear of carts and livestock. The enclosing bank stopped the beasts from straying into the precious arable. Detailed examination has even enabled the location of two circular corn driers of the type discussed above.

The rigs varied in wavelength from 4 metres to 8 metres and were on average 0.3 metres high. The long, sinuously curving rigs to the north and

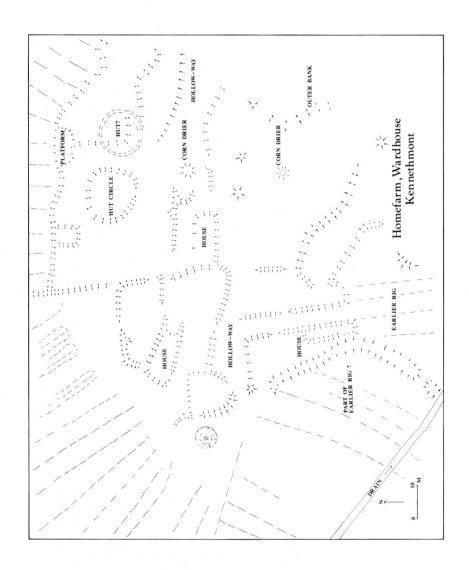

Homefarm, Wardhouse
Kennethmont

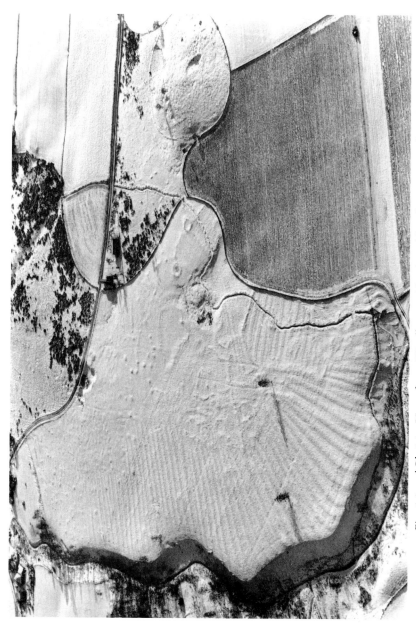

Fig. 6.1 and Pl. 6.1 Homefarm, Wardhouse, Aberdeenshire: fermtoun, earthworks and rig (Aberdeen Archaeological Surveys)

west radiate out from the fermtoun with which they are contemporary. Indeed the overall effect is strongly reminiscent of the classic deserted medieval sites of the midlands of England. A block of about eleven less well-defined, narrower rigs is visible to the south-west, cut by a later drain. These, along with traces of narrow rigs just visible beneath the fermtoun, appear to pre-date it, and some may even be associated with the pre-medieval settlement. These infield rigs were constantly cultivated, and may have been supplemented by blocks of occasionally cultivated outfield rigs, none of which survive in the poorer, higher ground to the east and north. It is also likely that the Wardhouse farmers had access to shieling lands for summer grazing on the Hill of Foundland to the north.

But why should this site be medieval rather than eighteenth century? The answer to this lies at least partly in the fact that much of this area known as the Garioch was within the great northern *dominium* of David, Earl of Huntingdon, during the late twelfth century. The historical framework of the settlement pattern has been expertly recreated by Stringer, forming a substantial and promising basis for future archaeological research (1985, 56). Basic documentary research has shown that the site does not feature on a pre-improvement estate survey of the 1780s executed for the landowner, the great Gordon family. This accurately depicts the plans of many nearby fermtouns, likely to be medieval or older in origin, along with their rigs. Almost all of these places now survive as hamlets and improved farms. It is similarly absent from Roy's survey, executed between 1747 and 1755, by which time the site would have been only a few hundred metres east of the landscaped grounds of Gordon Hall, a structure which no longer survives. The fermtoun may either have already been long gone or else was swept away during the building of the Hall. Whatever the date of desertion the site name does not survive, making research very difficult, but by the same token possibly indicating abandonment hundreds of years ago.

Economy and environment

The agrarian economy would appear to have been very limited and monotonous. Wool production was of universal importance, occupying large areas of upland grazing. The importance of cereal production cannot be stressed enough, for it was this along with dairy products that fed the farmers and their families through the winter, most cattle production being destined for the burgh markets where they were transformed into meat and hides.

Oats and bere (barley) were the chief grains, although wheat is frequently referred to in the charters of William the Lion (1165–1214), if rarely thereafter except when recorded as an import (Duncan 1975, 322). Yields were low by modern standards, between 1:3 and 1:5 with a proportion being kept back as seed corn for the following year (Duncan 1975, 324). An important by-product was straw, which would have been the main animal winter feed along with some hay and even weeds from the arable fields. Some of the latter are known to have been utilised as famine-foods by man.

Legumes — peas and beans — if cultivated would have been a good source of protein for man and beast, providing pea-straw for winter fodder, and helping to improve the fertility of the soil by fixing nitrogen (G. Sprott pers. comm.). The evidence for legume production, however, is far from clear; indeed Duncan suggested that legumes appear in documents only as imports, that is as purchases, not as rents (Duncan 1975, 324).

The techniques of environmental archaeology, and more specifically palaeobotanical studies, may yet provide the answers to such issues. If few sites of our period have been excavated in recent years, even fewer have benefited from proper environmental study. The difficult environment with which these expert farmers were in millennia-old partnership can be reconstructed to reveal information such as: tree species and woodland management; location, change and condition of arable and grazing land; crop types and production. More excavated data are yet to come from the publication of the sites at North Straiton and Springwood (see above), and at present only limited information is available from sites such as Strachan and Nethermills, both Kincardineshire. The Strachan motte produced evidence of barley, oats and wheat along with weeds of cultivation (Yeoman 1984, fiche 4). Rig and furrow above the mesolithic site at Nethermills produced a carbonised cereal-processing waste assemblage which included the first medieval archaeological evidence of ergot, the infamous food-destroying mould (W. Boyd pers. comm.). Large quantities of cereals (oats and barley), along with weeds and chaff, were retrieved and analysed from the Capo and Abercairney corn-driers (Gibson 1989, 227).

Soil science can also help: phosphate analysis and micromorphological examination could provide information concerning how fertility was maintained on fields under constant cultivation. This question was addressed at Rosal where a rich soil with very high phosphate levels had been artificially created (Fairhurst 1967, 159).

Discussion

The above is an unashamedly archaeological assessment of the subject of the medieval countryside, and no apologies are made for what the pioneers of other disciplines will no doubt see as the misapplication of their results. Some important aspects have been completely left out, including place-name evidence, which has a very important part to play. None of the questions posed at the beginning have been answered, nor can they be without further fieldwork. But this author is optimistic that answers can be found, although we must be aware that our primary resource, the sites themselves, is constantly being eroded by forestry and other land-use changes. This situation should be improved, however, as a result of the increase both in pre-forestry survey by the RCAHMS and in the number of regional archaeologists.

Archaeology may be able to resolve the biggest problems of all: what date are the sites which survive, and what were the origins of settlement? Where upland sites survive, they may reasonably be interpreted as pre-dating the climatic deterioration, but conversely they may relate to periods of economic growth such as during the late sixteenth–seventeenth centuries when many references to 'outsetting' — settlement enlargement or splitting — are recorded. Clearly, forces were in conflict as far as land use was concerned; for example, the pressures on the uplands at the beginning of our period when the needs of sheep farming and the chase ran contrary to those of established arable farmers. Problems of site identification can be overcome by the application of techniques such as Pollock's model by which the slighter traces of medieval cropmarks, at least in areas of gravel, may be separated from the stronger ring ditch forms (Pollock 1985, 397).

The questions of regional variation of agricultural practices and settlement forms can be addressed by the careful selection of sites to be excavated ideally within a university research programme. Sites which appear in historical documentary evidence, and with clear indications of a medieval or earlier origin, can be selected; the site at Wardhouse being one such candidate. The lack of a university archaeology department in Scotland specialising in this period does, however, make the implementation of these recommendations problematic.

Models for such studies exist in England and in Scandinavia. In Yorkshire the Wharram Research Project has taken over thirty years to investigate a deserted medieval village complete with manor-house, mill, fish pond, fields, peasant houses and parish church (Hurst 1986, 215). Changes to the fabric of the latter are a good indicator of the fortunes of the parish, and the people themselves can be examined, or at least their bones can, to provide information on diet, disease and longevity. Similar problems have been examined by the Scandinavian Deserted Farms and Villages Project since 1968 (Gissel et al. 1981, 50). The general lack of nucleation makes site selection more problematic in Scotland, although an interrelated complex of neighbouring fermtouns, kirkton, millton, medieval parish church, and seigneurial centre could be found. Ideally the church or chapel should be a site only, as surviving fragments have tended to be used as family vaults in recent times.

One project which has gone some way to achieving this is that at Rattray, Buchan, where not a fermtoun but a deserted burgh has been excavated by the Murrays from 1985–90 (Murray and Murray 1985–90). Rural burghs may shed much light on our subject — as the point of consumption and selling-on of much produce, as farms in their own right, and with better chances of archaeological preservation.

It is only proper that we should be trying to understand the archaeology of the medieval countryside, after all we share their preoccupations — climatic change, the environment, organic farming and a poll tax!

Bibliography

Adams, I. 1967 Agrarian landscape terms — a glossary for historical geography, London.

Baker, A. and Butlin, R. (eds) 1973 *Studies of field systems in the British Isles*, Cambridge.

Barrow, G. W. S. (ed) 1960 *The Acts of Malcolm IV King of Scots 1153–1165*, Edinburgh.

Barrow, G. W. S. 1973 *The kingdom of the Scots*, London.

Beresford, M. W. and Hurst, J. J. (eds) 1971 *Deserted medieval villages*, London.

Clough, T. and Laing, L. 1969 Excavations at Kirkconnel, Waterbeck, Dumfriesshire, *Trans. Dumfriesshire Galloway Nat. Hist. Archaeol. Soc.* 46, 128–39.

DES *Discovery and excavation in Scotland*, Edinburgh.

Dixon, P. 1988 Springwood Park excavation. Unpublished interim report.

Dodgshon, R. 1980a Medieval settlement and colonisation, in Parry and Slater 1980, 45–68.

Dodgshon, R. 1980b The origins of traditional field systems, in Parry and Slater 1980, 69–92.

Dunbar, J. and Hay, G. 1960 Excavations at Lour, Stobo. *Proc. Soc. Antiq. Scotland* 94 (1960–61), 196–210.

Duncan, A. A. M. 1975 *Scotland — the making of the kingdom*, Edinburgh.

Fairhurst, H. 1967 Rosal — a deserted township in Strathnaver, Sutherland, *Proc. Soc. Antiq. Scotland* 100 (1967–68), 135–69.

Fairhurst, H. 1968 The deserted settlement at Lix, West Perthshire, *Proc. Soc. Antiq. Scotland* 101 (1968–69), 160–99.

Fairhurst, H. 1971 Rural settlement in Scotland, in Beresford and Hurst 1971, 229–35.

Fenton, A. 1978 *The Northern Isles: Orkney and Shetland*, Edinburgh.

Frend, W. 1983 Archaeological remains on Clairinch, *Glasgow Archaeol. J.* 10, 125–29.

Gater, J. 1988 Wardhouse geophysical survey. Unpublished report.

Gibson, A. 1989 Medieval corn-drying kilns at Capo, Kincardineshire and Abercairney, Perthshire, *Proc. Soc. Antiq. Scotland* 118, 219–29.

Gissel, S. , Jutikkala, E. , Osterberg, E. , Sandnes, J. and Teitsson, B. 1981 *Desertion and land colonization in the Nordic countries*, Stockholm.

Grove, J. 1988 *The Little Ice Age*, London.

Hurst, J. 1986 The medieval countryside, in Longworth and Cherry 1986, 197–236.

Laing, L. 1969 Medieval settlement archaeology in Scotland, *Scottish Archaeol. Forum* 1, 69–77.

Lerche, G. 1986 Ridged fields and profiles of plough-furrows, *Tools and Tillage* 5.3, 131–56.

Longworth, I. and Cherry, J. (eds) 1986 *Archaeology in Britain since 1945*, London.

Marshall, D. 1964 Excavations at Little Dunagoil, *Trans. Buteshire Nat. Hist. Soc.* 16, 3–69.

Mercer, R. J. 1980 Field survey and settlement location in Northern Scotland, in Morrison 1980, 21–34.

Morrison, A. (ed) 1980 *Rural settlement studies*, Glasgow.

Morrison, I. 1990 Climatic changes and human geography: Scotland in a North Atlantic context. Unpublished paper.

Murray, C. and Murray, H. 1985–90 The deserted medieval town of Rattray. Unpublished interim reports.

Newall, F. 1965 *Excavations at Knapp, Renfrewshire*, Paisley.

Parry, M. L. 1976 A typology of cultivation ridges in southern Scotland, *Tools and Tillage* 3.1, 3–19.

Parry, M. L. and Slater, T. R. (eds) 1980 *The making of the Scottish countryside*, London.

Pollock, D. 1985 The Lunan Valley Project: medieval rural settlement in Angus, *Proc. Soc. Antiq. Scotland* 115, 357–99.

RCAHMS 1990 *North-east Perth: an archaeological landscape*, Edinburgh.

Stevenson, R. B. K. 1940 Medieval dwelling sites and a primitive village in the parish of Manor, Peeblesshire, *Proc. Soc. Antiq. Scotland* 75 (1940–41), 92–115.

Stringer, K. 1985 *David, Earl of Huntingdon*, Edinburgh.

Whittington, G. 1973 Field systems in Scotland, in Baker and Butlin 1973, 530–79.

Whittington, G. 1980 Prehistoric activity and its effect on the Scottish landscape, in Parry and Slater 1980, 23–44.

Whyte, I. undated The historical geography of rural settlement in Scotland: a review. Unpublished paper.

Yates, M. 1977 The excavations at Polmaddy, New Galloway, *Trans. Dumfriesshire Galloway Nat. Hist. Archaeol. Soc.* 53 (1977–78), 133–47.

Yeoman, P. A. 1984 Excavations at Castlehill of Strachan, *Proc. Soc. Antiq. Scotland* 114, 315–64 and fiche.

Yeoman, P. A. 1988 Mottes in northeast Scotland, *Scottish Archaeol. Rev.* 5.1 and 2, 125–33.

Acknowledgements

I am most grateful to Geoffrey Barrow, Gavin Sprott and Ian Morrison for their time spent in discussing some of the contents of this paper, and especially to the latter who lent me many books and who kindly read and commented on the draft. Piers Dixon has also offered very helpful editorial comments. The fieldwork has been enabled by the assistance of Philip Duthie and David Easton, and I am indebted to the Department of Physical Planning, Grampian Regional Council and the Society of Antiquaries of Scotland for their financial support. The Wardhouse plan has been expertly produced for publication by Marion O'Neil.

7

SURVEYING FOR THE FUTURE: RCAHMS ARCHAEOLOGICAL SURVEY 1908–1990

S. P. Halliday and J. B. Stevenson

The last fifteen years have witnessed not only radical developments in the techniques of archaeological field-survey but also in the demands on, and the objectives of, field-survey. In this paper we will examine the effects that these changes have had on the archaeological survey of the Commission, and we will discuss the historical context of the Commission's work.

From a relatively straightforward archaeological programme preparing county inventories, the Commission has now expanded into numerous roles: aerial survey, Ordnance Survey mapping, pre-afforestation survey, and rapid survey programmes, to say nothing of the architectural programmes covering threatened buildings and industrial monuments. The survey kit has developed from a notebook, tape and plane table to a multiplicity of electronic instruments, staffs and tripods that fill half a Land Rover, and an inventory is now seen as a two-year project rather than a commitment to a single county for a period measured in decades.

With these changes, the Commission, as a part of the wider archaeological community, has acquired a broader understanding of what can be achieved through survey. Part of this broader understanding is, perhaps, no more than a sense of realism about the limitations of survey and untested field observations. With these limitations in mind, however, we are also beginning to explore aspects of archaeology undreamt of by previous generations of fieldworkers and excavators. Today, surveys and excavations are no longer solely concerned with the recovery of detailed plans and descriptions of individual structures; the emphasis has shifted to the landscape and its component parts. Indeed, other than as an administrative convenience, it is now far from clear what constitutes a unitary archaeological monument. In the Commission's surveys this shift in emphasis can be seen by comparing the volumes of the *Inventory of Argyll* (RCAHMS 1971–88) with the recently published survey of *North-east Perth* (RCAHMS 1990). In the former, the illustrations are concentrated on detailed plans of individual structures, while in the latter greater emphasis has been laid on maps of the archaeology in the landscape. Of the c.450 km² covered by the *North-east Perth* survey, 210 km² are illustrated at a scale of 1:25,000, 27 km² at 1:10,000 and 5 km² at 1:5,000. The comparison is somewhat simplistic and should not be overstated, and it could be argued, for instance, that a traditional inventory of north-east Perth might have been forced to adopt a similar approach, and in *South-east Perth* (RCAHMS forthcoming), where relatively little ground has survived modern agricultural improvement, the differences will be less easy to detect. Nevertheless, where extensive archaeological remains survive in the landscape, they are now both approached and dealt with on an entirely different footing.

The aim of the present paper is not simply to try to explain what lies behind these changes, but to place them in a historical context, and then to look in more detail at the approach to the Commission survey in *North-east Perth* (RCAHMS 1990). Some might regard the backward glance as unnecessary, but we hope to show that, before further advances in archaeological survey can be made, it is necessary to understand the processes that have led to the present position. To a considerable degree, the practice of field-survey is still rooted in the nineteenth century and, in the case of RCAHMS, the Inventory is the most persistent reflection of this phenomenon. In the closing decades of the last century David Christison, Fred Coles and Romilly Allen were systematically recording specific types of sites and monuments in descriptive lists and, against this particular background, it is easy to see the origins of an all-embracing survey programme. The term 'inventorisation', despite its modern mid-Atlantic ring, was coined in 1905 by Professor Baldwin Brown, Professor of Fine Art at the University of Edinburgh (Brown 1905), who was concerned about the increasing rate of destruction of archaeological and historical monuments. He contended that such work was a necessary preliminary to any scheme for the protection and care of ancient monuments, and three years later he was to be appointed a Commissioner to the newly established Commission.

The Warrant for the Royal Commission on the Ancient and Historical Monuments of Scotland was issued on 7 February 1908. The Commission was 'to make an inventory of the Ancient and Historical Monuments and Constructions connected with or illustrative of the contemporary culture, civilisation, and conditions of life of the people of Scotland from the earliest times to the year 1707 . . . and, to specify those which seem most worthy of preservation' (RCAHMS 1909, iii). The *modus operandi* by which this inventory was to be achieved was set out in the First Report:

> It was further decided to take advantage of the notification of antiquities made on the maps of the Ordnance Survey, and from there to prepare preliminary lists according to the counties and parishes for the purpose of distribution to the ministers of the Gospel, schoolmasters, and such other individuals as might be able to supplement these lists from local knowledge.

> [And that] the Secretary should visit each county in turn, with the object of personally inspecting each monument so as to satisfy your Commissioners as to its true character and condition. (RCAHMS 1909, v)

At the outset fieldwork was concentrated on recording details of a list of 'known' monuments, compiled on a county basis from sites depicted on the OS 6–inch maps, and it was not concerned with prospection for unrecorded sites. Similar patterns of fieldwork are detectable in the work of both Christison and Coles and, with one notable exception (see below), there is little sign that anyone considered that there might be large numbers of monuments that had escaped the notice of the OS Surveyors. The Second Report, however, notes that 'the monuments and constructions of Sutherland were found to greatly exceed in number and importance those previously known to exist', and it goes on to express the belief that others remained to be discovered (RCAHMS 1911b, v–vi). Similar sentiments are expressed in the Third Report for the County of Caithness (RCAHMS 1911a).

The pattern of the county Inventories was established in 1909 with the publication of Berwickshire (RCAHMS 1909). Alexander Curle, who had been appointed Secretary of the Commission in 1908, took his family down to St Abbs for the summer and, by rail and bicycle, worked his way across the county. His notes, together with a delightful journal, are lodged in the National Monuments Record of Scotland. In effect, the early Inventories are archaeological and architectural commentaries on the County Series 6–inch maps, even though in the wake of Sutherland there was clearly an expectation of encountering unrecorded monuments en route to the known sites. Nevertheless, there is little sign of deliberate prospection in any systematic manner and, given the level of staffing, it would, in any case, have been impractical. This continued to be the pattern of work throughout the 1920s and 1930s, and may have remained so had the Second World War not interrupted the Commission's activities. At the outbreak of hostilities much of the County of Roxburgh had already been examined and the volume was in a fairly advanced stage of preparation. Work resumed on the volume after the war, but the pattern of survey was never to be the same again. By a happy coincidence a number of factors coalesced to alter radically the previous pattern of survey. Several members of staff had been involved in air photographic interpretation as part of their military service and they were more aware of the existence of unmapped sites (Steer and Keeney 1948, 138–9). Shortly after the war much of the country was photographically surveyed from the air using underemployed RAF squadrons. The resulting stereoscopic and vertical National Air Survey photographs had a dramatic impact upon the Roxburghshire survey, not only revealing hundreds of unrecorded monuments, but also providing the first examples of the slight earthworks of palisaded settlements and enclosures (Steer 1951). The Fourteenth Report was able to claim that 'It has been possible to make so full a record of the earthwork monuments, many of which are scarcely visible — or even invisible — to observers on the ground . . . [that] . . . we have been able to prepare an Inventory which is much more complete than any other as yet produced' (RCAHMS 1956, xxvi).

With the publication of Roxburgh the Inventory had become a list of monuments appearing on OS maps, monuments found while visiting the 'known' monuments, and additional earthworks observed on aerial photographs. It is curious that no inclination to carry out systematic patterns of prospective reconnaissance is apparent, even though the palisaded homestead on Greenbrough had been recorded in this way (Steer 1951). Perhaps even more surprising, given the success of Cambridge University Committee for Aerial Photography sorties into Scotland, is that there was no apparent wish to exploit the medium of oblique aerial photography as a means of prospection or to broaden the field into a search for cropmarks. With the notable exception of Roman military studies, archaeological air photographic interpretation in Scotland remained primarily a prospective tool for above-ground monuments until the mid-1970s.

The delay in the development of prospective aerial reconnaissance in the Commission may well reflect a belief in the all-seeing eye of the vertical aerial camera, but it was probably also influenced by the advent of the Survey of Marginal Lands at the end of 1950. In order to undertake this pioneering rescue survey, the Inventory programme was postponed for a period that eventually ran to eight years 'in favour of emergency survey of marginal lands in all parts of Scotland where an expansion of agriculture or forestry may be expected' (RCAHMS 1956, xxvi). To achieve this in so short a time now appears unrealistic for any programme of systematic prospection, and it is, after all, a problem with which we are still wrestling today. The prospective element of the survey was provided by existing vertical aerial photographs, and the survey spent its eight years visiting three hundred new monuments located in this way, as well as numerous others already shown on OS maps.

The first signs that ground prospection formed a deliberate element in a survey comes with the *Inventory of Peeblesshire* (RCAHMS 1967). The recovery of the distribution pattern of unenclosed platform settlements was clearly achieved by fieldwork around the characteristic locations that these settlements occupy. Subsequent fieldwork in Peeblesshire suggests that this fieldwork was highly selective and there cannot have been any systematic attempt to cover the ground. The rows of platforms only came to light by chance and they had not been picked up on the aerial photographs. Fieldwork was also extended into the neighbouring counties to establish how far this new type of settlement spread (RCAHMS 1967, 22). Another stimulus for prospective work was probably derived from the architectural component of the surveys. With the amendment of the Warrant in 1948 to allow discretion to survey monuments of more recent date than 1707, the architectural investigators needed to look more widely than the buildings noted as antiquities on OS maps. Indeed, the working maps for Peeblesshire show quite how widely they ranged from standing buildings to the foundations of shielings tucked up small side valleys. Thus, with the publication of Peeblesshire (RCAHMS 1967) the Inventory had become a list of monuments on OS maps, monuments found while visiting those monuments, earthworks observed on aerial photographs, and monuments recovered by selective reconnaissance.

The amount of ground prospection increased steadily through the 1960s and 1970s as the surveys of Argyll and Lanarkshire progressed, but it remained selective. By the mid-1970s, however, swathes of the landscape were disappearing beneath coniferous plantations, and it was clear that considerable numbers of unrecorded sites and monuments were being destroyed. Furthermore, it was clear that the slow progress of county inventory survey was unable to provide a solution to this problem. The first SDD pre-afforestation surveys were taking place and the present generation of Scottish fieldworkers were becoming aware of the archaeological possibilities afforded by the landscape. The success of a survey was to be measured in numbers of new monuments found per man-day, and intensive fieldwork on known monuments was regarded as an expensive luxury. It was in this climate that in 1974 the Commission appointed two new investigators and that the Society of Antiquaries Field Survey was set up in 1977. The latter was of greater significance for the development of Commission working practices, for while the investigators were tied to the existing structure and practices of the Commission, the Society of Antiquaries Field Survey was given greater scope to develop its own style of work. The brief of the Antiquaries field-surveyors laid stress on the discovery of new monuments through prospective fieldwork. The survey also cast its net more widely than the Inventory, embracing all surviving rural settlement that had been abandoned prior to the publication of the first edition of the OS 6–inch map (c.1849–60). It thus took an inclusive approach to shielings and pre- and immediately post-Improvement farmsteads, a topic dealt with only in outline by the architectural side of the Inventory programme.

During the 1970s and 1980s developments were not only taking place in the scope of Commission archaeological surveys, but survey techniques were also undergoing radical change. The plans in the Roxburghshire and Peeblesshire volumes were surveyed with tapes and a plane table, a daunting task on a large or complex fort such as Eildon Hill North (RCAHMS 1956, 306–10) or the 30-acre field-system at Tamshiel Rig (RCAHMS 1956, 426–7). In 1976 the Commission acquired a self-reducing microptic alidade (SRA) which could measure distances of up to 150m and gave true horizontal readings on sloping ground. The SRA remains one of the essential tools of the Commission surveying kit, particularly for small unitary plans, but much of the work previously plane-tabled with the SRA is now carried out using a theodolite mounted Electronic Distance Measurer (EDM). These machines have the capacity to measure distances of up to 2 km to a tolerance of 20 mm. The first EDM was bought in 1983 as a consequence of the transfer of responsibility for mapping antiquities from the Ordnance Survey to the Commission, and it was designed to be used to improve the Commission's ability to plot sites accurately on to the OS basic scale map. We were also aware that Commission techniques for surveying large sites with the SRA allowed the possibility of invisible compound errors creeping into a survey. The EDM solved both these problems. We originally envisaged using the EDM to fix the plane table stations and map control, while the SRA filled in the archaeological detail, and it was with some satisfaction that after six man-days' work we completed our first survey of this type, Glenton Hill, Kincardineshire (RCAHMS 1984, 24; NMRS KCD/137/2), using three stations and four points for control (a job that now might take only two man-days).

The first generation EDM consisted of a laser unit mounted on a conventional theodolite. It was laborious to use, taking about two minutes to obtain a series of booked readings which then had to be drawn up manually. Nevertheless, it functioned satisfactorily and did the job for which it had been bought. Before long, however, we were asking for more. Here was a machine that could accurately measure distances of up to 2 km, surely we could start mapping all the archaeology in stretches of landscapes some 4 km across. Our first experiment with this sort of survey was at Meikle Tongue, Wigtonshire (RCAHMS 1987, 42–3) taking in a series of burial-cairns, hut-circles and small cairns scattered across a strip of moorland some 1,500 m long and 800 m wide. The cumbersome workings of the machinery, coupled with the time taken to move between the points to be surveyed (a surprisingly large element in any survey), imposed a limit of about 120 points in an average working day, but there was little doubt of the potential that this technology offered.

The Commission's second generation EDM was linked to a small computer. This not only allowed much greater speed and flexibility in the field, but the data could be transferred to an office-based computer and automatically plotted out as crosses and straight lines. It was on the strength of this level of development that in 1987 we approached the survey of north-east Perth, where we anticipated meeting extensive archaeological landscapes. The complexity of the archaeological remains in north-east Perth led to the acquisition of a more sophisticated data gathering system which incorporated a coded library of symbols and the facility to record curves. Inexorably we are moving towards a machine plot-out that resembles a hand-drawn archaeological survey, with the additional ability to blend files of archaeological detail with data digitised from OS maps and from aerial photograph transcriptions. The technological upgrading outlined above has been a vital development because, to a great degree, it has determined the Commission's ability to treat the landscape as an archaeological site, to survey the landscape itself, and finally to ask questions of that landscape.

Landscape archaeology was a fashionable concept in the late 1970s when a series of seminars were held in Edinburgh to discuss the direction of survey in Scotland. There was universal condemnation of unitary monument surveys and a call for landscape archaeology. Today it is easy to see that the late 1970s concept of landscape archaeology was naive. What is more remarkable, however, is that, a decade or more later, we still do not have any published examples of that essential tool of landscape archaeology, the landscape survey. With few exceptions, archaeologists have continued to present survey data in terms of spots on maps, together with detailed plans and descriptions of those spots. Little attempt has been made to place the spots in the context of their surrounding landscape or understand the landscapes that link them. The reasons for this are four-fold. In the first place, without sophisticated instrumentation it is both difficult and time consuming to map archaeology that covers areas measured in square kilometres. Secondly, many of the surveys have taken place within the framework of a training exercise for undergraduates, aiming to teach simple techniques of recognition and survey. Thirdly, we all now realise that the landscape is highly complex, and its archaeology does not necessarily lend itself readily to interpretation through survey. Finally, the mechanisms for the preservation of monuments are still geared to lists of spots on the maps, as it was when the Commission first embarked on the 'inventorisation' of Scotland in 1908. We are all trapped by our history, and further hamstrung by the 'numbers game', whereby a survey presents its value for money by a numerical quantification of its newly discovered monuments, not by the quality of its exploration of a single site, namely the landscape.

In the light of the above comments it is clear that the Commission must also be enmeshed by the constraints of the past. Nevertheless, the point has now been reached where the Commission recognises the problems — academic, technical and practical — inherent in landscape survey. On the technological side the Commission is adequately kitted out to cope with landscape survey, and the extent to which we apply the technology is governed by a delicate balance between objectives, time, and money. It is with these factors in mind that we have to examine the practicalities of landscape survey as, for instance, it would have been impractical to attempt a total survey of north-east Perth, an area of about 450 km^2, within the framework of a two-year project. We must, therefore, be selective when choosing areas for landscape survey and have a clear objective in mind. This leads on to the academic problems posed by the landscape. Every landscape contains a series of layers of destruction, some of them invisible, and it is only by understanding the sequence of those layers that we can hope to understand the distribution of remains within that landscape. In itself, however, survey should not be expected to explain the landscape or even to identify all the layers of destruction. The survey is the essential preamble to further exploration using the sort of invasive sampling techniques that have been developed by the Archaeological Operations and Conservation Unit of Historic Scotland (Lowe and Barber 1988).

In view of this discussion it is legitimate to ask what the contents of the *North-east Perth* survey represent (RCAHMS 1990). Its brief was to identify, accurately locate, describe, interpret, and selectively illustrate the archaeological sites and monuments with an upper chronological limit set by the first edition of the OS 6-inch map. Fundamentally, however, it is still the descriptive list with which Christison, Coles or A. O. Curle would have been familiar. But, in a small number of areas we have attempted to illustrate the archaeology in its landscape. The practical problems that this posed for a publication should not be underestimated. Even with an A4 page size it is possible to fit only a relatively small area on to a page:

Scale		Surveyed area
1:2,500	—	680m x 420m
1:5,000	—	1,360m x 840m
1:10,000	—	2,640m x 1680m
1:25,000	—	6,800m x 4200m

At a publication scale of 1:2,500 the archaeology can be depicted with a certain degree of subtlety; it is possible to illustrate all the archaeology in its correct spatial relationship as a line drawing. At 1:10,000 much of the archaeological detail has to be generalised, while at 1:25,000 it is only possible to use symbols. When faced with a single group of small cairns spread over a square kilometre, or a series of hut-circle groups extending up a side valley for a distance of 4 km, there is little room for manoeuvre. Rather than say yes we can, indeed, produce a landscape survey, but that it is unpublishable, we formulated an approach to the landscape based on a series of 'windows' which should carry the user from the general to the particular. All the monuments and the major windows are depicted on overall end-maps of the area which, for the sake of clarity, have been divided between the medieval and prehistoric archaeology. The 1:25,000 windows show the spatial relationships of the medieval or prehistoric archaeology; these may then lead to further windows at 1:10,000 or 1:5,000. At the latter scales it is possible to bring the medieval and prehistoric archaeology together without creating an incoherent jumble. In order to show individual monuments there may then be further windows at 1:1,000, 1:500 or even 1:250. In this way about 40 per cent of the entries in the inventory are depicted at 1:25,000; 12 per cent at 1:10,000; 2 per cent at 1:5,000; 3 per cent at 1:2,500; 2 per cent at 1:1,000, 4 per cent at 1:500; and 2 per cent at 1:250. For individual types of monuments, eg hut-circles, the percentages can be even higher: 70 per cent appear at 1:25,000, 11 per cent at 1:10,000, 8 per cent at 1:5,000, and 15 per cent at 1:2,500. In an ideal world there would have been a higher proportion of 1:10,000 and 1:5,000 windows but, within the framework of a two-year project, the process of selection was, of necessity, constrained.

With hindsight there are a number of more detailed plans that could have been sacrificed in favour of landscape block-plans (1:10,000, 1:5,000). The process of selection was, in part, determined by the structure of the landscape of north-east Perth, which breaks down relatively neatly into three major layers of destruction, each with its own set of surviving archaeological remains. The most recent layer of destruction is provided by the present arable land and the enclosed fields that date to the period of agricultural improvement in the late eighteenth and nineteenth centuries. This zone is almost sterile for prospective reconnaissance and, coincidentally, takes in most of the areas of primary medieval settlement. A second layer of destruction was wrought by the upper limit of medieval and pre-Improvement agriculture and settlement; farmsteads, many of them still occupied in the late-eighteenth century, and a small number of prehistoric monuments are the characteristic sites in this zone. The third layer of destruction was created by the upper limit of prehistoric settlement; here subsequent exploitation appears to have been largely limited to grazing, and this is the zone of the maximum survival of prehistoric monuments. This picture is, of course, a gross simplification, but the topography of the glens with their steep sides tended to emphasise the boundaries or high tide marks left by the respective layers, both reducing the areas of overlap between medieval and prehistoric remains and concentrating each set of remains into recurring topographic locations. In parts of Strathardle, for instance, the surviving hut-circle groups are concentrated on the shoulders of the glens high above the later settlement that occupied the floor of the valley. There was little to be gained by surveying examples of landscapes where the second and third layers of destruction overlapped. These did not produce the best examples of pre-Improvement farms and fields while, by definition, the prehistoric remains were partly destroyed. Accordingly, we concentrated our 1:5,000 and 1:10,000 surveys on the apparently most representative or interesting groups of remains from each of these two layers.

The techniques adopted to illustrate these landscapes varied with the nature of the archaeology, but all were designed to fit on to a map base, be it an OS 1:10,000 map extract or redrawn locational and topographical material derived from the 1:10,000 map. The fermtoun at Easter Bleaton, for example, was plotted from air photographs and then ground checked with a tape, while at other sites all the buildings, banks and cairns, as well as map control, were surveyed by EDM. At these scales it is not cost effective to survey rig-and-furrow cultivation on the ground, and furrows are normally plotted from aerial photographs. Indeed, the choice of landscape to be surveyed is influenced by the quality and availability of aerial coverage. Vertical photographs are the easiest to use, but obliques can be rectified by a computer-aided plot, and surveys often combine data from both vertical and oblique sorties. These major sources of material — map, survey, and aerial photographic — are best-fitted together manually to produce the illustration for publication. The prehistoric material readily lends itself to this approach as it all consists of banks and mounds of stones. The level of interpretation possible at these scales, however, gives a positive/negative picture; equal weighting has to be given to all features and there is no room for subtleties of interpretation, these must be accommodated at larger scales or in the accompanying text.

In contrast to earlier inventory volumes, and in order to illustrate the landscapes to greatest effect, a less rigid approach was taken to the use of standard scales in *North-east Perth*. The determining factor, apart from the practical question of how big an area would fit on the printed page, was which scale would most economically demonstrate the particular point in question. Thus, for the medieval material the 1:10,000 maps illustrate the remarkable pre-Improvement landscapes at the head of Glen Shee and in Gleann Beag, while 1:5,000 surveys were prepared for the rig-and-furrow systems around the farmsteads at Sheriffmuir in the Forest of Clunie and for the fermtouns of Easter Bleaton and Invereddrie in Glen Shee. For the prehistoric settlements 1:10,000 surveys were carried out on the ridges of Middleton Muir and in the valley of the Pitcarmick Burn. A further 1:5,000 window was surveyed on the Pitcarmick Burn and others at Balnabroich and Knockali. Between these surveys and those of sites at 1:2,500, it is possible to show that each of the major layers of destruction contains evidence of other destructive episodes. The cultivation terraces beneath rig-and-furrow at the Spittal of Glenshee come to mind or the hut-circles built across a trackway leading though the prehistoric field-system at Drumturn Burn.

Clearly, *North-east Perth* is not a landscape survey in itself, but (and this echoes the report for Roxburghshire) we have explored the archaeology of the landscape more fully than in any previous inventory survey. There is, then, some considerable irony in the realisation that this position had been reached by Sir Alexander Ogston some eighty years ago, at precisely the time of the Commission's foundation. Ogston was a pioneering surgeon and research scientist with a keen interest in the archaeology around his estate in Aberdeenshire. His approach to archaeological field-survey placed him head and shoulders above his contemporaries, but he is little known today, possibly because, although he completed his survey of the Howe of Cromar in 1911, he did not publish the results until 1931, and by that time the impetus had been lost. He was challenged by the landscape of the Howe 'where the structures to be interpreted extend continuously over an area of many square miles' (1931, xi). He analysed the problem and took a series of methodological steps so that he might view the archaeology more clearly and direct his enquiry more rigorously. Disillusionment with Abercromby's crude excavations at Kinnord (1904) lead Ogston to write:

> While one would not undervalue excavation . . . it was yet evident that it could by no means exhaust the possibilities of obtaining information; that for a complete examination of such remains more was required, and that better results were to be obtained from a survey capable of yielding a panoramic view of all these structures in their topographical relations to one another. (1931, xi)

It would be tedious to quote the development of his methodology (1931, xi-xii), but it mirrors our more recent deliberations. Suffice it to say, he opted for selected examples from his landscape drawn on to a map base to produce illustrations that would not be out of place in *North-east Perth*.

Sir Alexander Ogston's work is a timely reminder of the repetition of history and it demands that, as professional archaeologists, we think carefully about the future of our discipline. Undoubtedly we are standing on the brink of realising the potential and possibilities of landscape archaeology. Landscape surveys are the starting points for sampling the visible archaeology, as well as sampling to establish the parameters of the 'invisible' archaeology, providing contexts in both time and space in the overall development of the landscape.

Bibliography

Abercromby, J. 1904 Exploration of circular enclosures and an underground house near Dinnet, on Deeside, Aberdeenshire, *Proc. Soc. Antiq. Scotland* 38 (1903–4), 102–22.

Brown, G. Baldwin 1905 *The care of ancient monuments*, Cambridge.

Lowe, C. E. and Barber, J. 1988 Strath of Kildonan: a large area prospective survey, in *Central Excavation Unit and Ancient Monuments Laboratory, Annual Report 1988*, Edinburgh, 21–6.

Ogston, A. 1931 *The prehistoric antiquities of the Howe of Cromar*, Aberdeen.

Piggott, C. M. 1951 The Iron Age settlement at Hayhope Knowe, Roxburghshire, excavations 1949, *Proc. Soc. Antiq. Scotland* 83 (1948–9), 45–67.

RCAHMS 1909 *Inventory of monuments and constructions in the County of Berwick*, Edinburgh.

RCAHMS 1911a *Inventory of the monuments and constructions in the County of Caithness*, Edinburgh.

RCAHMS 1911b *Inventory of the monuments and constructions in the County of Sutherland*, Edinburgh.

RCAHMS 1956 *An Inventory of the ancient and historical monuments of Roxburghshire*, Edinburgh.

RCAHMS 1967 *Peeblesshire: an inventory of the ancient monuments*, Edinburgh.

RCAHMS 1971–88 *Inventory of Argyll*, vols 1–6, Edinburgh.

RCAHMS 1984 *The archaeological sites and monuments of Scotland, no. 21: North Kincardine*, Edinburgh.

RCAHMS 1987 *The archaeological sites and monuments of Scotland, no. 26: East Rhins*, Edinburgh.

RCAHMS 1990 *North-east Perth: an archaeological landscape*, Edinburgh.

RCAHMS forthcoming *South-east Perth: an archaeological inventory*, Edinburgh.

Steer, K. A. 1951 The identification of palisaded enclosures from surface indications, in Piggott 1951, 64–7.

Steer, K. A. and Keeney, G. S. 1948 Excavations in two homesteads at Crock Cleuch, Roxburghshire, *Proc. Soc. Antiq. Scotland* 81 (1946–7), 138–57.

Acknowledgements

The authors are grateful to Mr. R. J. Mercer and Dr. J. N. Graham Ritchie for commenting on an earlier draft of this paper.

8

THE SURVEY OF A HILLTOP ENCLOSURE ON BEN GRIAM BEG, CAITHNESS AND SUTHERLAND DISTRICT, HIGHLAND REGION

R. J. Mercer

Background

In May 1988 during the execution of the long-established annual field season of survey in Caithness it was decided to investigate the feasibility of carrying out a detached, detailed survey of the hilltop enclosure set at 2,000 feet OD on Ben Griam Beg on the new Caithness/Sutherland District border. Originally this boundary was that between the parishes of Kildonan and Farr, both in the old county of Sutherland. Even today the majority of the site lies outwith the county of Caithness and therefore does not sit quite happily in a publication purporting to illustrate monuments of that county (see Mercer forthcoming a). In keeping with the title of this volume the writer will use the text of this survey account to form the basis for some comments upon trends in Scottish archaeological field survey as he sees them emerging over the next decade.

Ben Griam Beg is situated at NGR NC 83004125, 6 km west–south–west of Forsinard Railway Station and 41 km north–west of Helmsdale in Sutherland District, Highland Region. Access to the site is gained by an unmetalled track which leaves the A897 (a single track road at this point) at NGR NC 88008776. Gated access to this track is today kept padlocked and keys are held by the Kinbrace Estate Office at Achentoul Lodge. The track crosses the Allt na h-Airemh, north of its debouchment into Loch an Ruathair, on a timber bridge (estimated maximum loading 2 tonnes) whence it passes to the steading (now a shooting lodge) at Greamachory set 3 km to the west of the A897 at a height 500 feet OD. Thence approach is made to the site on foot, heading in a steady climb in a west–north–westerly direction for 2 km before turning due north for the steep ascent to the summit, a total climb of 1,500 feet. About one and a half hours should be set aside for this walked ascent, which should not be attempted in other than reasonably clement weather conditions.

Ben Griam Beg and Ben Griam Mor, with the stretch of land that lies between, them comprise an absolutely isolated massif of middle old red sandstone with the two eminences composed of the conglomerates that lie superimposed upon these and which, elsewhere, create the eminence of Morven 24 km away to the south-east. The absolute isolation of this 'island' is demonstrated by the fact that Morven is the nearest location of similar rocks, with the broader distribution on the Caithness plateau being 25–30 km to the east and north-east. Set between this isolated exposure and the main body of middle old red sandstone to the east are intrusive granites, moine schists and quartzites, rocks of an infinitely less hospitable nature to the farmer. Clearly this isolated pocket of rock had been located by early communities and recognised for its quality as a base for farming activity. The relatively gentle south-facing slope of Ben Griam Beg, with its long exposure to the sun's warmth, comprises a niche of land of relatively high agricultural potential. One can but admire the precision and acumen of the people who first located and developed it.

The reconnaissance of this mountain top in May produced adverse impressions. The weather deteriorated steadily through the day. The mountain was shrouded in cloud/mist which ultimately brought visibility down to about 20 m and the wind rose to a velocity where it was difficult not to be pushed from one's feet. This, combined with a horizontal wet-lashing, saw the party glad to regain its vehicles, although by that time a number of important decisions had already been taken.

The mountain top is, indeed, today a terribly hostile environment. Active cryoturbation ridges are, at present, undergoing formation in the seasonally sub-Arctic circumstances of the summit. Vegetation is restricted to mosses and lichens — heather will not survive on the summit area. Cryoturbation has led to distortion and disruption of the man-made features and had given cause for very considerable doubt about the authenticity, or the original form, of features known on the site from the RAF vertical aerial photographs (ie RAF 10GG/Scot/UK 76: 3, 355–7) and, indeed, of a wide range of features set to the south of the hilltop enclosure, of which more will emerge. It became apparent that ground survey was essential to elucidate and validate these features. Furthermore, it was apparent that a considerable augmentation of data, over and above that visible on the aerial photographic record, would be possible by ground survey, as well as an evaluation of prevalent soil conditions on the hilltop, with a view to suggesting further lines of enquiry on the site.

The site has not figured largely in the literature. The first published account, as one might expect, was that by Alexander Curle, the first Secretary of RCAHMS, who visited the site on 18 September 1909 during his prodigious coverage of the two northern counties. His description, which can be compared with the current plan (Fig. 8.1), runs as follows (RCAHMS 1911, 108–9):

Two main lines of defence fortify the summit. Approaching from the south, between the 1500 feet and 1600 feet elevations, a solid stone wall, some 5 feet thick, and in places still as much in height, runs down from the summit at the southeast, and is carried westward along the edge of the shoulder of the hill for what appears to be a distance of some 500 yards, terminating at the edge of a mossy hollow, beyond which a precipitous rocky face (Creagan Iolair) forms a natural defence to the west. Through the wall near the centre of its course is a gap, which has probably been an entrance. In rear of it, to the east in the interior, is a circular depression. The absence of the wall across the short stretch of wet peat that fills the hollow at the western end is not remarkable, as there would be a difficulty in obtaining a firm foundation on such material. A wooden palisade may have been used as a substitute. To the east of the centre of the course of this wall there is a space of about 150 yards, over which there is an almost complete absence of stone on the hillside and where only the foundation of the wall is apparent. On the slopes below it, except at the gap mentioned, there is a perfect network of ruined walls or piled stones enclosing irregular spaces and forming an outer defence. At the western end of the hill, above the mossy hollow, and passing round towards the north, the same system of defence is repeated, but at a higher level than on the south face. Between the lower edge of this defence at its southern end and the wall along the edge of the shoulder, an open space is left, varying from 20 to 60 yards or thereby in width. Around the more or less level portion of the summit, towards the west, runs another wall, 4 feet to 5 feet thick, and at highest some 3 feet high, forming an enclosure, sub-oval in outline, about 500 feet in length by 200 feet in breadth (OS measurements). A break in the upper wall, just below the summit on the north side, 6 feet wide, seems to have been an entrance. This wall appears to terminate to the west of the actual summit, which is a rocky peak. Beyond the peak, some 40 feet distant, are visible the remains of another wall flanking the intervening space on the east and running for a short distance (about 50 feet) westward. Some 100 feet below this appears a network of ruined walls, from which starts the wall first described running along the shoulder. The northeast flank of the hill is precipitous, and the north is also very steep. The actual top of the hill within the upper enclosure is windswept and barren, with little vegetation on it. There is no spring of water visible in the fort, but there are several on the hillside just below it.

Lying among the ruins of the lower wall, roughly 150 feet below the summit, at the extreme east end, is a round mill-stone of the native sandstone, broken in halves. It is 4 feet in diameter, 5 inches thick, and is pierced in the centre with a hole 5 inches in diameter. To lessen the amount of piercing the stone has been previously flaked towards the centre in a circle of 1 foot 7 inches diameter, reducing the thickness to 2 inches. Neither face of the stone is worn regularly smooth by friction but there are depressions across the line of its revolution. Two other similar mill-stones are said to have lain on the slopes of the hill below the fortifications. One of them has now been rolled to the bottom.

A more lucid and competent description would be difficult to find. But it is one that looked almost exclusively at the hilltop enclosure — a view which unless impeded by cloud (which it might well have been) largely ignored another, less ordered, built landscape below.

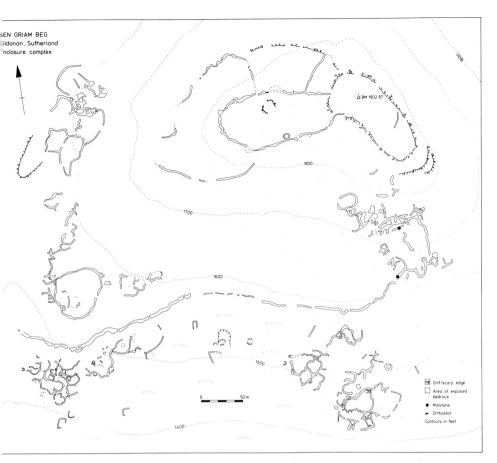

Fig. 8.1 Ben Griam Beg, Kildonan, Sutherland: enclosure complex

No further description of the site was made until May 1960 when it was visited by Jim Davidson and briefly described, as well as a 'sketch' survey undertaken. In 1963 R. W. Feachem published a very brief account of the monument (1963) in which he suggests tentatively that 'below (the fort) on the southern flank of the hill there lie the remains of other linear walls and of walled enclosures which, if they are contemporary with the fort and are of Early Iron Age date, may represent an expansion of the true fort into a much larger defended and occupied area'.

A further visit by Ordnance Survey personnel took place in 1977. Keith Blood appears, in his brief descriptive remarks, to take issue with Feachem's model of development on the site. His description reads:

> The fort . . . occupies the flattish summit of the hill. Its wall is crudely constructed of slabs and is of unusually slender proportions, though the steep rock-strewn hill slopes afford a good natural defence. The enclosures abutting on the west and northeast sides and the crude wall extending southwards from the southeast corner before turning west, are of similar construction to the fort, except that the wall of the northeast enclosure is more slight. These appendages to the fort do not

appear to be outer defences; they do not utilise any natural defence that may exist.

The several small, irregularly-shaped enclosures at NC 828409 are visible as platforms set into the slope on average 12.0 m across, with their lower edges retained by bands of stone. The interiors are noticeably clear of stones compared with surrounding rocky ground. In no way do they resemble hut-circles. There are other enclosures of similar type, those at NC 831409 being largely obscured by scree, and others at NC 828410 occurring on more level ground.

Blood goes on to say, however: 'the fort and complex of walls and enclosures below it appear contemporary. The extremely remote and exposed situation of the complex probably indicates a temporary refuge for men and beast under threat of attack, rather than a permanent settlement' (NNIR NC 84 SW 1). After visiting it in 1981, Ian Ralston and John Smith drew further published attention to this under-appreciated site (1983). The focus of their comment was upon the high altitude of the settlement below the hill-fort, set between 1,400 and 1,600 feet (420–75 m) OD, which was mentioned briefly in the accounts of Curle and the OS. Their description offers more detail of these subsidiary features which can now be substantially enhanced. The onus of their comment, however, rested upon the degree to which soil-creep and peat-growth over the site suggested an early date and they commented upon the parallels between the settlement on this site with the so-called platform settlement below the summit of Tap O'Noth (Gordon district), also c. 1,500 feet (456 m) OD. Their remarkable prescience in this matter is thrown into relief by the work of David Sanderson whose thermoluminescence dating of vitrified material from this site has suggested a calendar date 4.1 Ka ± 0.4 BP (2160 ± 400 BC) (Sanderson et al.1988).

Survey

It was decided to set aside one week for the survey of the site in late June 1988. A team of five experienced surveyors, plus the writer, were invited to carry out the task — Miss Jane Blair, Miss Karen Elder, Mr. Charles LeQuesne, Mr. Gordon Thomas and Miss Angela Wardell. Angela Wardell drew the plan of the surveyed area shown in Fig. 8.1. The equipment base, apart from routine surveying equipment (tapes, prismatic compasses, arrows etc) was two theodolites (with tripods and staffs) and one Topcon Total Station EDM (with tripod and prism), radio sets, painted bamboo canes and ranging rods. Photographic gear was also taken. All personnel were clad in waterproof/windproof clothing, neck to ankle, with headgear, gloves and boots. Day 1 comprised a transportation and reconnaissance trip. Heavy gear, eg tripods, was lifted using a framed manpack carrier, the remainder being carried in rucksacks or by hand. Heavy-duty survival bags were carried so that less delicate items of equipment could be stored on the hilltop during the course of the survey. All instruments, cameras, prisms, radio sets etc had, of course, to be imported each day. Spare tripods, staffs etc were retained at base to enable work to take place at a lower level should work at the higher levels prove impossible due to weather conditions. This proved a wise precaution.

The progress of the survey was intermittent with only two and a half days on the mountain top possible out of seven. Day 2 was effectively a half day with weather closing in to a visibility of 25 m by 2.00 pm. Days 3 and 4 were non-starters (during which a survey was conducted of the pre-improvement and post-improvement farmsteads at Greamachory itself). A reconnaissance trip to the summit was conducted on Day 4, only to confirm that conditions were impossible. Day 5 dawned promisingly but most of the day was spent in relatively unpleasant conditions with, however, useful survey results. Day 6 was a washout, with Day 7 dawning fair. Work on that day was frenetic — by 4.00 pm the weather was closing very rapidly and the last party reported survey completed at 5.20 pm. At precisely that point an extremely violent thunderstorm broke out. The writer still senses the tension created by that storm and congratulates his colleagues upon the coolness and business-like manner with which they greeted that contingency — during which all equipment had to be removed from the mountain.

The survey was undertaken as a series of five units — the hilltop enclosure, the eastern settlement complex and the south-eastern, south-western and western settlement complexes. Much of the internal survey within each unit was accomplished by theodolite survey with baselines developed by EDM. Finally key points over the whole survey were checked and tied together by EDM measurement.

Description of the site

The hill-fort can now be seen as a unitary defensive conception of probably two phases or, at least, two functional conceptions (Fig. 8.1). To the east is a naturally defined area edged by steep crags. No walling defines this eminence nor would it ever have been necessary. The one point where an assailant might have gained a foothold and rallied on relatively level ground has been flanked by a stretch of walling and the south-east approach to this summit is naturally defended by three broadly concentric lines of natural crag-defence. On the south-west side a small weakness in the crag-face is strengthened by a short stretch of walling. This 'enclosure' centres upon the modern trigonometric point, which has been levelled by lightning strike (with fragments of its brick structure located at a distance of 150 m), although fortunately the levelling 'heel' of the station was apparently undisturbed. The interior of this 'enclosure' is now almost entirely bare bedrock surface with little archaeological potential.

Attached to the south-west flank of this summit eminence is a walled enclosure 130 m by an average of 60 m. Within this enclosure is another lower eminence surrounded by an area of bare bedrock. Elsewhere the internal surface is covered by shallow peat which deepens on the downhill side of the enclosure (the west side) to more than 60 cm. The walling of this enclosure would appear to have been gang-built in lengths of *c.* 25 m, with changes in direction and subtle changes in building technique visible. On the northern side of the enclosure the building style is predominantly a narrow wall base of *c.* 1.5 m defined by upright slabs which have moved outwards, their tops tipping over with the force of basal soil-creep around them. This technique is also used at the eastern end of the south wall. Towards the western end of the north wall and around the west end of the enclosure occurs massive coursed stone-work over a rather wider wall base, which changes in the south-west sector to a mixture of narrow- and wide- wall styles. Wherever peat is of any depth at all, it can be seen to have engulfed the base of the stones; more so in the western sector. The rate of peat growth in this extraordinarily exposed location may have been very slow indeed.

This enclosure exhibits three probable entrances, and a possible fourth. The latter is at the southeast extremity of the enclosure *c.* 10 m from the point where the wall of the enclosure departs from the crag-enclosed summit 'enclosure'. The gap in the wall is here *c.* 2.5 m wide and is approached across steep, rock-strewn ground. To the west an entrance occurs at a distance of 35 m. This entrance is 3 m in width with quite clearly expanded wall terminals to either side of it. Set 8 m to the west, in the interior of the enclosure, is a very clearly defined 'hut circle' *c.* 8 m in diameter featuring as a low embanked circle under peat-cover with no clearly apparent entrance. A substantial gap in the wall 55 m further to the west was rejected by the survey party as a possible entrance on the grounds that recognisable traces of the wall's total outward collapse were visible. No entrance was apparent in the western arc of the enclosure wall. The next probable entrance lies 12 m to the north-west of the rocky eminence that lies within the enclosure. This entrance, without any visibly expanded wall terminals, is *c.* 3 m in width and apparently gave access to two outer annexes (see below). Immediately to the east is a substantial gap in the wall apparently brought about by collapse. At a further distance eastwards of *c.* 40 m is a third probable entrance approximately 2 m in width with slightly expanded wall terminals on either side.

The internal area of the summit, crag-defined, 'enclosure' is approximately 5,500 sq m, while the western enclosure attached to it is approximately 6,500 sq m making an area of 1.2 ha in total. Taken together the writer has little doubt that the 'crag-enclosure' (with its man-made 'improvements') and the western enclosure may be considered a defensive structure. Where the walls are well-preserved they stand today to a height of 1.8 m and probably stood only a little higher at the time the site was in use. They would present, however, a serious enough obstacle if defended with vigour by somebody who has not just climbed 150 m.

Attached to the north and west sides of this central enclosure complex are two, and possibly three, annexes. The first, to the west, is defined by a low and fragmentary wall that runs from 15 m south of the western enclosure's southern wall down slope and round to the west to pick up the scarp edge of the mountain top, and then around to the north-west side before curving inwards. There are some indications that it may originally have run right up to the more westerly of the two northern entrances of the western hilltop enclosure. The wall of this annexe, following as it does the scarp edge of the summit and being relatively slight construction, has disappeared without trace at a number of points, either as a result of total collapse or perhaps through engulfment by peat. The wall has been built evenly of relatively small boulders set upright and can never have been of great height. The area of the western annexe is approximately 8,000 sq m. No coherent traces of entrances exist within the extant wall-line.

On the north side of the western hilltop enclosure there is the strong likelihood of a further annexe of 4,200 sq m. Its outer limits are defined by the same crag-edge that forms the summit crag-enclosure. Its existence is, however, asserted by the length of wall, again relatively slight, that runs north-east to south-west over c. 50 m to join the western hilltop enclosure wall. Not even the most enthusiastic or hopeful eye could detect any evidence of chronological priority at the point of juncture. This wall is of similar composition and construction to that of the western annexe enclosure.

The continuation of the natural crag-line to the south-east to join the craggy massif of the summit enclosure suggests the existence of what may have been regarded as the third annexe of the north-east side of the central enclosure of about 1,000 sq m extent.

Thus this hilltop enclosure complex comprises four, possibly five, sub-enclosures covering a total area of c. 2.5 ha. Springs yielding water are extant on the south slope of the hill immediately outwith the enclosure, although no spring was recognised within it. Today the environment of the enclosures can be, as has been indicated, most inhospitable even in mid summer. Vegetation is minimal and largely restricted to moss and stunted heather. Even birds were a relatively scarce sighting and other animal life was not observed. Still, although only one circular house foundation has yet been detected within the central enclosure, this is presumably sufficient to indicate that human activity took place there, if only on a periodic basis. There the argument for the use of the hilltop would rest were it not for the extraordinary features visible below the hilltop that represent apparently prolonged economic use of the area (although not necessarily, it must be said, at a period synchronous with the use of the hilltop enclosure).

Further archaeological investigation of the hilltop enclosure complex can only ever be of limited extent and intention, within the framework of present archaeological technique. Nevertheless with simple pit-digging in the western sector of the central enclosure it would be possible to extract a peat column of c. 60 cm depth — and perhaps more — in direct association with the enclosure wall foundation. From this might emerge an environmental statement relating to the period at the immediate onset of peat growth. A linked radiocarbon date might also provide a *terminus ante quem* for the enclosure construction.

The external features are situated to the west, south and south-east of the enclosure complex and clearly exploit the unique geological and micro-climatological environment based upon the sandstone rock. In this area there is the maximum range of sun-strike, and the mountain provides shelter from the prevailing north-west wind.

The principal feature of this complex is the great linking wall running obliquely across the 1,600–1,500 feet contour from the north-east to south-west. This is a truly monumental structure at either end, and particularly at the south west end, standing to a consistent height of 2.0–2.5 m with cyclopean slabs piled one on top of the other. In reflecting the outer form of the hilltop enclosure complex, this wall is doing no more than reflecting the form of the mountain. In terms of ground plan, its diminished proportions in its central section are simply a feature of the vastly greater peat growth within this re-entrant situation, with both the presence of springs and of natural drainage leading to an accelerated growth. Inspection and extrapolation must indicate that in this area, by the wall itself, as much as 2–2.5 m of peat growth is extant. Here, in brief, lie important archaeological opportunities which, by means of comparison with results obtained within the hilltop central enclosure, might allow useful chronological and environmental contrasts between the two, although the palaeo-enviro-chronometer can be expected to be much more sensitive in the wall area.

The wall is of massive construction throughout its length, and exhibits numerous clear entrances/exits — often quite close together as, for example, at its west end. Here a succession of three 'entrances' occur within 50 m of one another, with the easternmost exhibiting what appears to be an intra-mural cavity 10 m to the east of it. Further to the east three very clear gaps in the wall appear before its form becomes incoherent as it drops into the peat-filled re-entrant wherein only the uppermost parts of its structure can be detected for a distance of nearly 100 m. Emergent once again and standing to its former stature, it proceeds but a short way (c. 30 m) to an extensive gap c. 15 m wide which does appear to be 'real'. Thus to the east four 'entrances' occur over a length of c. 150 m with the second among these also, apparently, exhibiting an intra-mural chamber. The fourth entrance leads the wall into an integral enclosure complex at its east end which will be described separately below. The micro-format (with intra-mural cavities entered from the north side and its clear gang-building lengths bowing out from the north side — each length losing a little height before necessarily regaining it to meet the next) and the macro-format (with its convex extensions dropping across the contour) suggest that this wall was built as a boundary cutting off south from north. Such a judgement is little more than subjective, but may be minimally sustained by suggestions made below.

This wall divides two groups of structures. The group to the south-east and south-west of the wall are very probably more apparently separate than actually so. The impression of separation is almost certainly created by the deep peat burying a conjoining series of structures. These structures, as can be seen from the plan (Fig. 8.1), reflect themselves by isolated structural elements that show above the bog surface (and within the spring washout at the focus of the re-entrant).

To the north of the wall lie two groups separated by the increasingly steep hillside — a division that is almost certainly real enough. To the west the components of this enclosure complex lie within, and on the east side of, a steep-sided very sheltered (in comparative terms) re-entrant lined on the western side by steep-sided crags that lie outwith the area of survey. This western component may be divided into two sections — a southern and a northern. The northerly of the two comprises a series of conjoined enclosures with, at their focus, a series of small cellular structures varying from 10 m by 5 m to 3 m by 5 m in size. The nature of the construction of these structures, carried out with large boulders, rendered their precise form difficult to assess, but six or seven separate small units of likely human accommodation could be seen as cell units integral with the construction of the main enclosures.

To the south, what is probably a continuation of the northerly group exists, precisely similar in its construction, and comprising at least two larger enclosures with more small cellular units (again six or seven) disposed around the area and, once again, cognate with the enclosure walls. The southerly limit of this enclosure complex does appear to conform to the line of the major east — west wall discussed above.

At the eastern end of the great wall stretching for 500 m lies a further group of structures, in this instance apparently joined to the wall. Here the structures would appear to be of a different form and are certainly located in different circumstances. Unlike those structures to the west, the eastern complex is built on steep, rock-strewn hillside, quite unlike the relatively sheltered and hospitable circumstances of the western complex. Its form is also somewhat different. Here large enclosures are lacking. Instead we observe an essentially rectilinear system with, at the focus of the complex, long, broadly rectilinear (or trapezoidal) structures with in one instance a central trapezoidal structure having, apparently, a transverse subdivision. The presence of small circular cellular structures in this complex may well suggest that the situation here is complex, but to the field archaeologist there is a 'lateish' look about these rectilinear structures. It is, therefore, perhaps interesting that here and not elsewhere the survey located (as had indeed been observed by Curle in 1909) two perforated millstones which have been produced from local sandstone and which, being damaged or broken in the process of manufacture, have been abandoned as unworthy of removal.

To the south of the 500–m wall lies a further series of structures. There are apparently two complexes which, however, are almost certainly united by further concealed structures lying beneath the 2 m or more of peat that has accumulated within the re-entrant on the south side of the hill. These two complexes are similar to each other in two principal respects. First, they comprise walls of similar boulder construction (though different from either complex north of the main wall) and they are composed of small irregularly shaped enclosures, which contained within them (but not cellularly within the walls) very small, 5 m or less, round stone houses built within or against walls of very irregular outline, and lesser stature, enclosing a series of conjoined small enclosures. The second common feature of these structures is that at all points they appear to be curtailed, and perhaps destroyed, by the construction of the main wall.

If one follows the logic of the above observations then it might prove possible to erect the following interim, field observed, sequence:

1. Those structures south of the wall. Small, relatively slightly built enclosures with very small round houses built within, but not integrally with, those enclosures. The whole complex is apparently broken and curtailed by the construction of the main east–west (500-m) wall.
2. The 500–m wall itself and possibly (although this could be a separate development) those elements at its western end and to the north side of it that conform with its position.
3. The settlement at the east end and north side of the main wall where rectangular/trapezoidal structures might anyway suggest later date, and which is cognate with the previous or current existence of the main wall in its disposition.
4. Over and above this separation of phases (based upon the axis of the main wall) lies the hillfort with its various sub-enclosures which lies in an uncertain relationship with all three 'phases'.

Thus at an altitude of 1,900 feet, in the most exposed circumstances, we observe a complex hill-fort of unknown date with a range of settlement around it, possibly multiphase, all of it at a height in excess of 1,400 feet above sea level. None of this complex of the remains of human activity can be linked in any way to any known chronological horizon. Ralston and Smith (1983) constructed a courageous and valuable case which suggested that the very altitude of the hill-fort at Ben Griam Beg was to some extent a chronological indicator. They pointed out the other hill-forts in Scotland at an equivalent altitude had produced (some) early dates by thermoluminescence dating of vitrified rampart remains — an hypothesis which has since been further substantiated.

Conclusions

The focus of this book is the future of Scottish archaeology and the problems, soluble or insoluble, that face it. To the author, some of these problems are, to some extent, encapsulated within the field survey presented here, though further exploration of the difficulties inherent in upland field survey will be undertaken in a forthcoming paper based upon the writer's Wheeler Lecture to the British Academy (Mercer forthcoming b).

In Scotland we still have very many major sites and whole tracts of landscape that remain to be surveyed in any detail. Their survey will require not only a major commitment of simple physical resources, but also the best technology and the deployment of the most competent skills in order to achieve any adequate record. It is endemically unlikely that the survey of such unattractive monuments in such remote areas will attract commercial sponsorship on a long-term basis and it is, therefore, likely that the provision for such survey will probably find its origin in public bodies — the RCAHMS and universities — certainly for the foreseeable future. Climatic and access difficulties will frequently mean that such surveys cannot be pursued at the optimum level of efficiency: there will be inevitable time loss for transit and for the unworkable conditions that such adverse environmental conditions can create.

Once having located the sites, however, the problems change in their complexion if not in the challenge they offer. In the first instance, in Scotland, there exists as yet no readily referable or, indeed, communally understood chronological reference against which very large tracts of the ancient landscape can be plotted. Indeed, in the few areas where it was perhaps felt that a degree of consensus did exist, it is rapidly emerging that that measure of certainty no longer applies. It is not so long ago that we felt secure in locating brochs firmly within a very well defined period; similarly stone circles and certainly hill-forts. These certainties are now gone and the Scord of Brouster, Shetland (Whittle 1986) has warned us forcefully about making grossly simplistic assumptions about 'hut circle' groups associated with cairnfields. Rectangular buildings are yet another area where house foundations leave the field worker stranded in a 'no man's land' (chronologically speaking) between the immediately pre-improvement (or indeed post-improvement) period and that which immediately succeeds the brochs, of whose date we are in any case no longer certain.

In a sense, Ben Griam Beg, where field survey evidence might suggest that three or possibly four episodes of activity have taken place, makes this point supremely well. Yet not a single one of those phases, the writer would suggest, could confidently be assigned to any single millennium AD or BC on its own merits, and even the quasi-stratigraphy offered by field survey of the site really offers no multiple registration that could allow any chronological refinement.

Furthermore, the predominant building environment of Scotland, at least in the upland zone, that of stone-building, is in itself an enormous benefit. Yet, ironically, it can also pose a profound setback to our proceeding. Beneficial, of course, in the permanence of its survival, its frequent confinement to the isolated tracts of land of suitable fertility and location in terms of water, communications and sun-strike, has led to consistent retroactive dilapidation as a later structure or land use strategy reorganises or re-uses the fabric of earlier structures. This phenomenon can be seen to good effect again at Ben Griam Beg. It presents us with the danger of the recurrent over-simplification or undervaluing of the chronological range of the remains superficially visible to us through the agency of field survey. This difficulty has led to some disillusionment with the interpretation of archaeological field survey because field interpretation prior to some recent excavations has been shown by those excavations to be simplistic both chronologically and structurally. This disillusion has led to frequent expression of the view that the interpretation of field survey information is at best a premature, and at worst a misleading, exercise, and that the act of record is the extent of the surveyor's responsibility.

It will be apparent from the discussion above that the writer does not subscribe to this view. In fact he regards it as anathema. However intermediate any observations based upon field evidence may be, it is the duty of the field surveyor to endeavour to interpret what he or she sees in order to allow the accumulation of recurrent observations, which will in turn allow the construction of the research designs upon which the expensive tool — expensive both financially and in terms of the cultural resource — of excavation can be trained with the greatest accuracy and value for money. Once again, survey at Ben Griam Beg allows an intermediate interpretation that points the way to interventionist approaches and allows some measure of comparison with other, broadly similar, sites.

If we accept Christison as the father of scientific archaeological survey in Scotland, then we stand at the end of a 100-year tradition. Yet in all those years we have barely begun the detailed recording of our landscape. Many sites of remarkable stature remain to be adequately recorded and we have yet to mount the lower slopes of any clear understanding of the sequence of settlement types over the broad chronology of farming settlement in Scotland. With Sir Isaac Newton we can perhaps feel that, thus far, we seem 'to have been only like a boy playing on the seashore and diverting [ourselves] in now and then finding a smoother pebble, or a prettier shell than ordinary whilst the great ocean of truth lies all undiscovered before [us]'.

Bibliography

Feachem, R. 1963 *Guide to prehistoric Scotland*, London.

Mercer, R. J. forthcoming a *Archaeological field survey in northern Scotland Vol.IV, 1983–87*, Edinburgh.

Mercer, R. J. forthcoming b Archaeology and landscape development in Scotland, *Proc. Brit. Academy* 1991.

Ralston, I. B. M. and Smith, J. S. 1983 High altitude settlement on Ben Griam Beg, Sutherland, *Proc. Soc. Antiq. Scotland* 113, 636–8.

RCAHMS 1911 *Second report and inventory of monuments and constructions in the County of Sutherland*, Edinburgh.

Sanderson, D. C. W., Placido, F. and Tate, J. O. 1988 Scottish vitrified forts: TL results from six study sites, *Nuclear Tracks* 14, 307–16.

Whittle, A. (ed) 1986 *Scord of Brouster*, Oxford.

9

THE ARCHAEOLOGY OF THE SCOTTISH LOWLANDS: PROBLEMS AND POTENTIAL

W. S. Hanson and Lesley Macinnes

The last fifteen years has seen a dramatic increase in the database for the Scottish Lowlands, but integration of this material with other forms of evidence and assessment of its contribution to our understanding of Scottish archaeology has failed to keep pace with the speed of its collection. This paper sets out to consider the potential of this evidence, identify biases in its collection, priorities for its assessment, and examine possible methods of approach.

The Lowlands are taken here to mean land subject to intensive agricultural use, either arable or pasture. In the main this means land below the 250 metre contour, with some local variations, and thus concentrates on the area to the south and east of the Highland massif, excluding the mass of the Southern Uplands. Within these areas the pattern of modern land use varies considerably, though in broad terms arable cultivation concentrates in the east with its higher proportion of grade 1 soils and lower average rainfall (Coppock 1976, chs 1 and 3).

With the exception of discrete monuments, usually of substantial proportions or of masonry construction and often located in pockets of unimproved or slightly higher ground, the vast bulk of archaeological sites in the Lowlands does not survive as recognisable upstanding monuments. Even Scotland's largest ancient monument, the 57 km long Antonine Wall, whose ditch was in places as much as 12 metres wide and 3.5 metres deep, is not visible for most of its length. The disappearance of the tangible remains of Scotland's long history of occupation from these most fertile parts of the country is a direct result of that fertility, for most sites have been ploughed flat. Such differential survival is well illustrated in some of the river valleys which penetrate the Southern Uplands, where the flat valley floor is currently intensively cultivated and there is little or no visible archaeology. But at the edges of the valley, at the margins of the ploughed land, archaeological sites do survive as upstanding monuments. There is an excellent example of this in the upper Clyde valley near Crawford (Fig. 9.1). Spread across no more than a kilometre and hugging the north side of the valley as the river bends eastwards, there is a group of at least five later prehistoric enclosures surviving as visible earthworks, two of which contain

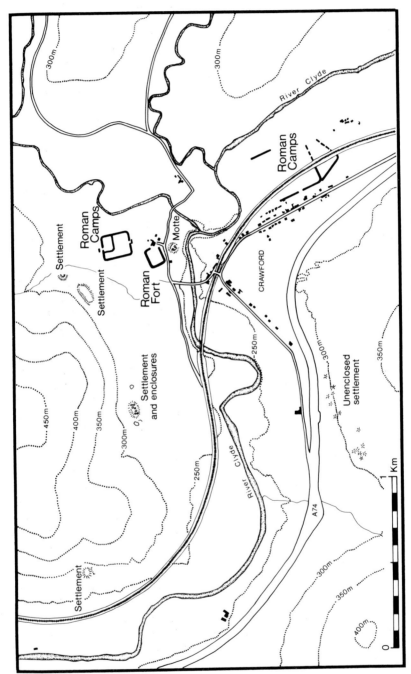

Fig. 9.1 Upstanding and invisible sites in the vicinity of Crawford

clear traces of internal structures (RCAHMS 1978, 86–97 *passim*). Yet less than 400 metres to the south in the centre of the valley the site of a Roman auxiliary fort is detectable on the ground only in ideal low light conditions, while only 200 metres away, and again a further kilometre upstream (RCAHMS 1978, 128–30), the remains of Roman temporary camps are visible only as cropmarks. Interestingly, this area also provides an example of the occasional survival of a well-preserved site within the plough zone: a motte with upstanding, though crumbling, masonry immediately adjacent to the site of the Roman fort.

The low level of archaeological visibility in the lowland plough zone is to some extent offset by the application of aerial photography, whose contribution to our understanding of the archaeology of the Lowlands is considerable. Indeed, it is no exaggeration to state that aerial reconnaissance has made the single most important contribution to our appreciation of the density, diversity and widespread distribution of archaeological sites in recent years. This is particularly the case for sites which survive only as cropmarks or soil marks. It is through aerial reconnaissance that we have come to recognise that these lowland fertile zones have always been, as they are today, the core areas for settlement in Scotland. The contribution of air reconnaissance lies in the first instance in the discovery of new sites. This continues each year and is perhaps most readily exemplified by the filling out of the map of Roman Scotland (St Joseph 1976) (Fig. 9.2). But more than just increasing the density and extending the area of distribution of familiar types of site, aerial photography is also responsible for the discovery of classes of monument, such as square barrows or cursus, previously unknown in Scotland (Maxwell 1983a) and, indeed, the recognition of entirely new types, such as the semi-subterranean structures recently excavated at Easter Kinnear (DES 1989, 17–18). Finally, by providing evidence of patterns of field boundaries and land divisions, it can demonstrate graphically that archaeology is concerned with the history of the landscape, within which archaeological 'sites' are merely foci, or concentrations, of past human activity.

Aerial reconnaissance for cropmarks or soil marks is not equally effective throughout the lowland zone. Because buried archaeological features are generally filled with dark silty or humic material, soil marks in recently ploughed fields show best against a brightly coloured or reflective subsoil. Such soils are not common in Scotland, with the result that soil marks have been recorded infrequently; though equally they have not often been sought. There is scope for improving the record here. A programme of flying specifically for soil marks may help to reveal sites in areas less susceptible to cropmark production. However, the financial constraints on such speculative work are considerable. The total annual budget for aerial reconnaissance in Scotland equates broadly with the cost of a single medium-sized excavation, and in terms of information-return provides, arguably, the best value for money in archaeology. Perhaps it is time for aerial reconnaissance to be given a higher priority than has been the case in the past.

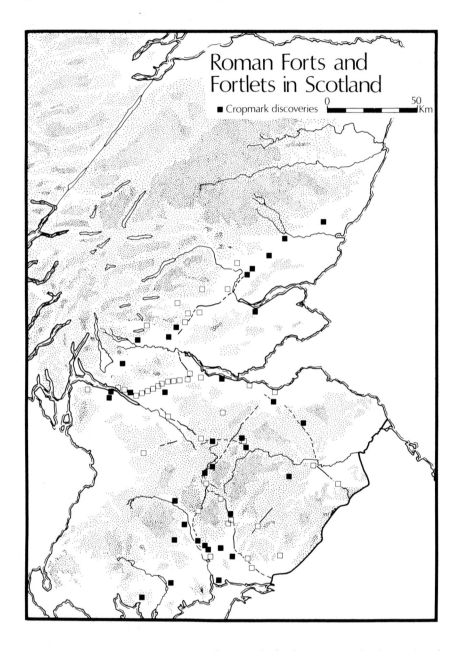

Fig. 9.2 Distribution of Roman forts and fortlets in Scotland: cropmark discoveries

The limited finances available for aerial photography tend to focus attention on summer reconnaissance for cropmarks or winter, oblique-light coverage of upland areas. Since the visibility of cropmarks is directly linked to the availability of moisture, mediated by soil type and depth, and by crop type, there is considerable bias in their recovery and, consequently, known distribution. In particular, there is a strong bias in favour of the drier eastern side of the country with its well-drained, fertile soils and greater concentration on arable agriculture, as opposed to the west with its generally wetter climate and much higher proportion of grazing land. It was noticeable in the relatively poor summer of 1990, for example, that cropmarks were almost totally absent from the west side of the country whilst still visible in parts of the east. This situation is exacerbated, however, by a natural tendency to concentrate reconnaissance in areas where there is the most obvious and immediate return. Thus even in a very dry summer such as occurred in 1984 or 1989, the bulk of flying has still tended to take place in the eastern regions, especially Lothian, Fife, Angus and Grampian. If we are to redress this balance in the recovery of aerial photographic data, there must be positive discrimination in terms of both finances and the deployment of personnel in favour of less productive areas. This is particularly the case in those rare, very dry years, occurring perhaps only once every decade, which may be the only occasions when some sites become visible in such areas. Indeed, the effect of the very dry summer of 1949 on the discovery of Roman sites in south-west Scotland has become almost a textbook example of the extreme circumstances sometimes necessary before sites become visible in the west (Evans and Jones 1977). Moreover, recent flying in Moray and Nairn has further demonstrated the potential of areas which are less frequently reconnoitred.

But aerial photography is also biased in terms of the types of sites detectable. It is largely constrained by the extent to which the archaeological remains involved cause physical disturbance of the subsoil, and thus ditched enclosures tend to predominate in the photographic record. As a result the technique is biased towards the recovery of settlement evidence of the historic and later prehistoric periods. The known settlement pattern of the Scottish Mesolithic, for example, is predominantly coastal, yet there are good reasons for believing that occupation of the interior was more extensive than is currently attested (Woodman 1989). Accordingly, alternative strategies for site discovery need to be more widely employed.

The nature in which most archaeological sites survive in the Lowlands largely precludes terrestrial survey, except on the margins of the cultivated area or in relation to the pockets of survival already mentioned. Nevertheless, ground checking of aerial photographic sites remains worthwhile if only to gain greater appreciation of the local topography and ecological setting.

However, there are other modes of survey which have been little applied in Scotland, but which have produced a considerable volume of information elsewhere. Fieldwalking after ploughing provides a speedy and non-destructive method of artifact recovery which can be further enhanced by the controlled use of metal detectors. Inevitably there is a bias towards the recovery of artifacts made from durable materials and from periods when the material culture was rich (cf Crowther 1983, 35), that is, principally, earlier prehistoric lithics and Roman, medieval and later pottery. Nonetheless, the exercise can offer valuable information about the past exploitation of the landscape provided the biases inherent in the data and the mode of their collection are borne in mind (Shennan 1985; Haselgrove et al. 1985). Indeed, the bias towards the recovery of lithics would go some way towards redressing that inherent in the aerial photographic record.

The technique is sufficiently simple and cost effective to be applied on a speculative basis across a wide area regardless of whether any potential sites have already been indicated by other methods of survey. Recent, systematic fieldwork by Colin Richards employed a strategy of runs 25 metres apart and 50 metres long across a transect through Sandwick, Stromness, Stenness and Orphir on mainland Orkney, designed to locate Neolithic settlement patterns. This resulted in the discovery of a previously unknown settlement of that period, at Barnhouse, which was subsequently confirmed by geophysical survey and excavation (DES 1986, 21–2). It is to be hoped that the promotion of fieldwalking by the Council for Scottish Archaeology and Historic Scotland will result in its increased application, especially as it is a procedure ideally suited to the involvement of local societies. Indeed, the technique has been employed for some years in Scotland by a small number of individual amateur archaeologists. What is now required is a more intensive and systematic approach.

Fieldwalking is also potentially useful for the dating of features identified through aerial photography, though the relationship between artifacts in the ploughsoil and structural remains beneath it is far from direct and does require the coverage of a sufficiently wide area to identify concentrations of artifacts against the background of material derived from the manuring of fields. This fact may be turned to advantage, for gaps in the distribution of particular materials might indicate areas of contemporary pasture (Crowther 1983, 40).

More specialised, but similarly little applied in Scotland, is geophysical survey. Until recently there was little resident expertise available and some doubts expressed about the widespread applicability of magnetometry in relation to the underlying geology of Scotland with its high percentage of igneous rocks. The first problem is slowly being remedied and facilities are now available in the Department of Archaeology at Glasgow University, for example, while the second is perhaps not as serious a problem as previously thought in the Lowlands, with their overlying drift geology and high percentage of alluvial deposits. Geophysical survey, particularly combining both magnetometer and resistivity, provides potentially valuable and relatively detailed information about site morphology. In principle this technique could help fill some of the large gaps in known site distribution, particularly in areas of improved pasture where neither aerial reconnaissance, terrestrial fieldwork nor arable fieldwalking are applicable. However, it is time-consuming and expensive to undertake over large areas and must, therefore, be applied selectively to locations where there is already some suspicion or indication of an archaeological presence. It was, for example, employed at Barnhouse to provide further information on the Neolithic settlement identified from the fieldwalking mentioned above, and has recently been used to provide enhanced knowledge of sites found from the air; for example, at a number of settlements in the Newstead area (Jones 1990, 112) and within the annexe of the Roman fort at Elginhaugh (Hanson and Yeoman 1988, 2–3).

Additionally, geophysical survey might usefully be applied on the fringes of, or to gaps within, cropmark complexes, as it recently was at Easter Kinnear, Fife (DES 1990, 16–7). The criteria for cropmark formation in relation to soil depth are now well understood (Evans and Jones 1977), and there are clear indications from excavated cropmark sites that only a small percentage of the surviving archaeological evidence is revealed in the photograph. This was well illustrated at Monktonhall, Inveresk, where none of the structural features or pits were visible (Fig. 9.3). Thus a strong case can be made for assuming that numerous sites lie undetected beneath deeper soils or hidden under alluvial deposits across much of the Lowlands. This is broadly analogous to the preservation of sites beneath peat deposits in the Highlands, as indicated at Achnacree (Barrett *et al.* 1976). Thus the checking of apparently blank areas by geophysics could prove most productive. Alternatively, such areas could be tested by trial trenching or ground based radar, though the latter is comparatively expensive (Stove and Addyman 1989). Given the doubts sometimes expressed about the wisdom of focusing excavation strategies on cropmark sites, since by definition they have been heavily degraded by ploughing, it is all the more important to identify sites within the plough zone which are potentially better preserved because of a covering of alluvium.

More speculative would be the application of sideways-looking airborne radar and multispectral scanner imagery which both have potential in archaeology because of their ability to detect differences in the surface moisture content of soil (Curran 1985, 107–8 and 128–9). This opens up the possibility of examining larger areas specifically for sites in improved pasture, one of the primary weaknesses of conventional aerial photography. However, there has been little attempt to develop or even test the archaeological potential of these techniques in Britain, presumably because of their relatively high cost and restricted availability.

With rare exceptions, the wealth and potential of the aerial photographic resource in Scotland has been grossly under-exploited. Archaeologists specialising in the Roman period, or more specifically on Roman military sites, have perhaps made fullest use of aerial discoveries, not merely in terms of the distribution of sites (Fig. 9.2), but also in detailed analysis of their morphology, perhaps best exemplified in the study of temporary camps (eg St Joseph 1969; Maxwell 1980). This may, in part, be a reflection of the specialist interests of the pioneers of aerial photographic work in Scotland. That is not to say that they have failed to record sites of all periods in the course of flying, but rather that they have more readily appreciated the potential and broader significance of that data in the context of their

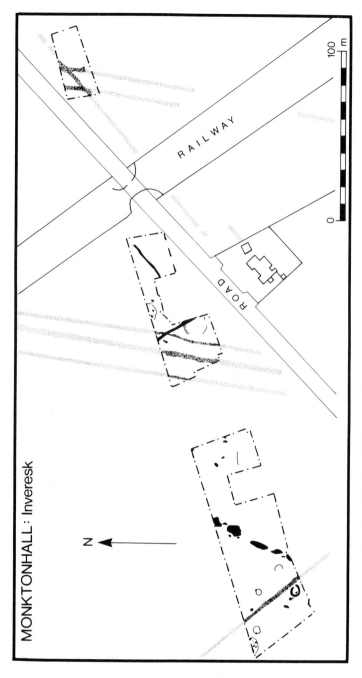

Fig. 9.3 Monktonhall, Inveresk: cropmark and excavation discoveries compared

own research specialisms. Wider appreciation of the full potential of aerial photographic data could be achieved by the routine transcription of sites onto a suitable map base, since in the limited areas where transcription has been undertaken in Scotland it has proved to be of immense value (eg Macinnes 1982). But this suggestion is not universally accepted, and some practising archaeological aerial photographers have argued that this procedure should be only a secondary, long-term objective (Ralston and Shepherd 1983, 54–5). Such procrastination has not been the case in England and Wales, and major programmes of transcription have been undertaken with very valuable results notably in the central Welsh Marches, the lower Trent valley (Whimster 1989) and central Wessex (Palmer 1984). Moreover, it is also widely undertaken as a matter of course within Sites and Monument Records in England.

Transcription provides a topographical context for the data; facilitates the combination of information from a number of photographs, perhaps taken over several years, to provide a composite picture which can be continuously updated; and provides the most effective method of aiding the objective analysis of aerial data by providing consistent and metrically accurate plans. Given the increasing availability and simplicity of computerised mapping systems, capable of providing plots at whatever scale is required, the problem is now merely a question of resource priorities. Plots are being produced both for regional authorities and Historic Scotland in the context of planning and scheduling requirements, but the process is piecemeal and is not carried out with research aims in mind. There is a pressing need for the comprehensive plotting of aerial photographic sites as a routine procedure, not only for specific ends such as monument protection (cf Edis et al. 1989), but also for research oriented analysis of the material (Macinnes 1983b).

There is also scope for considerable enhancement of the available aerial photographs to maximise their potential. It is quite possible, as has been demonstrated in Germany, to take panchromatic photographs and enhance them by computer to the extent that in some examples even the position of posts within the post holes of timber structures become identifiable. The information recoverable can be further increased by combining aerial photographic and geophysical data (Becker 1990).

The scope for analysis and interpretation of aerial photographic evidence in Scotland is vast and has barely been tapped. It can be approached in a number of potentially overlapping ways. Since aerial photographic data is primarily two-dimensional, it lends itself well to classification by morphological analysis, one of the basic methods of studying archaeological material. The classification of aerial photographic data has long been a matter of concern with, at the extremes, objective descriptive procedures (eg Ralston and Shepherd 1983) seen in opposition to more traditional interpretative approaches (eg Maxwell 1983b). Such methodological debate is largely sterile as it becomes increasingly obvious that both approaches are necessary and should be seen as complementary. It is quite legitimate to equate aerial photographic sites with established categories of archaeological monuments. Thus particular types of sites have been identified, whether Roman camps, as noted above, henges (Harding 1987) or pit alignments (Mackay 1980), and their varieties of form and distribution examined. Clearly, however, the possibilities for further such thematic studies of recognisable site types are far from exhausted. But this should not preclude either objective assessment and comparison within such types, or the recognition and classification of types not otherwise represented in the archaeological record on the basis of objective descriptive criteria.

An alternative approach, perhaps more in keeping with current research trends, is the examination of an area or region, placing the sites into their broader landscape context and integrating the data with other archaeological evidence in order to produce a wider synthesis (eg Macinnes 1983a) and facilitate statistical assessment of the results, such as rank-size analysis. Though this is basically a multi-period approach, some general chronological limits can be set (eg Driscoll 1987; Jones 1990).

In broad terms the threat of the complete destruction of archaeological remains is most severe in the Lowlands because they represent the more densely occupied and more intensively developed areas of Scotland. As a result, one distinctive feature of lowland archaeology, which has arisen particularly since the 1970s (eg Harding 1982 *passim*), is the rescue excavation of large areas, exemplified most recently at Elginhaugh where over two seasons some 2.4 ha of the Roman fort and annexe were examined (Hanson and Yeoman 1988). There are strong arguments for the selective continuation of such an approach, particularly in relation to the examination of settlement sites. The justification here is both pragmatic and methodological. Where sites are to be completely destroyed, there is clearly good reason to excavate as much of them as time and resources will allow. Moreover, for many lowland sites, where the main building tradition is of timber construction, structural remains are slight and difficult to detect. This is particularly true of most prehistoric settlements. This problem of limited evidence is exacerbated on prehistoric sites by the scarcity of artifacts. Accordingly, unless a sufficiently large sample of a site is examined the level of information recovered could be very restricted. Moreover, a single major excavation can have considerable impact on the understanding of the period or periods involved. For example, even though still unpublished in detail, the large scale excavation of the hill-fort at Broxmouth has resulted in a fundamental reassessment of the late Iron Age period in southern Scotland (Hill 1982). However, the result of a policy of encouraging large area excavation is two-fold: increased pressure on available and limited resources and, as a consequence, a concentration on sites deemed to be especially important.

To deal first with the resource problem. Excavation is an expensive process and growing more so, largely because of its increased complexity and the scale of operations. But at the same time resources are further stretched by their commitment to post-excavation analysis in order to clear the backlog of unpublished sites, a trend which is likely to continue for some time. This commitment will inevitably absorb a higher proportion of finite funds, yet the number of sites threatened by development remains undiminished. One way in which this resource shortfall may be at least partly overcome is the growing acceptance of the principle that 'the polluter should pay', which in archaeological terms means the funding of rescue survey and excavation by developers. This process, already strongly encouraged by Historic Scotland and relatively commonplace in England, has been enhanced by recent European legislation, and in particular the requirement for the Environmental Assessment of development (see Macinnes this volume). This puts the onus upon the developer to consider, and take steps to remedy, any detrimental impact upon the environment, including its archaeological component, caused by the proposed development.

A concentration of resources on sites deemed to be important demands that a series of research strategies be outlined and regularly updated so that decisions are seen to be based on current academic consensus (cf Roman Society 1985; Prehistoric Society 1988). Indeed, Historic Scotland have already approached the main period societies in Britain to put forward such strategies for their areas of interest. There is, however, a number of readily identifiable gaps in our knowledge, as well as general priorities, which research strategies should address regardless of period bias. High priority should be given to the examination of sites with the potential to produce good environmental data, both bones and the less frequently preserved organic materials. The modern excavation of a well preserved crannog, though likely to be expensive, would provide a particularly appropriate example since such sites, in addition to their waterlogged state, are often relatively long-lived and artifactually rich, as was the case at Buiston and Lochlee (Munro 1882; DES 1990). Indeed, wherever possible pollen columns should be taken from suitable locations, adjacent to excavated settlements and areas of intensive survey, to provide a broader environmental picture into which results from detailed site analyses can be fitted. A sequence of C14 dated pollen cores from suitable bog deposits in lowland contexts could have a dramatic effect on our understanding of landscape development by demonstrating changes in land use and occupation over time (cf Turner 1979).

But despite the importance of major set-piece excavations, there is still considerable scope and value in small scale sampling, provided it too is conducted within an established research framework and has limited, specified aims. In particular this should help to provide a counter-balance to the site specific approach of major excavation projects and place greater emphasis on the investigation of sites within a landscape context. This would involve more limited examination of sites for specific purposes, such as the elucidation of sequence, the provision of an approximate date or the acquisition of environmental samples. Such strategies have already begun in certain areas: in the vicinity of the Roman fort at Newstead, under the aegis of the University of Bradford, concentrating on the Roman and native interface (Jones 1990), though currently this has excluded the major hill-fort on Eildon Hill North; in the Leuchars area under the Scottish Field School of Archaeology, investigating an extensive multi-period cropmark complex (DES 1990); and in the Esk valley, mainly concerned with sites of the Iron Age and Roman period, though this programme suffers from a lack of overall coordination since it is not part of a single coherent research project. One important addition to this list should be the hinterland of Traprain Law. The artifactual record from this hill-fort, the largest in Scotland, indicates occupation from at least the Bronze Age to the post-Roman period. Thus, as a focus for settlement, it has one of the longest histories of any site in Scotland and provides a reference point of considerable importance for the study of the development of the landscape in one of the richest agricultural areas in the country. Indeed, there are large numbers of cropmark sites known in the immediate vicinity whose relationship with Traprain Law remains untested (cf Maxwell 1970).

In general, however, what is needed in Lowland Scotland is more emphasis on non-destructive assessment, particularly the integration of aerial reconnaissance, geophysical survey and fieldwalking, including the controlled use of metal-detectors, to provide a framework within which research strategies can be established and against which excavation strategies, whether sampling or on a larger scale, can be set. The primary tool of such an approach must be aerial photography which can provide a multi-period regional framework. The end result, however, must be to seek the integration of upland and lowland archaeology, uniting this complementary evidence into a total landscape study.

Bibliography

Barrett, J. C. , Hill, P. and Stevenson, J. B. 1976 Second millennium B. C. banks in the Black Moss of Achnacree: some problems of prehistoric land-use, in Burgess, C. and Miket, R. (eds) *Settlement and economy in the third and second millennia BC*, Oxford, 283–7.

Becker, H. 1990 Combination of aerial photography with ground magnetics in digital image processing technique, in Leva, C. (ed) *Aerial photography and geophysical prospection in archaeology*, Brussels.

Coppock, J. T. 1976 *An agricultural atlas of Scotland*, Edinburgh.

Crowther, D. 1983 Old land surfaces and modern ploughsoil: implications of recent work at Maxey, *Scottish Archaeol. Rev.* 2.1, 31–44.

Curran, P. J. 1985 *Principles of remote sensing*, London.

DES *Discovery and excavation in Scotland*, Edinburgh.

Driscoll, S. T. 1987 *The Early Historic landscape of Strathearn: the archaeology of a Pictish Kingdom*, unpublished PhD thesis, University of Glasgow.

Edis, J. , MacLeod, D. and Bewley, R. 1989 An archaeologist's guide to classification of cropmarks and soilmarks, *Antiquity* 63, 112–26.

Evans, R. and Jones, R. J. A. 1977 Crop marks and soils at two archaeological sites in Britain, *J. Archaeol. Sci.* 4, 63–76.

Hanson, W. S. and Yeoman, P. A. 1988 *Elginhaugh: a Roman fort and its environs*, Glasgow.

Harding, A. F. 1987 *Henge monuments and related sites of Great Britain: air photographic evidence and catalogue*, Oxford.

Harding, D. W. (ed) 1982 *Later prehistoric settlement in south-east Scotland*, Edinburgh.

Haselgrove, C. , Millett, M. and Smith, I. (eds) 1985 *Archaeology from the ploughsoil*, Sheffield.

Hill, P. 1982 Broxmouth hill-fort excavations, 1978–79: an interim report, in Harding 1982, 141–88.

Jones, R. F. J. 1990 The Newstead project: the archaeological search for acculturation, *Scottish Archaeol. Rev. 7*, 104–113.

Macinnes, L. 1982 Pattern and purpose: the settlement evidence, in Harding 1982, 57–73.

Macinnes, L. 1983a *Later prehistoric and Romano-British settlement north and south of the Forth: a comparative survey*, unpublished PhD thesis, University of Newcastle.

Macinnes, L. 1983b 'The view from the bird's eye' — the dilemma of aerial archaeology, *Scottish Archaeol. Rev. 2.1*, 60–2.

Mackay, G. A. 1980 *A study of pit-alignments in Scotland*, unpublished BA dissertation, University of Edinburgh.

Maxwell, G. S. 1970 Early rectilinear enclosures in the Lothians, *Scottish Archaeol. Forum 2*, 85–90.

Maxwell, G. S. 1980 Agricola's campaigns: the evidence of temporary camps, *Scottish Archaeol. Forum 12*, 25–54.

Maxwell, G. S. 1983a Recent aerial survey in Scotland, in Maxwell, G. S. (ed) *The impact of aerial reconnaissance on archaeology*, London.

Maxwell, G. S. 1983b Cropmark categories observed in recent aerial reconnaissance in Scotland, *Scottish Archaeol. Rev. 2.1*, 45–52.

Munro, R. 1882 *Ancient Scottish lake-dwellings or crannogs*, Edinburgh.

Palmer, R. 1984 *Danebury an Iron Age hillfort in Hampshire: an aerial photographic interpretation of its environs*, London.

Prehistoric Society 1988 *Saving our prehistoric heritage: landscapes under threat*, Leeds.

Ralston, I. B. M. and Shepherd, I. A. G. 1983 Archaeological air photography — the classification of results, *Scottish Archaeol. Rev. 2.1*, 53–60.

RCAHMS 1978 *Lanarkshire: an inventory of the prehistoric and Roman monuments*, Edinburgh.

Roman Society 1985 *Priorities for the preservation and excavation of Romano-British sites*, London.

St Joseph, J. K. S. 1969 Air reconnaissance in Britain, 1965–68, *J. Roman Stud. 59*, 104–29.

St Joseph, J. K. S. 1976 Air reconnaissance of Roman Scotland, 1939–75, *Glasgow Archaeol. J. 4*, 1–28.

Shennan, S. 1985 *Experiments in the collection and analysis of archaeological survey data: the East Hampshire survey*, Sheffield.

Stove, G. C. and Addyman, P. V. 1989 Ground probing impulse radar: an experiment in archaeological remote sensing at York, *Antiquity 63*, 337–42.

Turner, J. 1979 The environment of north-east England during Roman times as shown by pollen analysis, *J. Archaeol. Sci. 6*, 285–90.

Whimster, R. 1989 *The emerging past: air photography and the buried landscape*, London.

Woodman, P. C. 1989 A review of the Scottish Mesolithic: a plea for normality!, *Proc. Soc. Antiq. Scotland* 119, 1–32.

Acknowledgements

We are grateful to Dr. D. J. Breeze for his comments on an earlier draft of this paper and to Lorraine McEwan for the line illustrations.

10

An Insular View?

Raymond Lamb and Val Turner

Orkney and Shetland are reckoned to belong together, usually in a half-scale box in the Moray Firth. Together they have been within the Kingdom of Norway for longer than under Scottish rule. They shared, until the eighteenth century, closely related variants of a West Norse language, and their farm, hill and coastal names are overwhelmingly Norse, to the extent that a visitor from Norway, once accustomed to some curious Scottish-imposed spellings, will recognise many of them from his own home surroundings. The speech of the people throughout retains a Scandinavian intonation. Boat-building traditions remained firmly Norse-based down to the present century. The common Norse heritage is so strongly the outsider's first impression, that the fundamental differences can escape notice. This is especially true in archaeology.

Orkney's archaeological resource resides in individual sites; Shetland's in landscapes. Sites such as Skara Brae and Maeshowe are well known; they represent the distinctive condition of Orkney archaeology, dramatically upstanding structures often associated with remarkably deep and rich stratigraphies. The circumstances which generate these conditions are quirkish: the upstanding structures, timber-deprived, are built of flagstone; the stratigraphies result from active soil formation processes and most notably from blowing sand, sand which is almost entirely composed of lime and so preserves bone and is kind to pottery. Timber-built equivalents of Skara Brae, complete with furniture and home comforts, presumably existed throughout Europe, but it is only where the timber supply failed and the local stone happened to provide so inviting an alternative to planks and beams, that the prehistoric builders obligingly made their handiwork so durable. The intractable metamorphics, which make up the even more timber-deficient 'Old Rock' of Shetland, lent themselves much less to architectural invention (Mousa broch, the obvious exception, occupies an island of flag stone), while the acidity of these rocks and of peat was unconducive to archaeologically good preservation conditions (Jarlshof being the exception, sealed under lime-sand).

To the student of the prehistoric farmstead or tomb, the Iron Age broch or the medieval church — to the practitioner of archaeology as the term was generally understood up to and through the 1960s — Orkney's attractions, therefore, were obvious and immediate. The perception, that Shetland's archaeology is basically a lower-grade version of the same, persists. This is a misconception: the archaeology of Shetland is radically different. Prehistoric structures were largely turf-built on a stone base, and set within a system of dykes which ran for miles. The subsequent low intensity of land use, crofting rather than farming (other than in the South Mainland), has ensured that these patterns of landscape still survive. Shetland today has strong links with Scandinavia, and its Viking past has become legendary, sacramentalised in the annual festival of Up Helly Aa. Viking-Age farmsteads in Shetland are archaeologically elusive; with the exception of one house site at Jarlshof, the few sites which have been excavated have turned out to be later. There was little development of vernacular architecture between the tenth and eighteenth centuries in Shetland; and, as yet, it is impossible in surface fieldwork to distinquish between the two extremes. The only Norse farmsteads which have been excavated are, by definition, those which have for some reason failed; otherwise the Viking house sites are beneath the later medieval, which, in turn, lie beneath today's inhabited croft houses. The placename evidence suggests that Shetland was a heavily populated Norse landscape. It is, therefore, to the serious student of prehistoric upland landscapes (for in the Northern Isles, statutory bodies deem that the uplands start at sea level) that Shetland has more immediately to offer; a fact which is still not widely appreciated.

In lowland England, considerable resources are devoted to the investigation of relict prehistoric landscapes, visible only from the air when conditions are exactly right (for example, on the Thames gravels in Oxfordshire). Without in any way wishing to denigrate the value of studying these landscapes, the extant proportion of the remains of such landscapes in Shetland is many times greater. Prehistoric house sites and burial tombs can be stumbled over, set within their original pattern of field dykes and tenurial divisions. The lowland archaeologist excavates and peers at gullies and pits in the subsoil; in Shetland one leans one's ranging rod against the wall and photographs it. The daunting work comes in getting the whole onto a plan; typically several square kilometres of landscape in which nothing can be related to the Ordnance Survey map, unless the prehistoric dykes, the most prominent features visible, happen to have been incorporated.

The individual tombs and houses in Orkney are likely to be better built and richer in contents — Orkney's rich farming landscape always has offered a more comfortable living than Shetland's rocky hills — and within themselves are likely to be better preserved, although usually needing to be dug. But apart from Eday and a few places like it — one valley in Hoy and a number of uninhabited 'pasture islands', Auskerry, Linga Holm, Muckle Skerry — the Orkney landscape within which the antiquity sits, will be a modern one. We have become used, without questioning it, to the 'archaeology reserve' — the neat square of chain-link fencing enclosing a turf of a miraculous chemically-manicured verdancy, conveying to the visitor the message that only that which is within is Archaeology. Although this style of presentation encourages the feeling of alienation, it has to be admitted that, even without the fence, the surrounding scene of neatly squared fields filled with contentedly munching beef cattle has very little to do with the agricultural landscape of the Neolithic or Bronze Age in which the tomb, stone circle or whatever it might be, was originally built. The student who wishes to study such features as integral parts of a landscape must be referred to Shetland, but if her interest is in the structure, its contents, the chronology of artifactual evolution, the faunal and floral remains which inform about prehistoric husbandry, it will be easier and more profitable to select an Orkney site to yield the desired results. What up to now has been less obvious is that the best structural and stratigraphic preservation is more likely to be found in the outer isles — to those who already know, and are impressed by, the quality of Mainland Orkney sites, the discovery of Sanday, Westray or Papay can be a revelation. These islands combine an original richness of prehistoric and medieval settlement with a preponderance of shell-sand giving optimal preservation — in Sanday, stratigraphic thicknesses regularly exceed five metres, providing tell-like conditions. It is in these low-lying and readily-eroded islands that such sites are rapidly succumbing to the rising sea level, posing the most consistently serious rescue problem we face.

Orkney and Shetland historically differ from the Scottish Highlands in a significant respect: whereas the Highland landscape hindered access, so that General Wade after the '45 had to push through a ruthless policy of 'opening-up', the Northern Isles have always stood wide open to outside influences. The archaeologist who keeps his face too close to the ground does so at his peril. A recent illustration is the Neolithic carved stone from Westray (part of the structure of a previously unknown chambered tomb) with an association with Newgrange which is so immediately obvious that one forgets the hundreds of miles in between (Neil 1981). The patterns of prehistoric landscapes, including the massive long-distance linear earthworks or walls which in Orkney are known as treb dykes, not to forget the extensive field systems of the West Side of Shetland, are manifestations of a social phenomenon — the elaborate ordering of the landscape in the Bronze Age — which shows itself more widely in Britain (Dartmoor, Berwickshire, Cumbria, western Ireland) and probably throughout north-western Europe. The organisation of the early Church in Pictish Orkney, revealed by the systematic fieldwork of the last decade, turns out to be a close variant of, and arguably springing from the same source as, the system imposed in central Germany by the Anglo-Saxon-dominated missionary efforts of Carolingian times. When we then move into the Viking Age, the outside connections — Scandinavian — are taken for granted by everyone. Less well known, but undoubtedly significant, is Shetland's position on the periphery of the Hanseatic trading network of the later middle ages. Much closer to modern times, in the context of the politico-military strategies surrounding the high point and subsequent decline of the British Empire, new naval technologies suddenly placed the Northern Isles in a key position, with the result that the world-upheaving events of the early twentieth century are now archaeologically represented by naval guns on Vementry, a sizeable portion of von Tirpitz's High Seas Fleet under the waters of Scapa Flow, and an enormous corpus of fortifications (few of them ever recorded on paper) from 1939–45. Viewed from a centralist perspective, Orkney and Shetland may seem to be on the periphery of new developments: clearly the reverse is true, lying as they do in the middle of busy seaways.

Some of the non-realisation of the potential of Orkney and Shetland is unfortunately due to a quality of insularity in British archaeology, including Scottish archaeology, which has been slow to acquire a European perspective. It should hardly be surprising that the medieval archaeology of Orkney and Shetland should be Norwegian, but those charged from the centre with dealing with it, have not always shown full awareness of the implications. Whole classes of field monument which have been established in Norwegian archaeology for a generation or more — the enormous, and instantly eye-catching 'farm mounds' of Orkney's outer North Isles, and the nausts (boat-shelters) which are ubiquitous coastal features throughout the Northern Isles — found no place in Scottish-controlled Orkney and Shetland archaeology until the 1980s, while the status of Kirkwall, as probably the best archaeologically surviving example of a medieval Norwegian town plan, has hardly been taken into account. At the same time, the assumption of the early medieval period under the heading 'Viking', has obscured the considerably wider, mainstream-European milieu in which, for example, twelfth-century Orkney found herself; the Cathedral of St Magnus is the obvious statement of the cosmopolitan character of the court which produced not only it, but, it now seems, some of the key advances in literature and music of that age (Crawford 1988). Archaeologists do not help when they persist in applying the term 'Late Norse' to this period, which is the high middle ages in all their glory.

The fact that Orkney and Shetland are series of islands, within often treacherous seas, has repeatedly led ships to founder off their coasts. Any ship going around the north of Scotland, sometimes a safer route than the journey through the easily controlled English Channel, would run the risk of bumping into Shetland, or the North Isles of Orkney. Each shipwreck is a time capsule, fossilising as it does the very moment when the ship went down. There are over 1,500 known wreck sites around Shetland alone, reflecting the cosmopolitan nature of the sea routes in which it lies (for example, the *Kennemerland* — a Dutch East Indiaman; *El Gran Grifon* — an Armada ship; and the *Evstafii* — a Russian man-of-war). Realising the archaeological potential of such sites early, prompted by the then Shetland Museum Curator, Tom Henderson, Shetland Islands Council took the initiative of protecting fourteen wreck sites by taking out a lease of the sea bed. Whilst storms have ensured that most of the ships themselves have long since broken up (those in deeper water may have received protection from sand or gullies) the contents remain, and the value of examining them is currently being demonstrated by Chris Dobbs' work on the *Kennemerland*. If wreck sites must not be overlooked in considering the archaeological potential of the Northern Isles, there is the additional potential of discovering previous landscapes which are now under the sea: that there appears to be no Mesolithic surely is due to the fact that Orkney and Shetland are sinking, while the sea is rising.

All field surveys up to and including the Ordnance Survey fieldwork in the 1960s followed the pattern first set by the OS in its primary large-scale mapping of the Northern Isles in the 1870s. The surveyors — military engineers — used the triangulation which had been set up in the 1840s and 1850s to produce mapping at scales of 1:2,500 for populated areas and 6 inches to the mile (1:10,560) for uninhabited regions. The original surveyors were not expected to record place-names. At the OS headquarters in Norwich, tracings of the maps were made and men — ordinary sappers — were sent out into the countryside armed with these and with sheaves of pro-formas on which they were to find out and record the local place-names. Each name was to be verified by three local people — 'authorities' — each of whom gave the spelling as he understood it — and whose names and social positions were recorded against each entry. These local informants also were asked to give information about the area's antiquities. Back in Norwich, the information was collated, a definitive form of each name decided upon, and the pro-formas bound up in book form for preservation in the archives as the *Original Name-Books*.

The thoroughness of this original survey depended first of all on the degree of interest shown by each individual soldier. Some of these men evidently became quite dedicated to this unusual work, and listened carefully to what their informant had to tell about the local antiquities, sometimes composing a minor essay on a particular broch or cairn. Secondly, and more seriously, the idea of who constituted an 'authority' was too heavily influenced by Victorian social mores — very often we find that the three sources for a given piece of information are the laird, the minister and the schoolmaster, all three unlikely to have been brought up in the district, and whose Latin literacy too often shows through in the name-forms adopted. Less reference was made to the tenant farmers or crofters whose local upbringing and daily contact with the land, and their oral tradition which as often as not preserved place-names in unadulterated medieval Norse forms, would make them the immediate priority of a modern folklorist; needless to say, female opinion on no account could be admitted. Many a prominent and well-known cairn or burnt mound thus failed to get into the records, simply because the surveyor never asked those best qualified to inform him.

The name-books therefore provided the documentation behind the marking of antiquities on the first series 6–inch and 1:2,500 maps published in the 1880s, and the haphazard procedure of the original information collection created distortions which became perpetuated in subsequent re-workings. Some map sheets show a dearth of antiquities, for no other reason than lack of enthusiasm on the part of a particular private soldier of the Royal Engineers. Given these circumstances, the overall result was a remarkable achievement; the subsequent problems arose when the world of academic archaeology began to treat the material as definitive. The name-books remained shut up in Ordnance Survey headquarters (the Scottish ones mercifully being transferred to Edinburgh and so escaping the ultimate fate of the English books, destroyed in the blitz on Southampton), and clearly did not impinge on the awareness of those who were charged with the compilation of the Royal Commission Inventories.

The Royal Commission began their work in the Northern Isles in 1928, with Orkney. It took until the mid 1930s for the work to be completed. The Investigators involved were John Corrie and Charles Calder. Of the two, Corrie carried out the more thorough field work, whilst Calder's strength lay in his more academic approach. Corrie carried out much of the work in Orkney, but by 1934 his health was failing, not helped by his constantly getting soaked when cycling between sites in the rain. Calder completed the survey. One result of this is that the Orkney volume offers a fuller account than is contained in the Shetland volume. An additional factor was that sites in Orkney tend to be more readily accessible than those in Shetland. By the mid 1930s the scale of the job in Shetland overwhelmed the available resources and work petered out, with Calder all too aware of what had not been accomplished. Corrie died in 1938, leaving others under the arbitrarily decisive Secretary, Sir George Macdonald, to assemble his material for publication, a job which was on the point of completion when war broke out. The quality of Corrie's field records was such that many a text in the 1946 *Inventory* is taken verbatim from his miraculously neat notebook; unfortunately, editorial decisions had been taken to save time by excluding or reducing some extremely important material, which the academic world consequently lost sight of for over thirty years. The burnt mounds, of which Corrie had written meticulous descriptions, were relegated to mere lists of locations. The whole class of early prehistoric linear earthworks known in Orkney as treb dykes, which, it transpired, Corrie understood and recorded in detail, was omitted altogether, and had to be virtually rediscovered in the 1980s (Reynolds 1984, 102).

Corrie, whose appointment was at a fairly junior level, worked to the instruction of visiting all antiquity sites marked on the 6–inch map — for this purpose he carried the map sheets in a specially contrived tube attached to his bicycle. The flaw of course was the underlying unawareness of the constraints of the Original Name-Book survey; although he sometimes did so on his own initiative, Corrie had no brief to look at areas where no antiquites were marked on the map.

Calder had become keenly aware of the large number and remarkable preservation of prehistoric sites, particularly houses, on the uncultivated hills of Shetland's West Side. The published *Inventory* (RCAHMS 1946) appeared with many of these unnoted or unsurveyed, so Calder returned to Shetland in the 1950s in order to rectify the situation. The results of his survey and excavation were published as a series of papers (Calder 1950; 1956; 1961; 1963) and included investigations at Stanydale, and at Gruting, and also at 'the Benie Hoose' on the island of Whalsay. Like his predecessors, however, Calder did not question the fact that some areas appeared to be devoid of sites, according to the maps.

As a prelude to carrying out a revision, in the 1960s the Ordnance Survey re-examined all the sites which had been included on their earlier map sheets, or had been discovered subsequently and published in academic papers, which were carefully searched. Yet again, it was only already known sites which were the objects of visits. As it happened, the excellence of the personnel involved in the exercise resulted in large numbers of previously unrecorded sites being observed by the way, while many more were added by the systematic use of air photographs, but aerial photography often fails to reveal sites under heather, so the corpus was greatly enlarged while still leaving some areas misleadingly devoid of mapped antiquities.

The OS work had a particular intention — the feeding of information into the map-making process — so the new material, much of it inviting exciting new research lines, remained in the format, a card index, which the OS found most convenient to use. One of the writers had the privilege of consulting that index, when the new material was still fresh, at an early stage of his post-graduate research, and not only extracted much important information, but got a lot of ideas by talking with the field-experienced staff in the old Rose Street office. It would have been refreshing had there been in the late 1960s, that age of optimism, a Scottish university with both the resources and the will to throw itself wholeheartedly into the archaeology of Scotland. Professor Alcock's achievement from his arrival at Glasgow in the mid 1970s, in building up the department there, drew attention to the potential of the Highlands and injected welcome self-confidence into Scottish archaeology.

The essential issues encountered when we look at the specialised geographical and cultural environments of Orkney and Shetland were provocatively touched upon in Fowler's (1987) article reviewing a series of popular regional guidebooks put out by the Commission. In England since the late 1970s there has been a long-running debate over the relationship between county Sites and Monuments Records (SMRs) and the National Monuments Record (NMRE) being established by the English Commission. Fowler's experience as English Commission Secretary during much of this debate inevitably has coloured his perception — he is clearly a centralist, and seems inclined to suspect the quality of regional SMR data (Fowler 1987, 14). He regards 'centralised control of data-generation and curation' as a Good Thing, and perceives Scotland as a place where 'the relevant operation is small and simple'. In terms of archaeological data already held on paper, this relative assessment may be valid, but in terms of archaeology extant on the ground, any visitor to Shetland who has taken a walk in the West Side will question it.

What may be regarded as a small sample of a Shetland-style archaeological landscape has recently been under discussion in the Orkney island of Eday, which was used by Fowler (1987, 12) as a testing-ground for Anna Ritchie's excellent popular guide in the RCAHMS series (Ritchie 1985). Fowler would have liked more details than Ritchie offers of the prehistoric 'sub-peat dykes' which form the matrix of these landscapes, and he found what he wanted in the Eday 'List' in the RCAHMS *Archaeological Sites and Monuments of*

Scotland series, which he gratifyingly praises. These brief, rapidly-produced mini-Inventories, originally the work of staff appointed to the Commission for the purpose, have provided archaeological coverage for many areas, particularly in southern Scotland, where it was urgently needed, although in Orkney the mechanism of their production has been essentially different. The Orkney 'Lists' have been generated from the SMR, using the data put into it as the result of systematic field work by the Orkney-based joint writer of this paper, although Fowler does not take account of this in his assessment of regional SMRs as an institution. Fowler was specially interested in the prehistoric dykes in Eday, and may well have come across a previously unreported one, but unfortunately he did not make use of the SMR with its more complete details of the 'List' sites, and with its inevitable additions since the 'List' appeared in 1984, although an invitation to do so prefaces each 'List' (RCAHMS 1984, 6). As a working document, the SMR will always be the fullest database of available information at any given moment. Fowler was impressed by the quality of the Eday dykes, which he compares most favourably with those of Dartmoor and County Mayo: however a comprehensive assessment of this class of monument, given equal awareness of all relevant landscapes, would be dominated by Shetland.

It is becoming steadily more difficult for any archaeologist to remain widely informed, as the sheer quantity of information being published increases. This is not the place for yet another discussion of 'levels of publication' of excavation reports, but the problem persists; more is being published than is possible for an individual to assimilate, assuming, of course, that the individual physically has access to all the publications. This point must be considered. We hear that a long-awaited report is 'published', when all that has happened is that copies are offered for sale at a price which precludes most individuals buying them, and indeed restricts their acquisition to a very few academic libraries. Can the purpose of publication be claimed to have been achieved when no copy is held by any library within three hundred miles of a scholar with good cause to want regular access to it? (Would English archaeologists be happy if they had routinely to travel to Dresden to consult English material?). To tell Orcadians and Shetlanders that they have access to central services in Edinburgh is arrogance, even if unwitting: the statement would be valid if Scotland had a national transport policy giving people at the periphery easy and affordable access to the centre. Not only is that not so, but those working furthest from the centre are likely to enjoy lower incomes than those in central positions; and a comparison of railway maps of England and Scotland shows immediately that Scotland actually has no obvious and universally-accessible centre comparable with London. Norway is a more extreme example of a country where communities are widely separated by difficult geography, and Norway has had the good sense to decentralise the fullest possible range of administrative functions and services to regional centres.

Fortunately, as Fowler (1987, 14) pertinently has pointed out, modern computer technology has the power to render irrelevant much of the debate as to where data should be stored. The distinction of where SMR data ends and an excavation or survey report begins is not, nor should be, a rigid one, and much of what an excavator now assigns (voluntarily or under editorial pressure) to 'archive' rather then 'publication' level, could quite happily be incorporated in the SMR. This is already happening in the case of Chris Morris's work at Deerness and Birsay, where the archive material which backs up the published reports is incorporated into the Orkney SMR (as well as into NMRS).

As Fowler says, the key word is 'network'. It is not accidental that enthusiasm for the possibilities offered by telecommunications technology is highest in the Highlands and Islands, for this offers to remove many of the drawbacks we have suffered through distance from centralised services. It is possible with a modem (an accessory costing a fraction of the price of the microcomputer with which it is used) to exchange data, over the ordinary telephone lines, with any other similarly equipped party. Orkney Islands Council has taken a lead in using this technology for 'distance learning' — enabling pupils in tiny North Isles schools to enjoy specialist teaching without expensive and time-consuming travelling. We need no longer argue over whether data should be held in the regional SMR (obliging a scholar based in the south to travel to Lerwick or Kirkwall to use it) or in Edinburgh (so that Shetland or Orkney material is accessible only to Shetlanders and Orcadians who have the time and means to travel), as the actual physical location of the databank can be decided purely on grounds of administrative convenience, when it can be consulted and read from any modem-equipped computer. It is worth noting here that the rural schools in Orkney routinely double up as community centres, and the computer-station in each island school can immediately become a terminal from which data, wherever held, can be read.

We should like to see the Scottish National Monuments Record (NMRS) developing a 'clearing-house' role in this field. At this time, copies of the Orkney and Shetland SMRs are maintained at NMRS, with the intention that their contents shall be as readily available to scholars in Edinburgh as in Kirkwall or Lerwick, but the facility to consult ideally should be more widely available — even for a student in Glasgow, for example, it would be better if the need to catch a train to Edinburgh could be eliminated. Where, in England, the National Monuments Record and the regional Sites and Monuments Records have existed in tension, the Scottish SMRs, a later development, have been supported both morally and financially by the Royal Commission, who have played a key role in their establishment. The option is available now for anyone to get data from the SMR in Kirkwall through the modem. It is desirable that each regional SMR in Scotland eventually will exchange data with any other, but many enquiries will be better met by NMRS — a scholar who, for instance, wishes to make a study of a particular class of monument or a selected period, throughout Scotland, will have her initial needs better met from one data base rather than many. The transmission of data between SMRs and NMRS needs to be two-way; it would be helpful if NMRS could develop a computer system under its own control, untrammelled by externally-imposed security constraints, as only thus can Fowler's vision of 'network' be realised.

Of course, a most significant aspect of the largely RCAHMS-sponsored initiative of the past decade, has been the attention to new and systematic fieldwork. The first effort went into Orkney's North Isles, an area where existing records were most obviously deficient, and the consequent notification of very rich and rapidly-eroding settlement sites, such as Pool in Sanday and Tuquoy in Westray, produced commendably rapid response from Historic Scotland, whose excavations on these sites set a new pattern of using SMR data to choose sites for rescue digging, on a careful assessment of academic research applicability, physical characteristics, and threat-appraisal, rather than moving in on one site which had happened to come to someone's notice, as inevitably happened in the past. Of course, we are still a long way from the ultimately satisfactory situation, of being able to assess priorities on an equal nationwide footing by bringing regional SMR data together (surely an appropriate task for NMRS) — at the moment, the threatened sites in Sanday, Orkney's biggest 'rescue problem island', are well documented, but we have no means of comparing them with possibly similar sites in the Outer Hebrides where parallel machair conditions prevail.

Rescue excavation however is only one, and a hideously expensive, method by which archaeology is advanced; the routine surface fieldwork constantly reveals new classes of sites and new directions of research. John Hunter's Bradford University team has seen through the excavation at Pool, but a more original departure has been their high-intensity surface surveys (working to a level of detail far beyond what is practicable for the initial overall SMR cover) on small islands, the extreme difficulty of access of which had ensured both that upstanding antiquities survived, often spectacularly, and that they have usually escaped notice. Work on the uninhabited islands beginning with Muckle Skerry, in the midst of Pentland Firth tide-races, and then moving through the small pasture islets of Scapa Flow, led to the invitation to John Hunter's team to undertake something on a larger scale in Fair Isle, Shetland. The results were astounding: an increase in the number of known sites from 23 to 746, on an island where the archaeology is far less spectacular than in most parts of Shetland.

New research lines are constantly presenting themselves to the writers as the routine field investigation proceeds, and most of these have to be left unexplored by ourselves, especially those which fall outwith our own areas of academic competence (the Shetland-based writer is a prehistorian with a special interest in landscapes, the Orkney-based writer is a medievalist specialising in the early Church). Not uncommonly, in reading some publication by a southern archaeologist, we are struck by the thought, 'If only this author knew about ... ', and then there are the topics, most obviously the Norwegian-oriented ones such as the relevance of boat-nausts to historical problems of medieval naval levies, which fall outwith the narrow British awareness altogether. The SMR work both reveals these research directions and provides for students a base from which to pursue them; we hope that universities' involvement in Orkney and Shetland will continue to grow, and that academic staff will guide their best research students in our direction. If the 1980s have begun to demonstrate the potential for archaeological research in the Northern Isles, the 1990s should begin to see this potential realised.

Bibliography

Calder, C. S. T. 1950 Report on the excavation of a Neolithic Temple at Stanydale in the Parish of Sandsting, Shetland, *Proc. Soc. Antiq. Scotland* 84 (1949–50), 185–205.

Calder, C. S. T. 1956 Report on the discovery of numerous stone Age house-sites in Shetland, *Proc. Soc. Antiq. Scotland* 89 (1955–6), 340–97.

Calder, C. S. T. 1961 Excavations in Whalsay, Shetland, 1954–5, *Proc. Soc. Antiq. Scotland* 94 (1960–1), 28–45.

Calder, C. S. T. 1963 Cairns, Neolithic houses and burnt mounds in Shetland, *Proc. Soc. Antiq. Scotland* 96 (1962–3), 37–86.

Crawford, B. E. (ed) 1988 *St Magnus Cathedral and Orkney's twelfth-century renaissance*, Aberdeen.

Fowler, P. J. 1987 The past in a foreign country, *Proc. Soc. Antiq. Scotland* 117, 7–16.

Neil, N. R. J. 1981 A newly discovered decorated stone from Orkney (with note by G. Daniel), *Antiquity* 55, 129–31.

RCAHMS 1946 *Twelfth report with inventory of monuments in Orkney and Shetland*, Edinburgh.

RCAHMS 1984 *The archaeological sites and monuments of Scotland, no. 23: Eday and Stronsay*, Edinburgh.

Reynolds, D. M. 1984 J. M. Corrie, archaeologist, *Trans. Dumfriesshire Galloway Nat. Hist. Antiq. Soc.* 54, 94–107.

Ritchie, A. 1985 *Exploring Scotland's Heritage: Orkney and Shetland*, Edinburgh.

11

THE MULTI-PERIOD LANDSCAPE

J. R. Hunter

Few archaeologists involved in excavation or field survey in rural Scotland can have failed to notice the extent to which traditional land use, subsistence methods and ethnographic data from the recent past have been of more than passing interest to their own interpretation of earlier societies. During the last decade research carried out from Bradford University throughout the Northern Isles (Fig. 11.1), a region of particularly high monument preservation in rural Scotland, has highlighted awareness of these factors. This paper gives the opportunity to make a considered overview of the extent to which tradition, landscape survival and certain types of record may be of archaeological significance.

One of the privileges of studying the archaeology and history of the Northern Isles is the excuse it offers to enjoy a collage of observations and records bequeathed by a succession of antiquarians and high-minded visitors of the later eighteenth and nineteenth centuries. Antiquarian investigation has played an intrinsic part in archaeological studies in the Northern Isles, partly because the state of monument preservation has been inviting and partly because island geography has traditionally inspired a type of museological study — a point to be considered below. This antiquarian contribution holds a significant place in excavation reports (eg Morris 1989), as well as in its own right (eg Reynolds 1985), while the history of investigation in a particular subject (eg brochs) is sometimes indivisible from the subject itself (Hedges 1985).

The origins of modern archaeology are firmly rooted in the activities of Farrer, Goudie, Petrie and others, but it is on the anthropological, almost pure literary side, that the contribution is most apposite from our point of view. Researchers consult, almost in ritual, a corpus of 'Tours', 'Visits' and 'Descriptions' undertaken by a formidable array of clerics, gentry and other individuals of private means whose writings constitute a unique dimension to the archaeological record. The more noteworthy of these belong to Hibbert, Low and Tudor and the list might also be extended to include the works of Sir Walter Scott whose professional activities provided the enviable opportunity for both travel and descriptive prose.

The colouring and bias of much of this literature rarely fails to obscure the sharp sociological distinction between the two parties involved: the southern professional classes on one side and the island communities on the other. The same distinction emphasises, in a manner which the twentieth century observer might define as patronising, island levels of social and economic behaviour which at best were considered curious and at worst primitive. From an archaeological point of view these observations are seen as having some potential, not because they fulfil some crude Victorian notion of anthropology, but because they appear to capture the character of a preserved landscape showing evolved subsistence economics, settlement characteristics and land forms in advance of a mechanised society. Wood's classic account of monuments enclosed within 'a chain of forts' on Sanday (NSA 1845, 136), Scott's disgust of the Shetland horizontal mill (Laughlan 1982, 29) and Hibbert's pedantic description of 'cottages', their layouts and construction (1822, 114–6) are all cases in point.

The value of this documentation, however biased or subjective it may appear, is simply that the landscape visited and described has since been substantially altered by agricultural changes, population movement and redevelopment in its many forms. By the mid-twentieth century the archaeological integrity of the landscape had diminished, appearing to survive best in isolated or marginal locations where a combination of chance, neglect and inaccessibility provided certain levels of preservation.

Study of this early modern period has benefited from ethnographic material in the form of traditional skills, crafts and pastimes (eg Baldwin

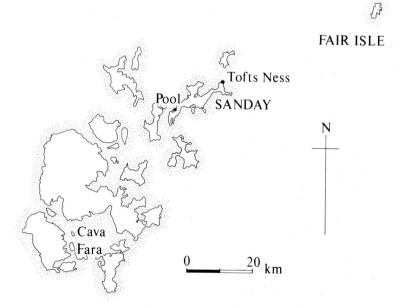

Fig. 11.1 The Orkney Islands and Fair Isle, showing locations discussed in the text

1978, Fenton 1978), and these might be seen as forming a clumsy link between document and landscape. It is not the place here to do other than reinforce the role of ethnography; retention of tradition is unsurprising among groups of remote but socially connective communities located peripherally to political and economic foci. In places where natural economic resources are restricted and where exploitation is patterned according to population size and seasonality, optimal subsistence strategies soon develop. In any remote area, man's response to the pre-technological nineteeenth century landscape is, in theory, likely to be little changed from that made one or even two thousand years earlier.

Conservatism of tradition also fosters attitudes of preservation, demonstrated in the retention of old buildings, trackways, place names, customs and even the timetabling of activities. This is particularly apparent in the seasonal cycle of the crofting year where adherence to well-tried and tested economic methods often indirectly involves a certain fossilation of the archaeological landscape. This type of preservation, taken together with persisting traditions and partial landscape survival, not to mention the vivid first-hand accounts of 'worthies', provides a remarkably well-faceted record of early modern society. In view of the minimal opportunity for change imposed by climate and limited resources, this record might justifiably be argued to represent a realistic insight not only into recent centuries, but also into earlier periods of settlement. The very nature of this conservatism begs the question as to how far back in time these economic systems might be traced; indeed, whether this spectrum of nineteenth century evidence could conceivably be interpreted as a valid perception of late prehistory.

One location where these elements satisfactorily combine is Fair Isle (Fig. 11.2), an island with an area of slightly less that nine square kilometres in a geographical position of some importance. Fair Isle lies midway between Orkney and Shetland, roughly 40 km from either landfall, and historically provided an important stepping stone with respect to the transmission of cultural influences from one island group to another. More fundamentally, a combination of its physical size and the sailing distances required for access has always necessitated a high degree of self-sufficiency among Fair Isle populations; this is an important factor to consider in any evaluation of its development. In archaeological terms it offers the rare opportunity for investigating a closed social unit which relied on a consistent (and largely quantifiable) resource base throughout antiquity. The island also has the benefit of being relatively well-documented by visitors in the eighteenth and nineteenth centuries. These descriptions, apart from noting the nature and habits of the contemporary population, often included valuable observations on land erosion (Sibbald 1711, 50), plant survival (Tudor 1883, 442) and geological exploitation (Heddle 1879).

The island divides itself neatly into two zones, a 'green' zone to the south which is populated and crofted, and a moorland zone to the north which is grazed and mostly unpopulated in historic times. The two are divided by a wall which follows the line of a great earthen dyke running from coast to coast. Such boundary dykes separating farm land from hill land also feature on other Shetland islands such as Foula, Papa Stour and Fetlar and are of indeterminable date.

On Fair Isle, as on other islands, the integrity of the archaeological landscape is best preserved on the moorland zone beyond the dyke. One area comprising field boundaries, cairns, burnt mounds and structural remains (Hunter 1985, Fig. 5) is analogous with an excavated landscape at the Scord of Brouster which holds a similar moorland position in Mainland Shetland (Whittle 1986), while a further Fair Isle example is partially buried under peat formation (Hunter 1985, Fig. 4). The dyke on this and other islands effectively divides traditional methods of land use, and thus provides classic separation between relict landscape on one side (moorland) and individual monument survival on the other (crofted).

There are additional, less substantial boundaries which appear to isolate specific headlands or nesses. It can be no coincidence that many of these have animal names (eg *Buness*, *Hestaness*), boundaries across peninsulas being the most economical way of stockading livestock. In common with most other parts of the Northern Isles the place-names of Fair Isle are almost 100 per cent Norse or Norse-derived attesting, among other activities, to the importance of fowling (eg *fugla* and *maava* elements in cliff locations). This aspect of subsistence is of long tradition, the presence and density of sea birds being a likely attraction to early settlers. Even at the time of Scott's visit in 1814 fowling was still carried out and he described how 'a fine boy of fourteen had dropped from the cliff . . . into a roaring surf by which he was instantly swallowed up' (Laughlan 1982, 53). The event was, it seems, greeted with an air of resignation within a community that had traditionally relied on 'mostly milk, fish, wild-fowl and wild-fowl eggs' (Hibbert 1822, 124).

The majority of place-names otherwise display an extra-ordinary obsession with topography. Unfortunately, the linkage of place-names and field systems, so plausibly demonstrated by Baldwin on Foula (1984) and on Faroe (1983) as a key to understanding the development of land use, is likely to be of less value on Fair Isle where the impact of open systems was greater.

The current field system which primarily defines crofting land is, nevertheless, a useful indicator of the effects of existing land use on the archaeological landscape. Within the fenced grazing area nineteenth century rig lines predominate, earlier narrower rigs only surviving outwith the fence in those few places where chance alignment of the fence has left them intact. The same applies to individual monument forms; the precise positioning of the modern fence effectively governs not only the degree of monument preservation in marginal land but also, indirectly, the extent to which they might conveniently provide material for modern shelters and walling.

Some monuments appear to have been unaffected by change of land use and land division. The surviving distribution of over 20 examples of burnt mounds on the island (Hunter and Dockrill 1990, Fig. 2) appears to reflect no such distinction in their preservation and might be regarded for most purposes as an original distribution with consequent implications for settlement organisation. At least part of the reason for their survival

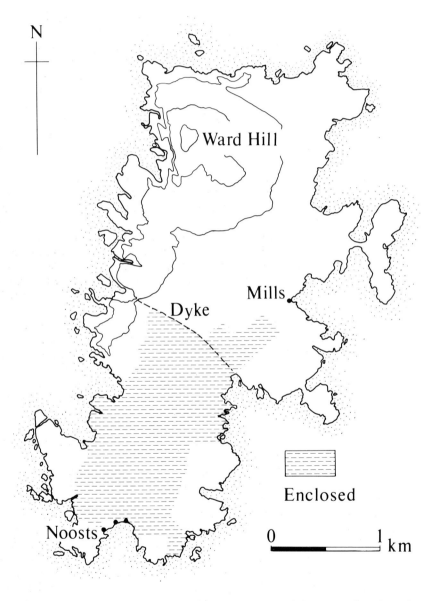

Fig. 11.2 Fair Isle showing current land division and locations referred to in discussion

must relate to factors of both composition and size. The small fractured stones constituting the mound are of no particular building value and are, therefore, unquarried; while burnt mounds on Fair Isle tend to be awkward to plough out or remove, and at the same time are mostly too small to pose a significant threat to formal agriculture. This is particularly the case within small island populations where the degree of respect afforded to the history of the community itself guarantees a certain level of preservation.

In Fair Isle (and other parts of Shetland) the landscape is characterised by isolated lengths of walling, often in an L- or T- shape, used as shelters for sheep. They seem incongruous on the landscape, those on Fair Isle being the subject of previous discussion (Hunter 1990a). It is interesting that these sheep shelters and, indeed, the plantiecrues (crubs) — small drystone square structures inside which seedlings are reared safe from the wind and grazing sheep — appear to have no obvious association with either habitation patterns or agricultural land. The locations of both types appear to be determined almost entirely by the presence of existing stone sources, natural or otherwise, thus indicating the possibility of early monuments close by. This at least goes some way to identifying former elements of the archaeological landscape. It also makes a potentially significant contribution to the location of past population centres, even of relatively modern date when the previous number of souls on the island was far in excess of the present total. The census for 1861, for example, lists a population of over 350 compared to the present (saturated) population of a little over 60. Identification of likely habitation sites is itself a potentially important aid to understanding those periods of change in the settlement record, particularly between the Norse and early modern periods.

Fieldwork has so far identified a number of foundation remains on Fair Isle, several in clustered arrangements, based on the above principle (Fig. 11.3). The extent of their antiquity is subject to excavation and may offer useful implications for future studies in the Northern Isles. One concentration of apparent structural remains on the west side of the island which had the appearance of Norse-type structures (and which on a promontory location might be referred to as a monastery) turned out to be a series of turf-based planticrues of a type identified by O'Dell earlier this century (1939, 78). This alone must cast some doubt on a number of interpreted monasteries elsewhere in the Northern Isles.

Others are of more plausible antiquity, for example a nucleus of foundations in the vicinity of Shirva (the modern post-office) bisected by the construction of a new road. This represents the location of one of only four tunships recorded in the First Statistical Account where the houses were 'confusedly thrown together as chance, whim, or conveniency directed' (OSA 19, 436). Other foundations were identified adjacent to standing buildings the names of which contained traditional Norse elements. For the latter, this presents the opportunity to test place-name-based settlement models of the Marwick (1952) type in an attempt to secure some insight into the nature of settlement evolution from Norse times to the present day.

Recent work on standing remains elsewhere in Orkney has confirmed

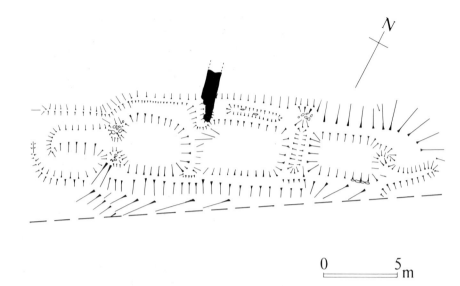

Fig. 11.3   Contour survey of a structural foundation on Fair Isle. The standing wall (blackened) is used as a shelter

rather than thrown light on this problem of structural continuity. The point was reinforced by an investigation of ruined structures undertaken in the region around Scapa Flow where deserted and derelict farm buildings provided the opportunity for an evaluation of structural change in a relatively undeveloped rural area (Hunter *et al.* 1982 and 1984). Islands such as Fara and Cava, now depopulated and mostly unvisited, represent fossilised landscapes complete with fields, farm units (tunships) and even surviving internal features within farmsteads.

The buildings examined belonged in the most part to the nineteenth century and lay in nucleated groups (Plate 11.1). Some were of tunship status like those on Fair Isle, and each group testified to alteration and expansion of both domestic and agricultural components, even the transfer of one to the other. The exercise involved the production of ground plans and elevations of individual structures of traditional Orcadian type, not to mention a record of trackways, boat noosts, jetties, wells, field boundaries and other elements of a functioning island community. Apart from creating a rare record of nineteenth-century vernacular architecture and social infrastructure, the investigation showed little visible in the structural evolution that might be construed as significantly closing the gap with Norse times. It did at least make the point that standing remains (or at least those examined in Scapa Flow), while ostensibly the product of Norse traditions, were not in themselves of any long-term duration.

It might be worth adding by way of a reminder of the effects of twentieth century activity that these Scapa Flow islands were intensively reoccupied

Pl. 11.1 Derelict *tunship* settlement at Peat Bay, Fara, Orkney. One of many abandoned farmstead complexes dating from the eighteenth and nineteenth centuries

during two World Wars, but in a manner which appears to have preserved the integrity of the existing landscape. Superimposed on the former social and agricultural patterning of the islands was a series of Nissen-hut groups, gun emplacements, barrage balloon supports and lookout posts — all worthy monuments in their own right, but with a clustering based on high ground vantage, access to other islands and with direct bearings on specific anchorage points in the surrounding waters. The distribution of military monuments and settlement remains respectively are almost wholly discrete. A similar phenomenon is evident on Fair Isle where the military remains are almost exclusively restricted to the highest point on the island (Ward Hill) at an altitude well above observed early landscapes.

Although the investigation of the Scapa Flow structures was to some extent disappointing the buildings offered other advantages; they represented a type of upstanding archaeology on the basis that the architecture, the materials and even the subsistence economies represented were little different from Norse times. They exhibited the last glimpse of Viking tradition, but by inference only. The project at least confirmed by lengthy and controlled experiment that the question whether the 'longhouses' of the eighteenth and nineteenth centuries were the product of an ongoing tradition or simply a reintroduction was still pertinent (eg Fenton 1982) and worthy of pursuit.

A similar problem is reflected on Fair Isle where other, more tangible traditions of Norse culture manifest themselves, the yole and the mill. The yole — a small boat constructed in the long tradition of Norse boat-building, is, in fact, of indirect tradition — a reintroduction of the post-medieval period from Norway with a variant specific to Fair Isle itself (Ostler 1983). While still authentically Scandinavian, the pedigree is not altogether unblemished. The associated boat noost (Plate 11.2), again a characteristic element of the Shetland coastline, may have followed a similar route and can at least be traced back to the late eighteenth century where, according to the First Statistical Account, the island's 'pitiful skiffs' were kept (OSA 19, 437).

Similar difficulties arise with the horizontal or click mill whose distribution in Scandinavia, Shetland, Faroe, Ireland and the Mediterranean has caused untold problems of interpretation. Its origins are traditionally ascribed to second-century BC Greece — its spread subsequently following a course which, according to Irish dendrochronology, took it to Ireland during the seventh — tenth centuries (Baillie 1980) at a time before Norse immigration and activity. Thus they are not strictly Norse mills according to accepted interpretation, but mills spread by Norse activity, presumably reaching Shetland from the west, not from the east. They are, nevertheless, Norse-derived and introduced as a by-product of Norse culture.

Horizontal mills have, as a character, a horizontal wheel normally fed by a moveable lade or trough system. They are unbelievably crude, cheap to build and can be constructed from easily obtainable materials. Unlike their vertical-wheeled cousins they have no gearing, the millstone being mounted directly above the wheel itself within a simple structure usually 'thatched with peats or strips of turf' (Evershed 1874, 197).

Pl. 11.2 Boat noosts and yoles on Fair Isle showing summer (lower) and winter (upper) arrangements

It is a mill system that has two particular requirements, firstly a narrow but steep mountain stream (found in Shetland rather than in Orkney) and secondly a peasant-based society such as that of the original Mediterranean setting in which feudalism played little part. The continued use of the horizontal mill is to some extent dependent on the absence of any imposed centralised system of authority for which the larger controlled vertical-wheeled mill, complete with archetypal evil miller, was more appropriate. Horizontal mills were essentially designed for individual families, or for small groups within a community, each mill being arguably 'little better than a handmill or a quern' (Low 1879, 74). Shetland mills were traditionally derided by visitors; Scott wrote how the mechanics were 'enclosed in a hovel about the size of a pigsty' (Laughlan 1982, 29), while Hibbert described the grinding machinery as being 'destined for a race of pygmies' (1822, 19). Gilbert Goudie, a distinguished antiquarian, was one of the few to recognise the cultural significance of the horizontal mill in Shetland. His pioneering work published in 1886 provides an important landmark in studies of this type.

The known Fair Isle mills are of the eighteenth or nineteenth centuries and belong to a complex system of drainage, dams and channels (Plate 11.3). There is, interestingly, no apparent fundamental difference between their mechanics and those of their predecessors some 1,000 years earlier. Indeed the nature of the crofting community which they served must have adhered to the same type of social structure as in Norse times. Recent excavation of these remains evidenced similar technical phenomena — wooden troughing, elaborately designed water coursing and the axle or tirl with angled recesses for the individual paddles. The problem, however, is in determining whether these Fair Isle mills (not to mention other mills in Shetland) belong to a lengthy tradition in the north or whether, like boat-building, they relate to a reintroduction and represent an impure pedigree.

This apparent absence of physical continuity from Scandinavian times through to the present day is particularly anomalous; Scandinavian culture is traditionally argued to have formed the modern social and agricultural system in Orkney and Shetland, a concept supported by ethnographic and

Pl. 11.3 New Mill, Fair Isle during excavation. The millstone is still *in situ*

linguistic evidence. With the possible exception of Jarlshof, Scandinavian sites of the Northern Isles do not appear to show any great degree of structural continuity through to the middle ages and beyond, although it should be added that research has not traditionally been directed to this end. Sites appear to be of relatively short-term duration, exemplified in Shetland at Underhoull (Small 1966) and in Orkney at Birsay (Hunter 1986), Buckquoy (Ritchie 1977) and more recently at Pool, Sanday. Norse remains from this last example represent the latest deposits from a multi-period settlement site which, for a number of reasons, had been a focal point for occupation since Neolithic times (Hunter 1990b).

Like these other sites, Pool leaves an emphatic question mark over subsequent settlement in the immediate area when archaeological evidence again seems to be at a premium. Adjacent to the Pool site lie the reused farm buildings of the late eighteenth–nineteenth centuries, and it might be argued that the continuity is to be found below these and other post-medieval farmsteads. The gap at Pool and elsewhere is otherwise remarkably difficult to fill and there are few physical links in either Orkney or Shetland to span the thirteenth to eighteenth centuries. Sites such as Tuquoy, Westray (Owen 1988), The Biggins, Papa Stour (Crawford 1985) or Sandwick, Shetland (Bigelow 1985) are important although detached links in Norse settlement chronology.

A problem of continuity in a period as late as this begs the question to what extent, if at all, the nineteenth century landscape and its associated traditions is a valid indicator of settlement and subsistence economics of the Norse period itself, yet alone earlier. The question requires knowledge of the extent to which land use and resource exploitation was optimised at a sufficiently early date (as suggested above) and remained conservative irrespective of any actual *lacunae* in the settlement record. It also needs to ascertain the extent to which such a major cultural influence as the Norse might have erased, or substantially modified, an existing set of developed economic traditions.

The logical recourse to excavated evidence is not an entirely satisfactory solution given that excavation methodology is itself a possible cause of this bias in the settlement record. Archaeological investigation has only recently evolved from a tradition of site by site investigation. This has a tendency to restrict research to specific stages within the overall sequence of man's settlement, often with single-period sites pinpointed by highly specific research designs. The stubborn retention of a 'three age' concept has a similar effect in designating sites into blunt period groups rather than visualising them as part of a progressive sequence. Chronological studies emerging from the archaeological record show precisely this type of patterning (eg Renfrew 1985), with breaks in settlement continuity occurring most consistently in the early second millennium BC, in the pre-broch period (mid Iron Age) and following later Norse settlement from the twelfth–thirteenth centuries.

It must, however, be established whether these apparent lapses are entirely an unfortunate by-product of methodology (including a bias in the type of material remains recovered) or partly the genuine result of social, economic or climatic phenomena. The latter is certainly attested; for example the Iron

Age utilisation of Neolithic burial monuments after lengthy periods of desertion (eg at Howe, Pierowall and Quanterness) points to the reality of shifts in population stability and land use. Irrespective of causes, however, the overall effect has been to minimise the opportunity to consider the evolution of subsistence economics and exploitation at evenly spaced intervals of time.

Whether this situation can be improved by the discovery of a control site remains to be seen; those sites which are longest in terms of settlement duration, for example Jarlshof (Hamilton 1956), Kebister (Owen 1986) and Howe (Carter *et al.* 1984), tend to reinforce rather than refute the behaviour pattern set by groups of individual, single-period sites. This has been reaffirmed subsequently by two separate excavations on the island of Sanday, Orkney, at Pool and Tofts Ness (Fig. 11.1); the Pool site contained major phases of occupation from the Neolithic and later Iron Age/Viking periods (Hunter 1990b), while at Tofts Ness settlement was identified from the Neolithic/Early Bronze Age and Late Bronze Age/Early Iron Age (Dockrill 1987).

The two investigations, although entirely different in their strategy, ironically produced a virtually complete overview from Neolithic to later Norse times. Whilst it would be incorrect to consider them together as a single site (approach methodologies, local landscapes and settlement types were in contrast), they did at least occur on the same small island and together might be cautiously used as a yardstick against which to measure the development of a local subsistence economy. The sites had the advantage of a cognate technological development and common access to similar resources throughout a period of some 4,500 years.

Continuity is attested in a number of broad ways, notably in the evolution of the circular or sub-circular structure from Neolithic to later Iron Age times — a development which has only recently been revolutionised on the basis of an early radiocarbon date at Bu broch (Hedges 1985, 167), now supported at Tofts Ness (Dockrill 1987, Appendix 5). Accessible building stone is a feature of each location. Both sites also share an expected level of local exploitation in their utilisation of other naturally available materials, outwashed flints, strand pumice and beached *cetacea* together with other fruits of the sea, including driftwood. Clay sources for pottery were local, and MacSween has shown (MacSween *et al.* 1988) that at Pool certain specific clays were used throughout all periods of occupation, despite the massive gap in settlement continuity at that site. The tempers used at both Tofts Ness and Pool reflect exploitation of the two different local geological resources respectively. Only with the exception of rare occurrences of ground steatite does this picture of the use of local resources change, presumably reflecting important external contact (with Shetland?) from the Bronze Age onwards.

As far as other materials are concerned the two sites continue to demonstrate common trends, for example the assemblages of Neolithic worked stone from both sites are consistent. Clarke (pers. comm.), however, has noted some idiosyncracies in the later material from Tofts Ness, particularly in the Iron Age assemblage which contained objects which would not appear out of place in a Neolithic context, notably pot lids and skaill knives; this may suggest a behavioural bias. The presence of quartz in considerable quantity at Tofts Ness and its apparent absence in the Pool record may be seen as further evidence of this, although it has to be added that the two flint assemblages have many features in common and that the technologies are similar.

The environmental record, however, is perhaps a more accurate long-term indicator of land use and resource exploitation; certainly the major trends are identical from both sites even taking into account local landscape differences. From earliest times the evidence points to an economy which included the growing of cereal crops, perhaps without sustained use of the plough, and the keeping of cattle probably for both meat and milk. Unlike Neolithic economies further south, sheep rather than pigs appear to have played an important part.

Specific anomalies such as the faunal assemblage associated with a late Grooved Ware building at Pool might justifiably be ascribed to ritual activity, but the overall trend is otherwise consistent, even to the extent of characteristic butchery techniques through into the later Bronze Age. Indeed, the Late Bronze Age cereal and weed flora from Tofts Ness are similar to those of the Neolithic from Pool. The overview suggests that limitations of climate and land utility may have fostered environmental adaptation and maximisation of resources at a relatively early date. Even the apparent practice of the early slaughtering of cattle in the Neolithic and elsewhere seems to have persisted and still occurred at Pool in the Norse period, presumably reflecting an interest in milk yields.

The use of two sites, rather than a single site, is not entirely satisfactory, but nevertheless appears to demonstrate a certain correlation of trend, subject only to the inevitable behavioural biases of each. The next point to consider is the extent to which this developed economy might be affected by a major cultural change (the second part of the premise) — an issue which evidentially, as well as from the point of view of this paper, is perhaps best considered from the Norse period itself.

In a previous paper (Hunter *et al.* 1990) the mechanics of Norse settlement on the site at Pool were discussed at length, the cultural influence being identified from structural, artifactual and to some extent from ecofactual standpoints. It seems clear that although colonisation had a major impact it did not entirely obviate elements of an evolved native culture, nor did it occur overnight. While diagnostic indicators such as steatite support the notion of Scandinavian supremacy (either politically or numerically), the persistence of earlier pottery traditions would tend to suggest not only that some degree of assimilation is to be considered, but also that a considerable period of overlap took place.

One myth to be broken at an early stage, and the focus for discussion here, is the assumed catastrophic nature of this ninth century AD Scandinavian colonisation. The widely held view that the modern (nineteenth century) agrarian economy of the Northern Isles was essentially of Norse inspiration is a far from satisfactory interpretation of the excavated evidence. While partly true, it is equally clear from Pool that the same basic type of economy was already being followed in the Iron Age and that, although some differences exist, taken over a longer-term view the change of cultural dominance was largely irrelevant.

It seems to be the case that Norse influences accentuated an existing economy. In the case of horses, for example, the present characteristic short, sturdy Shetland breed is seen as developing from the same stock as the Norwegian horse (Berry and Johnston 1980, 138). However, the use of horses is well attested in pre-Norse times from both faunal evidence and from symbol stones. They occur at Pool in the later Iron Age (Pictish period) although evidence of breeding, interpreted from remains less than 18 months in age, is demonstrated only from the deposits belonging to the Norse period (Hunter *et al.* 1990). The modern Shetland breed is not necessarily to be seen as resulting from a new emphasis on horses introduced by Viking colonists, indeed the species from Viking deposits at Jarlshof would appear to be greater in stature than the modern sheltie (Platt 1956, 214). It might also be added that characteristics similar to those of the modern Shetland breed are also to be found among other, unimproved breeds elsewhere in (non-Viking) Britain.

Similar problems of origin apply to the appearance of the field mouse *Apodemus sylvaticius*, whose interpreted Norwegian origins and subsequent spread in the Atlantic and Scottish islands is portrayed on the basis of the 'founder effect' theory of genetic evolution (Berry and Johnston 1980, Fig. 19). Its ultimate appearance on both Foula and Fair Isle is conveniently ascribed to 'chance colonisation from a Viking ship' (Berry 1974, 154). Other species where Norse influences might be seen to operate include the gannet, whose temporary disappearance has sometimes been attributed to Norse hunting (Berry and Johnson 1980, 131), although it has since been shown that other populations in other periods have also been responsible (Serjeantson 1988). The characteristic breed of Shetland sheep creates a further issue; the species shows certain affinities with the primitive feral Soay species found on St Kilda, particularly in the horns and in the moulting and colours of the fleece (Berry and Johnston 1980, 139), and its spread might be assumed to be caused by Norse maritime activity.

This assumption too, is probably ill-founded; the Shetland breed is indigenous and its modern characteristics may stem from apparent inbreeding in the eighteenth century when the flocks were allowed to roam wild. Hibbert observed that sheep were 'almost to be regarded as in a state of nature, since they range at large over the scattalds during the whole of the year' (1822, 436), while a generation earlier the First Statistical Account for Aithsting and Sandsting reported that the number of sheep 'cannot be properly ascertained as they go at freedom on the hills; and some of them are so wild as only to be caught by dogs' (OSA 19, 388).

Archaeological deposits in both Orkney and Shetland show sheep/goat remains to be prominent in the faunal assemblages even from Neolithic times, yet despite the weight of material there is no evidence to indicate that the primitive Soay breed evolved in Shetland. On the contrary there is evidence from a number of sites to suggest that it did not. At Jarlshof, for example, the Late Bronze Age levels contained remains of sheep similar to the long-horned Soay together with those of more slender stock (Platt 1956, 214). At Buckquoy, Orkney, sheep in the final Viking phase were virtually indistinguishable from Soay type, although their predecessors on the site were clearly different. Noddle ascribes this development to a process of selection caused by the environmental pressures to which the breed was subjected during those centuries (1977, 208). Modern Shetland sheep, therefore, might be seen as belonging to an entirely separate evolution to that of the Soay on St Kilda, although following a largely parallel process of selection for which the Norsemen can only partly be held responsible.

On this varied evidence it would seem that the Norse impact on an existing evolved economy may have been over-estimated, and that the landscape and its resources were sufficiently resilient to survive changes of management either at Norse hands, or by earlier populations. An overview of this nature raises more questions than it resolves, but it does at least point towards continuity of traditions from earliest times both from a subsistence point of view and, to a lesser extent, in material technology. The archaeological evidence, although not entirely satisfactory, appears to identify discontinuity in the settlement record — a phenomenon which seemingly has little effect on any subsistence traditions. If this discontinuity is a fact, as opposed to a simple response to archaeological method, it serves to confirm the strength of this economy against social or cultural change, as suggested by the data available from the Norse period. Settlement in the Northern Isles was, it seems, a process of adaptation to pre-established and proven methods. It was not so much a question of man's impact on the environment as his acceptance of its limitations.

In many senses the original question whether the nineteenth century traditions are relevant to earlier archaeological studies has been answered. They adhere to the same systems of economic awareness and exploitation as those of earlier societies in the Northern Isles and as such might be seen as a relevant insight to antiquity. The value of the nineteenth-century landscape utilising ethnographic tradition, and the vivid, first-hand accounts of antiquaries are an intrinsic part of this perception.

Bibliography

Baillie, M. G. L. 1980 Dendrochronology — the Irish view, *Current Archaeol.* 73, 61–3.

Baldwin, J. R. (ed) 1978 *Scandinavian Shetland. An ongoing tradition?* Edinburgh.

Baldwin, J. R. 1983 Structure in a community: the outfield, its use and its organisation in the settlement at Gasadalar, Faeroe Islands, *Northern Stud.* 20, 5–37.

Baldwin, J. R. 1984 Hogin and Hametoun: thoughts on the stratification of a Foula *Tun*, in Crawford B. E. (ed) *Essays in Shetland history*, Lerwick, 33–64.

Berry, R. J. 1974 The Shetland fauna, its significance, or lack thereof, in

Goodier, R. (ed) *The natural environment of Shetland*, Edinburgh, 151–63.

Berry, R. J. and Johnston, J. L. 1980 *The natural history of Shetland*, London.

Bigelow, G. F. 1985 Sandwick, Unst and late Norse Shetland economy, in Smith 1985, 95–127.

Carter, S. P. , Haigh, D. , Neil N. R. and Smith, B. 1984 Interim report on the structures at Howe, Stromness, Orkney, *Glasgow Archaeol. J.* 11, 61–73.

Crawford, B. E. 1985 The Biggins, Papa Stour — a multi-disciplinary investigation, in Smith 1985, 128–58.

Dockrill, S. J. 1987 *Excavations at Tofts Ness, Sanday. Interim 1987*, Bradford.

Evershed, H. 1874 *The agriculture of the islands of Shetland*, Edinburgh.

Fenton, A. 1978 *The Northern Isles*, Edinburgh.

Fenton, A. 1982 The longhouse in Northern Scotland, in Myhre, B. , Stoklund, B. and Gjaerder, P. (eds) *Vestnordisk byggeskikk gjennom to tusen ar*, Stavanger, 231–40.

Goudie, G. 1886 On the horizontal water mills of Shetland, *Proc. Soc. Antiq. Scotland* 20, 257–97.

Hamilton, J. R. C. 1956 *Excavations at Jarlshof, Shetland*, Edinburgh.

Heddle, M. F. 1879 The geognosy and mineralogy of Scotland. Mainland (Shetland), Foula, Fair Isle, *Mineralogy Mag.* 3, 18–56.

Hedges, J. W. 1985 The broch period, in Renfrew 1985, 150–75.

Hibbert, S. 1822 *A description of the Shetland Isles*, Edinburgh.

Hunter, J. R. (ed) 1985 *Fair Isle survey, interim 1985*, Bradford.

Hunter, J. R. 1986 *Rescue excavations on the Brough of Birsay, Orkney 1974–82*, Edinburgh.

Hunter, J. R. 1990a The sites and monuments of Fair Isle, Shetland, in Smith, B. and Turner, V. (eds) *Settlement in Shetland, continuity and change*, forthcoming.

Hunter, J. R. 1990b Pool, Sanday — a case study for the later Iron Age and Viking periods, in Armit, I. (ed) *Beyond the brochs*, Edinburgh, 175–93.

Hunter, J. R, Bond, J. M. and Smith, A. N. 1990 Some aspects of early Viking settlement in Orkney, in Batey, C. and Jesch, J. (eds) *Proceedings of the eleventh Viking congress*, forthcoming.

Hunter, J. R. and Dockrill, S. J. 1990 Some burnt mounds on Fair Isle and Sanday, in Buckley, V. (ed) *Burnt offerings: international contributions to burnt mound archaeology*, Dublin, 62–8.

Hunter, J. R, Dockrill, S. J. and McKinley, J. I. 1982 *The sites and monuments of Fara, Orkney*, Bradford.

Hunter, J. R, Dockrill, S. J. and McKinley, J. I. 1984 *The sites and monuments of Cava, Risa Little and Switha, Orkney*, Bradford.

Laughlan, W. F. (ed) 1982 *Northern lights: the diary of Sir Walter Scott*, Hawick.

Low, G. 1879 *A tour through the islands of Orkney and Shetland in 1774*, Kirkwall.

MacSween, A, Hunter, J. R. and Warren, S. E. 1988 Analysis of coarse wares from the Orkney Isles, in Slater, E. A. and Tate, J. O. (eds) *Science and archaeology, Glasgow 1987*, Oxford, 95–106.

Marwick, H. 1952 *Orkney farm-names*, Kirkwall.

Morris, C. D. (ed) 1989 *The Birsay Bay project*, vol 1, Durham.

Noddle, B. 1977 The animal bones from Buckquoy, Orkney, in Ritchie 1977, 201–09.

NSA 1845 *New statistical account of Scotland*, vol 15, Edinburgh and London.

O'Dell, A. C. 1939 *The historical geography of the Shetland Islands*, Lerwick.

OSA Sir J. Sinclair (ed), *The statistical account of Scotland 1791–1799*, Edinburgh.

Ostler, A. G. 1983 *The Shetland boat, South Mainland and Fair Isle*, London.

Owen, O. 1986 Kebister 1986, unpublished interim report.

Owen, O. 1988 Tuquoy, Westray, Orkney, unpublished interim report.

Platt, M. I. 1956 The animal bones, in Hamilton 1956, 212–15.

Renfrew, C. (ed) 1985 *The prehistory of Orkney*, Edinburgh.

Reynolds, D. 1985 'How we found a tumulus' a story from the Orkney Islands — the journal of Lady Burroughs, *Proc. Soc. Antiq. Scotland* 115, 115–24.

Ritchie, A. 1977 Excavation of Pictish and Viking-age farmsteads at Buckquoy, Orkney, *Proc. Soc. Antiq. Scotland* 108, 174–227.

Serjeantson, D. 1988 Archaeological and ethnographic evidence for seabird exploitation in Scotland, *Archaeozoologia* 2, 209–24.

Sibbald, R. 1711 *Description of the islands of Orkney and Shetland*, Edinburgh.

Small, A. 1966 Excavations at Underhoull, Unst, Shetland, *Proc. Soc. Antiq. Scotland* 98 (1964–66), 225–48.

Smith, B. (ed) 1985 *Shetland archaeology*, Lerwick.

Tudor, J. R. 1883 *The Orkneys and Shetland. Their past and present state*, London.

Whittle, A. (ed) 1986 *Scord of Brouster*, Oxford.

Acknowledgements

The author would like to express his thanks to Ann Clarke, Bill Finlayson, Ann MacSween and particularly to Julie Bond and Steve Dockrill (supervisor of the Tofts Ness investigations) for helpful advice and comments in the preparation of this paper. Work at Pool and Tofts Ness has been undertaken on behalf of Historic Scotland. Survey in Scapa Flow and Fair Isle has been funded variously by the British Academy, the National Trust for Scotland, the Shetland Amenity Trust, the Society of Antiquaries of Scotland and the Russell Trust.

12

PRESERVING THE PAST FOR THE FUTURE

Lesley Macinnes

Through interpretation, understanding; through understanding, appreciation; through appreciation, protection. (Tilden 1977, 38)

Fieldwork is recognised as an essential part of archaeology and the survey work of the Royal Commission on Ancient and Historical Monuments for Scotland (RCAHMS) is both well-known and widely used as a basis for research. In contrast, the protection of monuments in the field, the remit of Historic Scotland (HS) and the Regional Archaeologists, is not as fully appreciated by archaeologists in general. This paper attempts to redress the balance. It is in three sections: part one reviews the current provisions for the protection and management of field monuments in Scotland; part two considers the relationship between archaeological protection and nature conservation, which is appropriate at a time when there is increasing concern over environmental protection in general; and part three examines the ways in which public awareness of field monuments could be enhanced.

Monument Protection and Management

Archaeology in the landscape: the scope of the problem

Monuments are found throughout the Scottish landscape (Ritchie and Ritchie 1981). Although generally best preserved in unimproved moorland or marginal land, they also survive in improved land and even intensively cultivated land, where they have been reduced to cropmarks. Archaeologists are very familiar with the varying states in which monuments survive and the effect that differential survival has had on the accuracy of our distribution maps, but all too seldom consider the pressures of contemporary land-use which continue to erode the archaeological resource in the landscape. The landscape is in a state of continuous change and the preservation of our archaeological sites and monuments has to be actively pursued, not left to chance (cf Darvill 1986, for England and Wales).

Natural processes of degradation and erosion cannot be avoided, but many of the pressures facing the preservation of archaeology in the countryside are caused by human activity. These can be avoided, or at least minimised.

In Scotland it is agriculture and afforestation which pose the most severe threats, though a wide variety of developments are also damaging. It is worth considering some of these problems and the damage they can cause.

Ploughing gradually erodes both upstanding earthworks and below ground archaeological deposits. Shallow ploughing causes least damage and many cropmarks which survive in land regularly cultivated have proved on excavation to contain well-preserved archaeological deposits, such as at the Iron Age settlement of Broxmouth (Hill 1982). Indeed, the archaeology of large parts of eastern Scotland is known predominantly through cropmarks, representing the core of settlement on the better land through all periods (eg Macinnes 1982). In contrast to shallow ploughing, farming techniques involving deep ploughing, subsoiling and drainage can have catastrophic effects on archaeological features.

Grazing stock can also pose problems for monuments, principally through the trampling of earthworks and the creation of erosion hollows. This can be alleviated by sympathetic management which will maintain the most appropriate type of stock — generally sheep cause least damage — and, crucially, limit the number of stock. Similar problems are caused by burrowing animals, but these are more difficult to remedy, particularly since some species are protected by law. Over and above these problems, fencing, drainage and reseeding are all potentially damaging to ancient monuments, as they involve considerable disturbance of the ground.

Perhaps the single greatest threat to monuments in Scotland in recent years has been afforestation (Proudfoot 1989). This is not only a problem of scale, but also of technique, since the ploughing of large tracts of landscape — often previously undisturbed moorland — is a destructive process. Indeed, the whole forestry process from initial ploughing, through growth, thinning and felling is incompatible with archaeological preservation.

Afforestation can also affect archaeological sites indirectly: for example drainage of wetland areas may cause the loss of well-preserved archaeological deposits through drying out, even if they lie outwith the area actually afforested. Moreover, although specific monuments are protected under the arrangements instituted by the Forestry Commission, their wider setting will often be lost as a result of surrounding afforestation. Some upland forestry proposals cover several hundred hectares of land, affecting a substantial number of well-preserved sites, while recent changes in grant support have placed lowland cropmark complexes under increasing threat as well.

Other development problems occur in both upland and lowland areas, rural and urban contexts. These take a variety of forms: for example, quarrying and extraction works, road and trackway construction, pipelines, building works and associated services. All are damaging not only in their initial phases, but also during subsequent maintenance works. The escalating pace and scale of such activities poses a major problem for archaeological protection.

If the archaeological resource is to survive these modern pressures, it needs to be actively managed as a resource for the future, in the same way as areas of nature conservation interest (Walsh 1969, 38–9). Traditionally in Britain development seems to have been favoured over conservation, so choices will always have to be made about what to preserve and how much. Archaeologists accept that it is not realistic to preserve all archaeological features in the landscape (Lowenthal 1981, 218–23; Mercer 1989, 12). Nevertheless, the aim of monument protection is to preserve as much as possible, where land-use is not in conflict with preservation or can be adjusted to avoid such conflict. Where monuments under direct threat of damage or destruction cannot be preserved, other solutions have to be found. The principal alternatives to preservation are either rescue excavation, or survey, — euphemistically referred to as 'preservation by record' — or loss of the monument without record. As resources for rescue excavation are finite, there has to be continual selection of which sites to record in this way and, as a consequence, loss of sites without record happens by default. Given that resources are limited, there is a constant dilemma about whether to record as much as possible, or whether to concentrate resources on dealing with fewer problems more comprehensively. In an ideal world, no information should be destroyed without some degree of recording, since the distribution of known monuments is already a fragment of the original pattern and future work may demonstrate the significance of those monuments which seem of least significance to us at present. In the reality of the present and foreseeable future, however, the best that can be achieved is to seek to maximise preservation through all available options, while maintaining an awareness of the limitations of our database, the state of our knowledge, and changing archaeological perceptions and concepts.

A variety of legal provisions control development of the land, in both rural and urban contexts, although not all activities are subject to such control. These provisions have been described in detail elsewhere (Cleere 1984a; Proudfoot 1984; Breeze 1988; Macinnes 1990) and are presented here only in outline.

Archaeological legislation

The principal instrument for the protection of archaeology is the Ancient Monuments and Archaeological Areas Act 1979. This is the latest in a line of Acts which began in 1882, making the protection of ancient monuments the earliest conservation legislation in the country (MacIvor and Fawcett 1983; Cleere 1984a, 54–5). In the light of this, it is salutary to reflect that it is the conservation of the 'natural' environment, not the built heritage, that is most prominent in the public eye today.

Provisions within the 1979 Act allow monuments to be taken into public ownership or care (often called guardianship). This has most frequently been done by central government in the past, but local authorities are empowered in the same way. There are currently 330 monuments in the care of, or owned by, the Secretary of State for Scotland. Most are open to the public and are maintained and interpreted by HS (eg Breeze 1983).

Guardianship has rarely been invoked for field monuments. The principal form of protection for these sites is scheduling, supported by management agreements (see below). Through scheduling, monuments considered to be of national importance are added to a schedule maintained and periodically published by the Secretary of State for Scotland. All work related to scheduling is carried out on behalf of the Secretary of State by HS. There are currently around 4,700 scheduled monuments and HS aims to add approximately 300 to that every year.

The qualification 'of national importance' is significant, and means that not all monuments can be protected through this legislation. Nevertheless, the range of monuments that can be scheduled is very wide indeed, covering all periods from early prehistory to the recent industrial and military past, although a few categories of monuments are specifically excluded: occupied dwellings, ecclesiastical buildings in use as such and protected wrecks. The criteria for selecting monuments of national importance are the same as those recently discussed for England (Wainwright 1985, 23–4; Darvill *et al.* 1987, 395–401), with an underlying consideration in Scotland laid down by the Ancient Monuments Board (AMB), the Secretary of State's advisory board on archaeological matters:

> A monument is of national importance if, in the view of informed opinion, it contributes or appears likely to contribute significantly to the understanding of the past. Such significance may be assessed from individual or group qualities, and may include structural or decorative features, or value as an archaeological resource. (AMB 1983, 8–9)

An important aspect of this definition is that there is no provision for the protection of the setting or amenity value of ancient monuments, and the whole of the scheduled area must be considered to be of archaeological significance. In this respect the 1979 Act abrogated the amenity provisions of earlier ancient monument legislation.

Scheduled monuments are subject to strict controls which stand apart from planning controls. Essentially, this means that any works affecting a scheduled area require the prior approval of the Secretary of State for Scotland, obtained through the scheduled monument consent (SMC) procedure. Certain works are deemed to have prior consent, class consent, and are exempt from SMC: these relate principally to certain agricultural and forestry works, and safety matters. There are financial penalties, and even imprisonment, for unauthorised works leading to the damage of a protected monument. There has, however, been only one successful prosecution to date in Scotland under the 1979 Act, relating to the breaking of a condition attached to a scheduled monument consent. The recent appointment of monument wardens to monitor scheduled monuments throughout Scotland should help prevent such damage and unauthorised work.

Scheduling is largely based on data held in the National Monuments Record (NMR), with input from regional records. The selection of sites for scheduling is a difficult task, which needs to be carried out in full recognition of current academic thinking, debate and interpretation, since archaeological perceptions are constantly changing and developing. Scheduling decisions, therefore, need to be kept under constant review and an awareness maintained about the limitations of current knowledge and understanding. Since the scheduling of monuments is solely the responsibility of HS, it is incumbent upon its specialist staff, the Inspectorate of Ancient Monuments (IAM), to remain in close touch with archaeological research. However, input into the decision making process from those involved in research elsewhere, principally the universities, is also extremely valuable, and this has been encouraged recently by some learned societies who have provided guidelines on current research priorities in Britain (eg Prehistoric Society 1988). The academic weight this lends to scheduling is important, since, as monument protection becomes more widespread and successful, it is desirable to be able to point to supporting documentation for scheduling selections. Although HS has not so far issued any statements for scheduling along the lines of those prepared for rescue archaeology (AMB 1978, 12; Hanson and Breeze 1986), it has already increased its input into appropriate conferences and courses and thereby made possible wider discussion of the issues involved.

The concept which has primarily shaped monument protection to date is the site specific approach which has underpinned archaeological thinking until recent years. The strength of the 1979 Act has resulted in the adoption of very precise definitions of areas of archaeological significance, which can make the protection of dispersed archaeological landscapes difficult. Yet it is now recognised that such landscapes are one of the most crucial areas of study in field archaeology and are frequently recorded where modern survey is undertaken, as most recently in Perthshire (RCAHMS 1990). Part II of the 1979 Act, which allows for the designation of Areas of Archaeological Importance, has not been implemented in Scotland, and in England is used only for urban areas. In any case it acts only as a moratorium on development and is not a form of long-term protection like scheduling. The problem of the protection of archaeological landscapes can perhaps be addressed through a combination of scheduling and management agreements: since current legislation does not facilitate the preservation of the setting or amenity value of a site, additional protection might be achieved through the sympathetic management of a wider area. This would bring archaeological protection more into line with countryside designations, which operate largely through management agreements.

The current legislation has not kept pace with developments in archaeology and, indeed, there have been recent moves to review the 1979 Act. However, much can be done to apply the existing measures according to modern criteria: this has in fact always been done in practice as the discovery of different monuments and changing archaeological concepts have been brought to bear in the area of monument protection. Thus, the selection of sites worthy of protection has changed over the years. As an illustration of this, many sites scheduled in the 1930s-1950s protected no more than the physical features, while it is now standard practice to include an additional area in which associated deposits might be expected to survive below ground, as has been frequently demonstrated through excavation. Nevertheless, this practice falls short of the protection of the environment of archaeological sites, monuments and landscapes, which could only be achieved through more radical review of the current legislation to allow the protection, and control, of wider areas around monuments, in the manner of the 1931 Ancient Monuments Act.

Scheduling preserves monuments against external interference: it does not arrest natural processes of deterioration, nor requires the positive management of sites and monuments to keep them in the condition best suited to their long-term preservation (Morgan-Evans 1985; 1986). To achieve this there are management provisions within the 1979 Act: management agreements and grants to owners. The former can be applied to any monument which requires active land management, such as control of stock or burrowing animals, clearance of trees or vegetation, provision of fencing etc. Grants to owners are normally reserved for the consolidation and repair of upstanding masonry structures. Both HS, on behalf of the Secretary of State for Scotland, and Local Authorities are empowered to enter into such agreements. There are practical restrictions on the level of grant which should be paid, although management agreements usually cover the full costs involved. Agreements cannot be negotiated with other public bodies, such as the Forestry Commission, which has meant that a large number of the sites protected from afforestation have not been secured through management against self-seeding regeneration. However, the Forestry Commission itself has recently declared its intention of introducing management agreements which can be directed towards this end.

Planning legislation

The protective measures within the Town and Country Planning Acts have adopted the same site specific approach as scheduling. These measures allow the protection of archaeological sites and monuments through development and planning controls of both urban and rural areas (Baker 1983; Selman 1988). These can be used to provide a strategic approach to the protection of a region's archaeological resource through the Structure and Local Plans, which are regularly reviewed, as well as through specific measures for the protection or investigation of identified sites affected by developments. They can also lead to the designation of archaeological sites of regional importance, complementing the national designation of scheduling and providing the only protection for unscheduled sites; the identification of rural as well as urban conservation areas; and the protection of the setting of scheduled monuments. In practice these wide powers are not fully used generally in Scotland. Their application has instead been very similar to scheduling in placing emphasis on individual sites and monuments, although the potential of conservation areas in particular is great for wider archaeological landscapes.

The local authorities are advised on archaeological matters by their regional archaeologists, who maintain sites and monuments records as their regional databases. These complement the National Monuments Record, extending that record to encompass a greater range of local material. Archaeological protection within local authorities is increasingly linked to the protection of the natural environment, facilitating a more integrated approach to the landscape within the planning system (Shepherd 1988), as most recently demonstrated by the Fife Environmental Charter (Fife Regional Council 1990).

Since the protection of historic buildings also falls under the planning legislation, it is worthwhile considering at this point the links between their statutory protection and that of archaeological sites. Both HS and the local authorities have a role to play in each, but their roles differ for the two areas of interest. Historic buildings are protected (listed) under the Planning Acts not through separate legislation as in the case of ancient monuments, although listed building consent (LBC) is required for relevant works in addition to planning consent (HBM 1988). Listing is initiated within HS by the Historic Buildings Inspectorate, though its associated executive powers lie in the first instance with the local planning authorities. Nevertheless, the Secretary of State has the power to intervene and is consulted automatically where alteration to category A and B buildings, or demolition of any listed building, are concerned. Moreover, grants for the repair of historic buildings are approved, and paid, by HS. Therefore, two tiers of administration are involved in the listing of historic buildings, and a division exists between the designation and execution of the protective measures. In contrast, for ancient monuments, both scheduling and all associated executive functions are carried out exclusively by HS, and both operate independently of the planning legislation.

Ancient monuments and more recent historic buildings are distinct parts of the continuum which constitutes the built heritage. In view of this, it has been argued that their statutory protection should be more closely aligned than it is at present. Apart from the legislative and organisational differences indicated above, in essence the aims of their protection are much the same: indeed there is also considerable overlap in date and form between listed and scheduled structures. Historic buildings are normally, though not always, in current use and their protection is often concerned with maintaining the architectural integrity of the structure during the course of modern alterations. Archaeological sites, which generally survive in ruinous form in the landscape, are protected against active damage, primarily maintaining them in their present form. One major difference between them is the listing of historic buildings in categories, which affect the nature of control and form part of the assessment of their eligiblity for grant aid. Scheduled monuments are not sub-divided, but of equal standing as sites of national importance. However, sites which have been designated as of regional importance by local authorities could be considered analogous to lower graded listed buildings and protected principally through the planning framework, so in effect this distinction between the two is less than might at first appear.

Since the public and planners alike generally have more experience of historic buildings than ancient monuments, the distinct arrangements for the protection of ancient monuments are not always fully appreciated. There is, therefore, a need to clarify the different nature of the legislation protecting archaeological sites and monuments through appropriate training channels and ensure that each authority has an archaeological advisor (Breeze 1989, 20). To further this end, the Scottish Office is currently preparing a guidance note on archaeology for local authorities.

Environmental legislation

In the protection of ancient monuments additional provisions can be brought to bear, which, like the planning legislation, are not aimed primarily at archaeological ends. Foremost among these are provisions relating to agriculture and forestry, the twin mainstays of land management in Scotland.

The Agriculture Act 1986 facilitates the protection of archaeological sites in two ways at present: through section 17, which requires that archaeological features be taken into consideration, amongst other things, before new grant-aided agricultural developments are undertaken, and section 18, which allows the designation of national Environmentally Sensitive Areas (ESA) in which management methods sympathetic to conservation of archaeological features, among others, are encouraged. The former provision is essentially a balancing duty placed on the Scottish Office Agriculture and Fisheries Department (SOAFD), but it is an important innovation in that it gives conservation, including archaeology, a higher profile in relation to agriculture than has been the case in the past. In implementing the Act SOAFD consult HS, as the archaeological advisors to the Secretary of State for Scotland, and communication between SOAFD and HS is continually improving and widening. There remains a fundamental problem of identifying which grant applications involve archaeological features, but this problem is being addressed. A number of training seminars have recently been held for a variety of agricultural staff to acquaint them with archaeology in the landscape and the problems of its preservation and management. The practical effects of this initiative will not be measurable for some time, but it has at least heightened awareness among agriculturalists of archaeology in the modern landscape.

Closer cooperation is already implicit in the ESA designations, where land may be managed for a variety of conservation ends, including archaeological, instead of primarily for intensive food production. The scheme is voluntary so there can be difficulty in encouraging farmers to join it, and there have been problems in monitoring its effects, but its concept brings archaeological protection and management more into line with nature conservation. It is to be hoped that if the ESA scheme is eventually extended beyond the current five examples in Scotland, the new ESAs will include land which is considered to be sensitive as much for its archaeological significance as for its nature conservation value. The practice of this scheme has led to closer cooperation between agriculturalists and archaeologists than has hitherto been the case, which is providing a basis for closer links in the other areas of mutual interest.

Other agricultural grant schemes have a potential application to the management of archaeological sites. In particular farm and conservation grants, set asides and farm diversification grants can facilitate the sympathetic management of archaeological sites and monuments and create a more positive attitude towards their protection and presentation. In practice, however, the consultation needed to achieve this by the identification of suitable sites is still lacking, leaving this potential untapped. One difficulty lies in the relative roles of different organisations. However, the growing recognition that archaeological management, like that for nature conservation, is a legitimate use of the land which should be associated more with farming grants should bring a more integrated approach to the problem.

Forestry regulations also allow for the protection of archaeological sites in advance of afforestation. Regulations covering both the principal current grant schemes — the Woodland Grant and Farm Woodland Schemes — require the identification and protection of important archaeological features in grant applications (Breeze 1989). Moreover, unlike the agricultural schemes at present, the facility to ensure that this happens is provided: regional archaeologists receive copies of grant applications and notify the Forestry Commission of sites which should be protected. Under these present arrangements the protection for archaeological features within forestry is even better than for those of nature conservation interest. The Forestry Commission have stated their intention to introduce management grants in the near future which will be a valuable step towards an integrated approach to land management for conservation interests within areas of afforestation.

The other main provision which can facilitate archaeological protection is the Environmental Assessment Regulations. This covers both developments within the scope of the Planning Acts and afforestation. The Regulations are designed to ensure that environmental considerations are taken into account in development proposals and the protective measures to be adopted described. This, too, brings archaeological considerations into line with other environmental concerns. Implementation of the Assessment Regulations relating to development is at the discretion of the appropriate authorities: the planning authorities and the Forestry Commission. Environmental Assessments were initiated by a European Directive which allowed for their extension to agricultural development, where fresh land was being brought into cultivation. In Britain this provision has not been implemented because it was felt that it had little relevance. This decision has not aided archaeological protection in Scotland, since fresh land is still being brought into cultivation in the old crofting counties.

All these provisions apply the same site-specific criteria to monument protection as those under the 1979 Act and Planning Acts. They make no distinction between scheduled and unscheduled sites. There is no barrier to the protection of archaeological landscapes, though in practice the onus is on the archaeologist to demonstrate that an area to be protected is of archaeological significance in its entirety.

Conclusion

Thus it can be seen that provisions for archaeological protection and management are being brought more widely into the statutes or working regulations in Britain, albeit slowly. The signs are that this trend will not only continue, but be enhanced and become a matter of routine, and that archaeology will become even more widely acknowledged as a relevant environmental issue. Indeed, the benefits of this can already be seen: in England at least one archaeologist has been appointed by a River Authority as a result of the inclusion of archaeological protection within the Water Act 1989.

To achieve a fully integrated approach on environmental issues, we need to move towards an integrated approach to the land at a strategic level, which allows for its management for farming, forestry or conservation, including archaeological interest. Such an approach would require that archaeological grants come into line with agricultural and forestry grants on the one hand and a greater degree of integration or cooperation between the bodies responsible for each area of interest on the other. An integrated approach to the landscape is possible, as is evident from the Scandinavian countries, particularly Denmark (Kristiansen 1984, 21–7). In Britain much could be achieved by continuing to rethink the conservation aims of land management, by reallocating existing resources, improving consultation and promoting better cooperation between existing bodies.

Archaeology and nature conservation: towards integration

Consideration of the integration of archaeology into the conservation management of the landscape is particularly apposite at a time when the organisations primarily responsible for nature conservation are merging into a single new agency responsible for the conservation of the natural heritage in Scotland. This agency (Scottish Natural Heritage) is due to come into existence in 1992. It will incorporate the current functions of the Countryside Commission for Scotland (CCS) and the Nature Conservancy Council (NCC), which was itself split from a single British body into three national sections in April 1991. The new agency will thus be responsible for the promotion of public enjoyment of the countryside on the one hand, and its designation and protection on the other, including both landscape assessment and species protection. This will necessitate close consultation with other organisations concerned with countryside development, management and protection, including those concerned with the built heritage (SDD 1990). This consultation is particularly important, not only because archaeological protection and management is increasingly aligned with other environmental concerns, but also because it is now recognised that the 'natural' heritage has been substantially affected by human activity, past and present (eg Simmons 1989, 376–96; Sheail 1983). Yet, despite this acknowledgement, there is no integration between protection of the natural heritage and that of the built heritage, although collaborative projects have been undertaken, such as the *Inventory of Gardens and Designed Landscapes in Scotland* (HBM:CCS 1987). It is, therefore, worth exploring the areas in which the two concerns impinge on each other at present, and how they might develop in future (cf. Lambrick 1985).

It is often stated that the Scottish countryside is not entirely natural, but the extent to which this is true, or the manner of its alteration through time, is seldom considered. Those organisations dealing with the natural heritage do not generally seek to quantify the extent of human interference with the natural environment. Archaeology involves the study of the physical remains of the past, whether monuments in the landscape, artifacts or pollen grains. As part of this process it attempts to understand past environments and land-use, and this approach contributes to our understanding of the modern landscape and how it has developed. For example, recent work in the Strath of Kildonan has illustrated some of the dynamics which have destroyed some traces of past human activity and hidden others, resulting in a landscape which appears natural, but which has in fact been actively exploited in the past (Lowe and Barber 1988, 26; Barber pers. comm.). At Armadale in Sutherland, a large area which is designated as a Site of Special Scientific Interest (SSSI) for its semi-natural vegetation and which is under pressure from modern farming, numerous archaeological sites attest the past history of the land, indicating that it has been under similar pressure for over 3,000 years. The SSSI protects the nature conservation, but the area can only be properly understood with reference to its archaeology.

By providing the historical dimension to protection of the landscape as a 'natural' resource, archaeology complements nature conservation more closely than is usually appreciated. Both disciplines are concerned, after all, with understanding and protecting the landscape. Indeed conservation can only be properly undertaken if the processes by which the landscape has come to its present state are understood.

The landscape is not a single, easily defined, entity. It is the product of continuous use and change, and indeed of differing perceptions of it (Coones 1985). As a result, it is crucial that an assessment of the characteristics of the landscape take into account all the components which make up the modern landscape. All contribute to our perception of it. The physical remains of the past form an integral part of the modern appearance of the landscape, whether archaeological monuments, historic gardens or ancient hedgerows. This is particularly important in areas where extensive archaeological landscapes survive, since there the historical dimension to the landscape may be an eminent landscape characteristic. Through both its physical remains and its analysis of past landscapes, archaeology can contribute to our understanding of the form of the modern landscape, the characteristics of which we seek to assess, designate and preserve. It should, therefore, play a more important role in landscape assessment than has hitherto been the case.

The built heritage and natural heritage come together in their effect on the development and use of the land since both designate areas for protection. Although the legislations and procedures governing archaeological protection and nature conservation are entirely distinct, their effects are very similar in the perception of land-users and developers. The existing provisions for the protection of archaeological sites and monuments have been considered above. Other provisions protect land considered to be of importance for its nature conservation value or its natural beauty. The effect of these is to restrict and control the type of development which can take place, with a view to retaining those aspects of the land which made it worthy of designation. In the case of SSSIs, under the Wildlife and Countryside Act, the principal means of achieving this aim is through management grants and compensation payments (MacKay 1985). Management grants also form the basis of the ESA scheme, whose aim is to retain the character of the land through voluntary, sympathetic management. The provisions for the protection of scheduled ancient monuments are stronger than any other countryside designation, generally giving protection precedence over development, but in practice a balance is usually sought between preservation and the continuing use of the land. This is in recognition of the fact that the long-term aims of preservation are best served by sympathetic land management. The major practical means of achieving this balance in the case of ancient monuments, as in nature conservation, lies in management agreements. This is particularly crucial when dealing with extensive archaeological landscapes. The major difference between nature conservation and archaeological preservation is that the former depends on financial agreements to secure its aims, whereas the latter depends on prohibitive legislative powers, using financial incentives to improve sites rather than to prevent their damage.

Thus, although the respective designations are separate entities in concept and execution, there is nevertheless considerable overlap in effect between nature and archaeological designations. This overlap is not acknowledged to any real extent by working practice. Joint action on specific sites or projects does take place, but there is no strategic commonality of purpose between the various organisations to ensure that the overlap is viewed positively and even exploited. Some moves have been made in recent years to address this problem. Thus, discussions have been held between archaeological bodies and CCS, for instance, over the latter's approach to archaeology and areas where consultation may be fruitful. This has led to some informal practical results. Similarly, information is exchanged between HS and NCC about the presence of archaeological sites within SSSIs. Such exchange provides a mechanism for the identification, and thus resolution, of potential conflict. A recent series of seminars involving HS, NCC and CCS have been organised by SOAFD for its staff concerned with the balancing duties of Section 17 of the Agriculture Act. These have underlined some important points: that there is a fundamental relationship both between all aspects of conservation — landscape, natural and archaeological — and between conservation and agricultural use of the land, in that all seek to manage, to different ends, a single landscape; that the various organisations are gradually converging as public support for conservation aims widens; and that a proper integrated approach is only possible if financial incentives are brought more into balance. In the meantime there is still some way to go before a proper integrated approach to the conservation management of the land is achieved: the ESA model most closely approaches this aim at present.

An important step forward was taken during the passage of the Environmental Protection Act. NCC and archaeological bodies agreed a 'statement of intent' in which the need for consultation, both generally and in specific cases, is emphasised, as well as the need for reciprocal training. More recently, an amendment to the Natural Heritage (Scotland) Bill has been proposed, requesting the new agency to take archaeological interests into consideration. Together these provisions should open the channels for the close cooperation which is needed if we are to view the protection, management and interpretation of our national heritage in a properly integrated way. Existing contacts should thus be strengthened and extended following the establishment of the new agency.

Nevertheless, it seems unlikely that the new organisation will employ any archaeological staff, since the protection of the built heritage is the province of another national organisation, HS, although it is possible that there will be archaeological expertise on its overseeing board. There are, however, archaeological sites on land for which the agency will be responsible. Similarly, those responsible for the built heritage do not employ any nature conservation expertise directly, although there is need for this in the management of monuments, including those in state care, to ensure that management for archaeological purposes does not inadvertently damage nature conservation interests. However, steps have recently been taken by HS to provide such expertise for monuments in care, as part of the continuing integration of nature and archaeological conservation and management.

For the future, one may look towards single landscape designations which encompass natural and man-made interests; towards joint management strategies and agreements; and towards the integration of these conservation concerns with the major land developments of agriculture and afforestation. It will take a long time to alter deep-rooted perceptions of the land sufficiently to achieve such an aim, but such a goal would benefit conservation organisations and land-users alike.

Conclusion

Archaeology is important to the understanding and interpretation of the landscape. It gives proper time-depth to its modern appearance and adds the full human dimension. The contribution of archaeology lies in two areas: scientific analysis and physical remains, the former providing the background information, the latter the graphic illustration. The public are aware of the past through the publicly presented monuments and museum displays, but most people are less aware of the number and variety of monuments which exist throughout the countryside. There are exceptions to this rule, where groups of archaeological monuments are presented for the public as some form of heritage trail, but these are still relatively rare in Scotland. Rarer still are integrated trails incorporating both the natural and the historical dimension in landscape interpretation.

Yet there is great potential for uniting archaeology and nature conservation in a move towards the important educational aim of landscape interpretation and appreciation. Moreover, both have a similar recreational potential, as features in the landscape, and might provide economic benefits linked to tourism, not only on a national — and indeed international — scale, but also on a more local level. Such potential can be realised in three principal areas: presentation, recreation and education.

Presenting the resource: the potential for field monuments

Archaeology stands at the interface between the natural heritage and the wider built heritage. The built heritage includes archaeological landscapes and field monuments, as well as buildings of every period, whether protected by scheduling, listing or through local authority designations. All are part of the continuous human heritage. Yet there is a vast difference in the public understanding of a medieval castle and a prehistoric hill-fort. This difference relates to people's actual experience in the modern world on the one hand, and to their historical education on the other: castles and stately homes not only look more like modern architecture, but they are also concepts made more familiar through education and the media. Prehistoric hill-forts are unfamiliar in both senses. This problem exists throughout the field of monument presentation (Thompson 1981, 22) and related educational initiatives, but it could be addressed and remedied in a number of ways.

Presentation and interpretation

The presentation of archaeological and historical monuments is perhaps most traditionally associated with HS (and its predecessors) and the National Trust for Scotland (NTS). Both take site specific approaches to presentation, although their philosophies are rather different. HS seeks to 'conserve as found', while NTS not infrequently restores at least the furnishings of its properties to their former splendour. The two bodies care for different types of properties and their work tends to be complementary.

HS is directly responsible, on behalf of the Secretary of State for Scotland, for over 300 monuments, ranging from Neolithic settlements to major examples of medieval and industrial architecture. Different conservation skills are needed for different types of monuments: field monuments require land management, while upstanding masonry structures require continuous repair and maintenance of stonework. The latter are cared for by a direct work force of architects, skilled stone-masons and labourers who ensure that the structures remain standing as far as possible in the form in which they were inherited by the state: this necessitates the constant repair of mortar and stone, but every effort is made to maintain the nuances of the original structure and its historical modifications (Thompson 1981, 22–34). Field monuments are generally managed through grazing or grass cutting. As most monuments in care are open to the public, effort is also put into their presentation and interpretation. This work takes two principal forms: the production of on-site interpretative boards and authoritative guidebooks; and promotional marketing which involves, for example, audio-visual facilities, promotional literature and the staging of events on site. The thrust of the marketing side of HS is aimed towards those monuments which have custodians and for which, normally, the visitor pays an entrance fee. This trend is likely to continue in the effort to attract more visitors to monuments. Nevertheless, interpretative material is also produced for unattended, free monuments: for example, guidebooks covering a specific area, like Orkney (Ritchie and Ritchie 1990), or period and thematic volumes, such as *Scotland BC* (Ritchie 1988) or *A Queen's Progress* (Breeze 1987).

The interpretative material produced concentrates on the description and historical development of the monument, using reconstruction drawings to convey a visual impression of how a site may have looked and functioned. HS is currently completing the replacement of old-style metal plates with modern interpretative boards which incorporate colour illustrations and are both visually attractive and highly informative. In most cases the approach taken is site specific, concentrating on the description and history of an individual site rather than linking different sites, though in some cases a paragraph draws attention to other sites in the area. An integrated approach to monuments of the same period or those within a specific area is possible. For instance, HS's interpretative boards for the group of early prehistoric monuments in the Kilmartin Valley and Falkirk Museum's material for the Antonine Wall both adopt this approach. The same approach has also been adopted in some of HS's literature. It could be applied even more widely.

The wider question of historical interpretation has been thoroughly examined elsewhere (Lowenthal 1985), and is a highly complex and increasingly specialist discipline. It is perhaps most difficult in the area of prehistoric monuments, where interpretation depends on more limited evidence and where the field remains are usually less meaningful to visitors. If interpretation is to be successful, considerable effort needs to be put into trying to convey an impression of how such structures worked in a way to which the visitor can relate (cf Tilden 1977, 9).

The relationship between monuments in care and those in the landscape which require protection is important, and there is scope for using the former to draw attention to the latter. Some work is already being done in this area. For example, HS's recent period guides to monuments in care, such as *Scotland BC*, refer to all relevant monuments in the landscape. This link is important and deserves even more attention.

Indeed, concern for the protection and management of archaeological sites and monuments not in care has led to the production of information leaflets, cards and articles (eg Macinnes 1989). These are aimed at farmers and foresters, for example, seeking to widen their understanding of monuments in the landscape. It is intended that such literature will be increased to cover a wider range of topics, such as archaeology and farming, and different audiences. The same message is gradually being incorporated into specific interpretative boards and visitor centres at individual monuments and could be extended to other educational activities.

The composition of the estate has to be considered if this widening of scope in the areas of monument presentation and education is to be achieved. The range of monuments in care has built up gradually and primarily through happenstance rather than conscious strategy. This has meant that the full spectrum of monuments which survive in the landscape as illustrations of the chronological development of human activity in Scotland, spanning prehistory to the recent industrial past, is not represented among those open and presented to the public. In general attention has been focused on higher status sites to the exclusion of those associated with lower levels of society. At Staneydale in Shetland, for example, only the 'temple' was taken into care, not the adjacent contemporary houses and field systems. HS is, however, currently undertaking an exercise aimed at trying to produce a more balanced estate, reflecting the full range of archaeological sites of all periods.

Joint ventures are not new. HS has close links with NTS already and has undertaken joint projects with CCS. Nevertheless this could be broadened to achieve a greater integration of approach with the natural heritage in particular. A recent initiative to record, manage and enhance the nature conservation interest on monuments in care is a positive step in this direction, and might lead to the reciprocal recording and management of archaeological sites in national nature reserves.

The other organisation principally identified with the presentation of the past is the NTS, mainly through their stately homes, sometimes with associated gardens, and mountain properties. NTS undoubtedly owns a number of archaeological monuments within its properties, and now recognises the need for their management and their potential for presentation (cf Thackray and Hearn 1985; Thackray 1986, for England and Wales). Projects are already being carried out on Fair Isle and St Kilda, and a pilot, desk-based survey of the archaeological content of other properties has recently been initiated. It is to be hoped that a full archaeological inventory will gradually be completed, the management of the monuments secured, and the opportunity taken to present more of the sites for the public. This development will be invaluable in presenting to the public a fuller chronological picture of the development of the landscape.

Recreation

The recreational value of archaeological sites is now widely appreciated. Indeed, NTS is well-placed to link the built and natural heritage, as its properties embrace both areas of interest. A number of integrated heritage trails have been developed by the National Trust in England and Wales, a model for future developments in Scotland. The emphasis of these trails is recreational, but the educational potential is also important, for they provide information regarding the development of the landscape over time and the nature of human interaction with the environment. Similar work is done by the National Parks in England and Wales, and could perhaps be developed within any comparably designated areas in Scotland (CCS 1990).

The Forestry Commission is concerned with the recreational value of both natural and archaeological features. Ancient monuments are increasingly presented as positive assets within Forestry Commission land. Many are protected from planting: some are then provided with notice boards, as at Craig Phadrig, and others included in forest trails, as on Arran. The trails are accompanied by descriptive leaflets, which are normally site specific. The trails and leaflets also include natural features. A natural next step would be to widen such presentation to discuss the setting of sites in the landscape and the integration of archaeological and natural features. Comparable initiatives could be encouraged in private forestry, and might be stimulated as a result of the management grants to be introduced by the Forestry Commission.

Local authorities are also now widely recognising the recreational potential of their heritage. Some authorities own monuments and these are generally open to the public. Many have explanatory notices or interpretative panels, like those prepared for the Antonine Wall by Falkirk Museum. In addition, the idea of heritage trails is also more popular. In these public access is often secured through management agreements rather than direct ownership. Such trails may serve a number of functions: protection, by improving the condition of monuments through active management; recreation, by promoting public access for both local residents and tourists; and education, by demonstrating the time-depth to human occupation of a region. Such initiatives are increasing in Scotland, although the idea of integrated landscape interpretation is not yet often explicitly explored.

However, the recreational and wider tourist potential of archaeology has not been fully tapped in Scotland. Visitors come to monuments maintained by HS and NTS, or those presented by the Forestry Commission and local authorities, but they generally remain unaware of the wealth of sites surviving throughout the landscape. Yet archaeology could aid the local economy in a sustainable way: it is an intrinsic part of the landscape; it can be visually attractive; and it can be presented and maintained for the public without causing environmental disturbance.

Some possibilities have already been mentioned, but there is further scope to capitalise on the tourist potential of archaeology. This need not occur only on a large scale, involving national organisations such as the Scottish Tourist Board, but may also be explored by a variety of other means. For example, private individuals can make use of grants to promote individual sites; local residents can adopt a monument, a scheme proposed by the Council for Scottish Archaeology (CSA); private developers can incorporate archaeological sites within developments; local authorities can actively promote their archaeological heritage, as Falkirk District have already done for the Antonine Wall, and Highland Region are currently proposing to do through the preparation of a video; and countryside interpretative schemes, such as funded by the Countryside Commission for Scotland, can incorporate archaeological sites and the historical aspects of the landscape.

Such opportunities are slowly beginning to be realised. Thus, the Scottish Tourist Board have expressed interest in exploring with individual farmers the potential for presenting archaeology to the public through farm diversification schemes. Similarly, as more and more developers agree to fund archaeological work in advance of their developments, there is an increasing desire to display the information preserved or excavated. A good example of this approach is at Milton of Leys, near Inverness, where a combination of preservation and excavation was carried out in advance of a housing, hotel and golf course project. There the surviving archaeological features will be incorporated within a trail through the golf course, and interpretative material will be prepared for the public. This approach is increasing and the benefits of protecting archaeology and presenting it to the public are beginning to be recognised. This is particularly so when the existence of monuments is highlighted in large-scale developments at an early stage through Environmental Assessments. One may anticipate that this will become routine in large-scale leisure developments of the sort that appear to be increasing throughout Scotland at present.

There is clearly a danger of damaging the resource by encouraging its presentation for the public (Rumble 1986, 5–6) and visitor damage has occurred on many major monuments, primarily through erosion. All interpretation projects, therefore, need to take the vulnerability of the monument into account. Monitoring facilities to check on the condition of the site need to be built in from an early stage. Provided the dangers are borne in mind (cf Wickham-Jones 1988), the benefits to archaeology of initiatives like these are immense. They have the potential to present archaeology to a wider audience on the one hand, and, on the other, should lead to the improved perception and understanding of a range of archaeological sites and monuments, and an awareness of the need for their protection and management.

Education

The above considers a variety of contexts in which the presentation of monuments is being undertaken and their recreational value recognised. It also highlights their potential educational value for improving, extending and enhancing the protection and management of archaeology. Other opportunities also exist to further this aim.

Benefits would arise from the direct inclusion of archaeology as an academic subject in schools, where students could be introduced to the concepts involved in archaeology and so recognise the value of its preservation. This could lead not only to a better appreciation of the landscape by the general public, and a better understanding of its time-depth, but also to a greater respect for it. It could also improve and extend the teaching of history to those periods where the prime evidence is archaeological.

Benefits would also accrue from wider consideration of the whole area of monument protection and presentation within archaeological courses in universities. This already happens in the cultural resource management (CRM) courses which are now being set up, but such topics are only rarely incorporated into general archaeological degrees. Inclusion of these subjects is important to increase the awareness of the problems and potential that have been discussed throughout this paper. It would also bring such subjects into academic consideration and thereby enhance our approaches to protection and interpretation.

Moves have recently been made to incorporate archaeology into agricultural and forestry courses. There is also great potential for archaeology to be included in nature conservation and landscape courses. Here, however, the ultimate aim should be to achieve integrated courses on conservation in the countryside, in which archaeology takes its proper place beside nature and landscape issues.

Excavations can also be used to promote the protection of archaeological sites to a wider audience, whether at a public monument during the course of a rescue excavation, or as a way of raising money for private research work, as at Whithorn. Most excavations are short-term and do not link the process of excavation to the wider protection, management and presentation of archaeological sites and monuments. Yet because they can be extremely popular and well-visited, investment in interpretation is likely to be repaid. The best opportunities to use excavation for educational purposes are, however, presented at monuments in care, where excavations can be more long-term. In this context all aspects of archaeological work may be linked and used to promote the less well-known areas of monument protection and management.

Museum displays present a further educational opportunity. Artifacts are normally displayed outside the context of the wider archaeological landscape, though there are exceptions, such as the Royal Museum of Scotland's *Symbols of Power* exhibition and the few displays at monuments in Scotland. There is considerable scope for widening this approach to emphasise the link between artifacts and monuments. This would not only add a wider dimension to the educational and presentational value of the artifacts in the museum, but also help to increase the public's awareness of monuments in the landscape.

Summary: a vision of the future

This paper has attempted to consider areas where the protection, management and presentation of field monuments might develop in the future. The main themes are summarised here.

In monument protection and management, one improvement will be the closer integration of different aspects of the built heritage itself. Field monuments, historic buildings and monuments in care will be seen as more of a continuous whole than at present, with closer links being forged through education and presentation. This will help to overcome the current confusion between the protective measures for historic buildings and ancient monuments, and improve public understanding of the range of monuments throughout Scotland.

Archaeological protection and management will become still more closely integrated with nature conservation. ESAs have demonstrated a way forward, and there are provisions in various pieces of legislation which facilitate this further. These will certainly lead to closer working practices and joint approaches in the field and in planning, but may ultimately also lead to composite landscape designations which can acknowledge natural and historical characteristics and features in the landscape. It seems unlikely, however, that a single agency will develop. The reapportionment of resources available for land management and conservation would aid the public perception of the interrelationship between these different areas. Conservation, whether for archaeological, geological or botanical reasons, will be accepted as a legitimate aim of land management.

The recreational and tourist potential of archaeology will be more widely developed, in various ways. This will recognise the value of archaeology not only in its own right, but also as part of an integrated approach to the landscape.

In the area of education, archaeology should be seen as a more accepted part of historical education in schools. It will also play its proper part in land management and conservation courses. Issues of archaeological protection will be incorporated more widely into university courses.

At the basis of these opportunities is the concept of integration. Most importantly it should be recognised that all aspects of land-use are interrelated, and that the different uses need not be in competition. We are all dealing with a common landscape: appreciation of its unity is only a matter of perception.

Bibliography

AMB 1978 *Ancient Monuments Board for Scotland twenty-fifth annual report*, Edinburgh.

AMB 1983 *Ancient Monuments Board for Scotland thirtieth annual report*, Edinburgh.

Baker, D. 1983 *Living with the past: the historic environment*, Bedford.

Breeze, D. J. 1983 The Roman bath-house at Bearsden: making things public for the public, in Magnusson 1983, 29–32.

Breeze, D. J. 1987 *A Queen's progress*, Edinburgh.

Breeze, D. J. 1988 Planning and archaeology: the legislative framework, in Selman 1988, 1–4.

Breeze, D. J. 1989 Forestry and monuments: the role of SDD HBM for antiquities (Part 2), in Proudfoot 1989, 20–1.

CCS 1990 *The mountain areas of Scotland: conservation and management*, Battleby.

Cleere, H. 1984a Great Britain, in Cleere 1984b, 54–62.

Cleere, H. 1984b *Approaches to the archaeological heritage*, Cambridge.

Coones, P. 1985 One landscape or many? A geographical perspective, *Landscape Hist.* 7, 5–12.

Darvill, T. 1986 *The archaeology of the uplands: a rapid assessment of archaeological knowledge and practice*, London.

Darvill, T. , Saunders, A. and Startin, B. 1987 A question of national importance: approaches to the evaluation of ancient monuments for the Monument Protection Programme in England, *Antiquity* 61, 393–408.

Fife Regional Council 1990 *Charter for the environment*, Glenrothes.

HBM 1988 *Memorandum of guidance on listed buildings and Conservation Areas*, Edinburgh.

HBM:CCS 1987 *An inventory of gardens and designated landscapes in Scotland*, Glasgow.

Hanson, W. S. and Breeze, D. J. 1986 Elginhaugh project 1986: excavation strategy, *Scottish Archaeol. Rev.* 4.1, 44–5.

Harding, D. W. (ed) 1982 *Later prehistoric settlement in south-east Scotland*, Edinburgh.

Hill, P. H. 1982 Broxmouth hill-fort excavation, 1977–78: an interim report, in Harding 1982, 141–88.

Hughes, M. and Rowley, L. (eds) 1986 *The management and presentation of field monuments*, Oxford.

Kristiansen, K. 1984 Denmark, in Cleere 1984b, 21–36.

Lambrick, G. (ed) 1985 *Archaeology and nature conservation*, Oxford.

Lowe, C. E. and Barber, J. 1988 Strath of Kildonan: a large area prospective survey, *Central Excavation Unit and Ancient Monuments Laboratory annual report*, 21–6.

Lowenthal, D. 1981 Dilemmas of preservation, in Lowenthal, D. and Binney, M. (eds) *Our past before us: why do we save it?*, London, 213–37.

Lowenthal, D. 1985 *The past is a foreign country*, Cambridge.

Macinnes, L. 1982 Pattern and purpose: the settlement evidence, in Harding 1982, 57–73.

Macinnes, L. 1989 Ancient monuments in the countryside: their protection and management, *Landowning in Scotland*, 8–9.

Macinnes, L. 1990 Ancient monuments in the Scottish countryside: their protection and management, *Scottish Archaeol. Rev.* 7, 131–8.

MacIvor, I. and Fawcett, R. 1983 Planks from the shipwreck of time: an account of ancient monumentry, then and now, in Magnusson 1983, 9–27.

MacKay, K. F. 1985 SSSIs and the use of management agreements, in Lambrick 1985, 39–43.

Magnusson, M. (ed) 1983 *Echoes in stone*, Edinburgh.

Mercer, R. J. 1989 Why archaeology?, in Proudfoot 1989, 11–12.

Morgan-Evans, D. 1985 The management of historic landscapes, in Lambrick 1985, 89–94.

Morgan-Evans, D. 1986 The management of archaeological sites, in Hughes and Rowley 1986, 9–16.

Prehistoric Society 1988 *Saving our prehistoric heritage: landscape under threat*, Leeds.

Proudfoot, E. V. W. (ed) 1984 *Ancient monuments, historic buildings and planning*, Edinburgh and St. Andrews.

Proudfoot, E. V. W. (ed) 1989 *Our vanishing heritage: forestry and archaeology*, Edinburgh.

RCAHMS 1990 *North-east Perth: an archaeological landscape*, Edinburgh.

Ritchie, A. 1988 *Scotland BC*, Edinburgh.

Ritchie, A. and Ritchie, J. G. N. 1981 *Scotland: archaeology and early history*, London.

Ritchie, A. and Ritchie, J. G. N. 1990 *The ancient monuments of Orkney*, Edinburgh.

Rumble, P. 1986 The management of monuments: the overall context, in Hughes and Rowley 1986, 1–7.

SDD 1990 *Scottish natural heritage: the way ahead*, Edinburgh.

Selman, P. H. (ed) 1988 *Planning and archaeology*, Stirling.

Sheail, J. 1983 The historical perspective, in Warren, A. and Goldsmith, F. B. (eds) *Conservation in perspective*, Avon, 315–328.

Shepherd, I. A. G. 1988 Archaeology in environmental conservation in Grampian, in Selman 1988, 27–35.

Simmons, I. G. 1989 *Changing the face of the earth: culture, environment, history*, Oxford.

Thackray, D. W. R. 1986 Care and management of National Trust properties, in Hughes and Rowley 1986, 63–7.

Thackray, D. W. R. and Hearn, K. A. 1985 Archaeology and nature conservation: the responsibility of the National Trust, in Lambrick 1985, 51–7.

Thompson, M. W. 1981 *Ruins: their preservation and display*, London.

Tilden, F. 1977 *Interpreting our heritage*, North Carolina.

Wainwright, G. J. 1985 The preservation of ancient monuments, in Lambrick 1985, 23–7.

Walsh, D. 1969 *Report of the Committee of Enquiry into the arrangements for the protection of field monuments, 1966–68*, London.

Wickham-Jones, C. R. 1988 The road to Heritat: archaeologists and interpretation, *Archaeol. Rev. Cambridge* 7.2, 185–93.

Acknowledgements

I am indebted to Dr. D. J. Breeze, Dr. W. S. Hanson, Mr. F. Lawrie and Ms. C. J. Wickham-Jones for their helpful and critical comments on an earlier draft of this paper. They have considerably improved the final text. Any errors which remain are entirely my own.

13

MANAGING OUTPUT RATHER THAN INPUT? THE IMPLICATIONS OF COMPUTERISING THE NATIONAL MUSEUMS OF SCOTLAND'S ARCHAEOLOGICAL INFORMATION

D. V. Clarke

The National Museums of Scotland have responsibility for one of the largest integrated databases in Scottish archaeology. By integrated I mean that the stored data can normally be verified, within the varying limits of evidential value, in the museum without recourse to other agencies or confirmatory fieldwork. The objects and their associated records, either original documents or copies, are available for inspection, and the museum's outstanding archaeological library can normally provide the relevant published information.

Moreover, the quality and quantity of the archaeological collections — 120,000 catalogue entries covering some 500,000 objects — is such that within the museum's collecting area, principally Scotland, they have a dominance virtually unparalleled elsewhere in Europe. For almost any type of archaeological object the museum holds at least 50 per cent of the known examples from Scotland. In particular areas, such as objects made of precious metals or with a perceived high artistic element, the percentages are even greater. Nor is this importance restricted to Scotland. An analysis of D. L. Clarke's beaker corpus (Clarke 1970) shows the museum to have the single most extensive collection of this type of object in Britain, half as big again as the next largest. Indeed, in every artifactual area of British archaeology for which comprehensive lists of material are available, other than those represented only by specific regional groups, the museum's collections can be seen to contain major holdings judged in British, not just Scottish, terms.

Yet despite this, the museum's collections and their associated information remain one of the most under-utilised resources in Scottish archaeology. True, we have a steady stream of specialists looking at the collections but the majority are from England and Ireland or elsewhere in Europe, relatively few are from Scotland. The same pattern is observable with written enquiries. Of course, it would be easy to explain this as a reflection of the relatively small number of archaeologists working on Scottish archaeological problems.

Nevertheless, I am regularly amazed by the number of excavation reports on Scottish sites which are now appearing where the finds analysis seems not to have extended beyond a cursory literature search. The fact is that no serious artifact study involving Scottish material can be undertaken without consulting the National Museums' collections and the evidence of visits by specialists is that very little meaningful work in this field is undertaken by the Scottish archaeological community. This is all too clearly demonstrated by the absence of major artifactual studies by members of that community.

In part, this reflects the widespread lack of interest in artifacts currently to be observed in British archaeology. Whether this is part of what Carl-Axel Moberg characterised more than a decade ago in a broader context as 'the increasing importance of nonartifactually based archaeology' is more problematic (1978, 16). Perhaps it reflects, at least in part, the limited career opportunities in this area — the recent expansion in the number of posts for field monument survey and recording has found no echo in museums, which remain the principal source of posts for artifact specialists. Here, a mood of retrenchment has characterised the same period of increasing field archaeology posts. Yet equally important, at least for Scotland, has been a prevailing ignorance of the wealth of the existing artifact assemblages. Merriman in his review of the book accompanying the 'Symbols of Power' exhibition remarked that it used 'illustrations mainly from the excellent but seldom seen Scottish material' (1985, 225). In fact, since virtually everything in that exhibition was illustrated, the preponderance of Scottish material is nowhere near as great as his remarks might suggest. But the impact of these items, the product largely of their relative obscurity, is disproportionately greater than that of other more familiar objects; the perceptual biases resulting from the customary use of numerous photographers' work was, in this instance, almost wholly absent as more than 95 per cent of the artifact photography was the work of two National Museums' photographers, Ian Larner and Doreen Moyes, operating to a uniform brief. Moreover, the galleries in the Findlay Building in Edinburgh, where the Scottish collections are presently displayed, remain one of the last great displays for archaeologists. Virtually everything they are likely to have prior knowledge of is on display, crowded together in presentations accessible only to the serious student of archaeology.

Several factors have, in combination, insured that the Scottish collections of the National Museums have remained 'seldom seen', even by archaeologists. Although a diminishing number have, at least, continued to work on the very practical premise that everything they have read about in Scottish archaeology is likely to be in the national collections, the problem remains that the published material is only the tip of the iceberg. The last comprehensive catalogue — itself an event of unacknowledged importance in the history of British archaeology — was published in 1892 (Society of Antiquaries of Scotland 1892). Since then, the archaeology collections have more than doubled in size and the development of ever more rigorous publication standards has meant that the percentage of them adequately published is actually diminishing.

Allied to this overall weakness in publication is the legacy of the 1892 catalogue. It is all too easy now to forget that it was produced to mark the move of the collections to the building on Queen Street, which they still occupy, and that it was intended to be primarily a guide to the displays established in that building. As such it made no pretence at neutrality. The presentation, and the consequent subdivision of the collections into groups identified by letter prefixes and running numbers, was unavowedly, but legitimately, what the curators of the day believed to be considered statements about Scotland's prehistoric and early historic past as it was then perceived. The statements had considerable precision and clarity. These qualities may not have been quite so apparent to the average visitor who may have felt them to be almost submerged by the quantity of available detail — the concept of reserve collections had no real meaning at that time such that the catalogue was both a list of the holdings of the museum and a guide to the displays.

Although the presentation of prehistoric and early historic material might have changed, albeit not as much as many would now have wished, the sheer size of the collections even then, some 55,000 catalogue entries, meant that the cataloguing structure was bound to remain intact in the future. Such alterations as have been made to it are wholly in keeping with the original approach. As a result, changing perceptions, and the different questions that accompany them, have left the museum with a cataloguing system which has rendered the collections progressively more and more inaccessible. Without topographical, typological or materials indices and with insufficient staff to attempt their creation, access has become increasingly dependent on curatorial expertise and knowledge for anything except the well known. For example, spiral rings are now catalogued under at least 16 different categories and projecting ring-headed pins under at least 14 categories in the current register (for details see Clarke 1971, 45–54 — some of the unallocated items in those lists have now entered the national collections enlarging the number of categories).

All of these factors have contributed, in terms of artifact analysis, to the prevailing situation where data collection is still regarded as a research activity in its own right. To say this is not to slight the efforts of those few who have undertaken such work. Interpretation and explanation may accompany, or have stimulated, this data collection, but it is by no means universally the case. And because excavation remains the most glamorous form of data collection for the majority of archaeologists, ordering past assemblages in ways that make them accessible to current workers has received very little attention. Consequently, Scottish archaeology, in a mode by no means exclusive to it, continues to spend most of its disposable income on enlarging an ill-understood database. This reinforces existing paradigms, disproportionately rewards conservative thinking and penalises innovative approaches. The opportunities for waste and inefficiency do not need emphasising. Nor does the fact that this situation is largely the consequence of funds being spread among many agencies with uncoordinated, but important, remits. Certainly, the position is not helped by the oft unarticulated belief that data being collected now have greater evidential value than those assembled in the past even though the latter have not, by and large, been subjected to serious critical appraisal to determine their quality.

A major step towards resolving some of these difficulties has been the National Museums' decision to establish a Documentation Unit with the necessary resources to computerise the data held in the catalogues (an outline description of the whole programme, which embraces the archaeological collections, is provided in Burnett and Morrison 1989, 28–31). Turning this ambition into meaningful reality with relevance to the issues I have already outlined has so far involved a great deal of effort, given us long glimpses of the world-as-wished-for, but largely left us with the world-as-it-has-always-been. This characterisation is descriptive rather than critical. A key factor in the continuing disjuncture between ambition and achievement in the case of the Museums' archaeological information has been succinctly summarised by Burnett and Morrison:

> The single most significant reason for automating the NMS's documentation was to establish a proper basis for accounting for the collections. The aim of building up a large database of object records is to enable the NMS and its Director, as accounting officer, to demonstrate that they are properly accountable for the Museums' collections. This was one of the most important reasons for the Scottish Education Department funding this project. (1989, 30)

This goal, the importance of which is not to be gainsaid, can, of course, be realised without seriously addressing the academic, as opposed to the managerial, concerns of those charged with the curation of the collections. It has to all intents and purposes been achieved in the case of our archaeological information by entering the location index. While this has been no mean undertaking, the location index is the simplest of the twelve record systems in which information about items in the archaeological collections, amassed over two centuries, may be lodged. Its primary function is to enable any object to be found within the Museums' displays or stores and as such it gives only the register number, a brief description of the object, its general provenance and its position within the storage or display areas. Information as limited as this can be managed adequately in structures which are too simple to accommodate the full range of available data with a consequent diminution in its usefulness for research purposes. Certainly, in inputting terms there are good practical reasons for adopting restricted data structures in the first instance.

Nevertheless, what has so far been achieved, albeit primarily for accountancy purposes, appears to have some real potential for academic interests. It provides crude indices to material, type and place — the main deficiencies in the previous manual systems. But it is not as useful as it might have been because the records are largely unedited — such editing as has taken place or is programmed is necessarily determined by accounting requirements which have a poor fit with academic needs. Since the location index is the product of many hands over nearly a century, cumulatively the records reflect both the changes in terminology during that time and individual perceptions of the appropriate level of required detail. Moreover, it is important to remember that this particular information set was never intended to provide the principal access to the collections. It was designed to reveal the physical position of the object within the museum — most of the details have been provided merely as an aide-memoire for the curatorial users. Consequently, there is no evidence as yet that, faced with a particular query, searching the computerised information yields a greater number of relevant examples than the previous combination of manual search and curatorial knowledge. This is what I mean by the world-as-it-has-always-been.

What has changed, of course, is the speed with which we can acquire the information. This ought not to pose any serious problems or to be viewed as anything other than a major benefit. But curiously this seems not to be the case. The structuring of what is still essentially dirty data in a homogenised format has imparted a spurious sense of reliability to it. This occurs, I think, because this form of presentation removes all the visual clues to evidential quality that have been unintentionally embedded in the manually created records. Curators have necessarily interpreted these clues in terms of their own knowledge and experience whenever they have attempted to create a data set to satisfy a particular need. The problems caused by the loss of these guides are compounded by the ease of avoiding serious critical engagement afforded by the availability of virtually instantaneous data. This tendency to accord data different levels of evidential status solely as a result of the media form in which it is transmitted to us is a well recognised phenomenon and in no way restricted to computer generated information — the camera does not lie'. Nevertheless, when combined with a disconcerting absence of scepticism, most often manifest in archaeology through a willingness to treat as facts what are fundamentally interpretations, the problems of managing readily accessible and extensive blocks of information can become acute.

All of this may seem far too concerned with the familiar concentration on managing input rather than output. And it is not sufficient justification to parrot truisms that the quality of input determines that of output. In terms of information and analysis that has always been the case, even if we have previously had the mental acumen to dodge round the problems, for instance, of using words like 'pottery' as descriptors of both material and form. The lack of a rigorously structured terminology, so often the core element in considering the difficulties of achieving good quality input in computerised systems, can be overcome. This is only possible though, in my judgement, if the terminology reflects the view that the analysis of any artifact assumes a starting position of complete ignorance. It is all too easy to believe one's certainty that this particular object is a flat axe or that one a hipped pin is an incontestable truth. If the information systems we put in place merely encode our values and prejudices, few of which have yet been given explicit form, managing output will in many cases be very simple, but in a few key instances very difficult: simple where we continue to interrogate the data within the framework of our present set of questions; and difficult because innovative approaches are likely to have no meaningful data set to interrogate.

Clearly then, we cannot adopt, or even attempt to modify, available systems like the much vaunted Social history and industrial classification (SHIC) (SHIC Working Group 1983). Despite its claim to provide 'a broad interdisciplinary structure for . . . all . . . forms of museum material in the field of human history', one can only presume that history is here defined in the quite literal sense of those periods of the human past for which written documents exist. The structure is hierarchical 'with levels that run from the general to the more specific' so that 'as a rule the higher levels are conceptual whilst the lower levels are more directly object based'. Its aim 'is to relate objects . . . to their function in context with other objects' (SHIC Working Group 1983, vi). It should be noted that function is defined in this system in the most narrowly utilitarian terms, which perhaps says more about the creators' prejudices than it does about social history. To use such an approach would involve an unwarranted set of assumptions about prehistoric and early historic objects — for most pieces we have very little direct information on their actual or intended functions. It would impose a straitjacket of access only through functional (as defined by SHIC) context — the classification does not group material according to generic type or family similarities' (SHIC Working Group 1983, vi) — which is far too restrictive for archaeological purposes.

It is not clear to me whether it is really possible to create structures for information about archaeological artifacts which can be in any meaningful way independent of our current perceptions and values. We must, however, be able to make those perceptions and values clear and not leave them among the unspoken assumptions that guide our everyday practice. Many, I suspect, will not stand the test of the serious scrutiny to which they will be exposed in such circumstances. Otherwise, we will be engaged in constructing only an alternative version of the 1892 Catalogue, which will prove just as constraining as its predecessor and within much the same timescale. Indeed, it would stand a good chance of being obsolete before it was completed. Certainly, the redeeming factor will be that developments in computer technology may well make the reformulation of data a far less onerous task than has previously been the case.

Computerising our data does make explicit the multi-dimensional nature of the information which every artifact represents. This concept has resided far too often in the realms of intuitive understanding and consequently is open to disregard when recognition might prove inconvenient. It certainly seems to have passed by the SHIC Working Group. The resulting variety of access points available through a computerised system is generally assumed to make it qualitatively distinct from earlier modes of information storage, predominantly printed catalogues in one form or another. Ease of access is, regrettably, a mixed blessing. Investigation of the problems associated with the description, as distinct from the classification, of archaeological artifacts has been very limited. There is no discussion of the issue at all, for instance, in the most recent volume on archaeological curatorship

(Pearce 1990). Classification, whether seen in the form of the familiar typological/chronological studies or in more recent attempts to explore social patterning through artifacts (eg Miller 1985; Shanks and Tilley 1987, 135–240), remains the ordering of selected information for the purposes of explanation. Although they must take cognisance of such schemes, particularly those receiving widespread acceptance, museums should not be in the business of adopting individual classifications as the easy providers of structures for their information systems. In museological terms, classification has to remain distinct from description, not a substitute for it. Description, within the context of museum archaeology, has to aim at neutrality in its use of language. It has to have as its primary aim the maximising of opportunities in subsequent investigations of our data and so it must not give emphasis to one group of artifactual attributes at the expense of others. This is what classification in archaeology, quite properly, always does even on the rare occasions when the analysis involves the techniques of numerical taxonomy (eg Clarke 1962). Description, on the other hand, involves no expectation of a particular conclusion, or indeed any conclusion at all. Rather it seeks only to ensure that it can successfully contribute to the widest possible number of approaches.

I am well aware that the distinction which I am drawing between description and classification, and the consequent need to maintain a clear separation between the two sets of terms, represents a counsel of perfection which will prove unrealisable in practice. My ideal is that those consulting the collections for serious academic purposes should, as a matter of course, be required to identify what for them are the defining characteristics of the artifact types they wish to study. This would be a requirement in order to gain access to the collections and the museum's role would then be to produce all the material that conformed to those characteristics without imposing any judgements on their validity. But the myriad other aspects of curatorial existence beyond academic concerns would be made significantly more onerous without the benefits of existing classifications. Once embedded in the systems virtually all researchers will willingly use them despite the restricted data sets that will almost invariably be available to them as a result. Moreover, many simple descriptors, for example axe or knife, are themselves the product of earlier classifications but have now become so much a part of archaeology-speak that they are now descriptors of form and often independent of the interpretation of function that first prompted their adoption. Separating description from classification in these instances would now require much additional, unfamiliar terminology. Its invention, were it ever to be embarked upon, would no doubt involve much acrimonious debate, face clear problems in achieving widespread acceptance, and generally provide too attractive a diversion for a significant part of the creative talent deployed on archaeological issues for the exercise to be justifiable. In practice, then, complete neutrality in description is a chimera, but it must nevertheless remain an aspiration which influences our day-to-day practice.

In marked contrast to museum curators, the library profession has long wrestled with the problems of ordering information in ways which make it as available as possible (the whole exercise is conveniently summarised in Needham 1971). Clearly, the distinction between description and classification has been less problematic in the case of printed matter than is the case with museum objects. The SHIC Working Group certainly thought there to be a firm analogy between museums and libraries and, with the merest hint of vanity, implied that their scheme was comparable to the major library classifications — Dewey Decimal, Library of Congress and UDC (SHIC Working Group 1983, v). In a sense I suppose they were justified in making this claim but, even then, there was a growing interest, which they would have done well to pay attention to, in the possibilities of generating new knowledge through information retrieval systems (admirably reviewed in Davies 1989). An important aspect of this, with clear implications for our management of museum data output, is the concept which Swanson (1986) has christened 'undiscovered public knowledge'.

Swanson has developed this concept within Popper's framework of three worlds — World 1, the physical world; World 2, the world of subjective knowledge; and World 3, the world of objective knowledge (Popper 1979). He argues that 'knowledge can be public, yet undiscovered, if independently created fragments are logically related but never retrieved, brought together, and interpreted' (Swanson 1986, 103). To illustrate this he uses examples from three aspects of interpretation that reflect upon his theme. The first, the hidden refutation, is straightforward and involves the simple universal hypothesis. If current knowledge asserts, for example, that all swans are white, the claim remains an hypothesis which cannot be verified in the sense of proved to be true. Swanson argues that refutations of such hypotheses can exist in the literature — observations of black swans in a remote part of the world published in a local wild life journal, for example — without their import being recognised either by the observers or the wider world. The second, a missing link in the logic of discovery, involves the publication, in two separate areas of knowledge, of observations that process A causes result B and that B causes the result C. From this it follows that the proposition A causes C objectively exists, at least as a hypothesis. But its exploitation requires that both claims are known simultaneously to an individual with sufficient knowledge to appreciate the logical implications of them. The third, the hidden cumulative strength of individually weak tests, relies on the potential for a series of independent tests or observations, all of which can only be individually regarded as weakly demonstrating a particular theory, to provide an aggregate of support which is stronger than that provided by any single observation. The power of Swanson's arguments has been greatly enhanced by his ability to provide actual examples from the current literature (summarised in Davies 1989, 277–83).

Swanson is, of course, concerned with much wider areas of knowledge than the archaeological information from a relatively small geographical area. He recognises that no retrieval systems yet available offer guarantees of success in this area. But his concepts are the most dramatic demonstration of the flexibility needed to exploit fully the potential of computerised systems. It does not require too much imagination to realise that the factors affecting Scottish archaeology which I outlined above — lack of personnel, inaccessible databases, and data collection based on inadequate information and analysis — might make it a microcosm, loosely speaking, of Swanson's world. Computerising our data, of which the National Museums of Scotland's efforts are but one example, is only a first step towards the recovery of undiscovered public knowledge in our area of interest. But how effectively we manage the output from these new systems will be an important measure of our commitment to taking the chances for change and development which are inherent in such concepts. Equally important will be to ensure that our input structures do not constrain our exploitation of these new opportunities.

Nor should we regard these developments as of merely local concern. Centralising tendencies have always been a significant feature of Scottish archaeology and, although this pattern is now being weakened for the first time, there remains a remarkable concentration of data in the national agencies. The National Museums' collections are perhaps the demonstration par excellence of this situation. Consequently, computerising the data held by the National Museums will be a significant step towards the creation of a national inventory of portable artifacts. To suggest this may still be to wander in the world-as-wished-for, but for Scotland it is a realisable project. The recent survey by the Scottish Museums Council suggested that archaeological material was held by about 100 museums but only half a dozen, apart from the National Museums, claimed to have holdings in excess of 10,000 items. The vast majority have collections of fewer than 1,000 artifacts. Processing this level of data will not consume an inconceivable level of resources providing there is a widespread commitment to the goal. A first step down what will undoubtedly be a long road has been taken with the appointment of a member of staff attached to the National Museums' Documentation Unit specifically to advise and help local museums in their computerisation projects.

The creation of a national inventory would have a significant impact on collection policies and greatly facilitate loans and exhibition creation in both the national and local museums. But it will have the greatest implications for our understanding of the prehistoric and early historic past. It will, of course, remove from artifact studies the aura of research that has surrounded data collection. This will, in turn, force the emphasis onto source criticism (as defined by Almgren 1971) and explanation. Such a dramatic change of emphasis will have a number of unforeseen ramifications, as well as features which can be clearly anticipated. Of the latter, one of the most influential, at least in the early stages of interpretation, is likely to be combined quantitative and spatial studies. They certainly provide an admirable example of the potential to be derived from computerised data on a national scale.

Beyond the straightforward distribution map intended to document a particular point in an argument, quantitative and spatial studies have rarely been used in Scottish archaeology as the basis for making observations deserving of explanation. Professor Atkinson's study of leaf-shaped arrowheads from eastern Scotland (1962, 19–21), for instance, has provoked few imitators. I can well understand why; my own experience within the National Museums has shown me how many hours the collection of such basic data must have taken. Atkinson was, of course, concerned to examine whether patterns of Neolithic settlement might be indicated in broad terms by the number of arrowheads per 100,000 acres of arable land in various regions of eastern Scotland. This confirmed the north-eastern concentration suggested by other artifacts. Equally interesting though was the massive number of arrowheads from Culbin Sands in Moray. The only other comparable assemblage from Scotland is from the extensive sand dune systems at Glenluce in Wigtownshire. How are these finds to be explained? Atkinson noted that they might be the distortions of modern flint collecting, but qualified this by saying that 'collectors are most active and most successful precisely where flints themselves are most numerous' (1962, 21). This raises a number of important issues about the biases which the various methods of collection may have created. But they must not be allowed to obscure the archaeological implications. In the case of Culbin and Glenluce, either they are unusual glimpses into the overall density of arrowheads which would be revealed with comparably assiduous collecting throughout lowland Scotland or they truly are exceptional concentrations which collecting practices may have enhanced to some degree. Whichever position one chooses requires hypotheses which are not yet part of mainstream interpretations of Neolithic Scotland.

The opportunities, which a national computerised inventory would provide, to investigate such problems against the full range of artifactual data will lead us into quite new sets of questions and interpretations. This will be especially important in examining variations in patterning on a broad scale through time. This single group of examples does, I hope, demonstrate the potential of computerised data. It will not, alas, be available to us in the near future, but we should not believe that the benefits only accrue at the completion of input. The work that is now under way in the National Museums will progressively enhance the quality of the data and enlarge the number of ways one can interrogate it. The key point is that we remain aware of the enlarging consequences of this data explosion for our interpretations of the prehistoric and early historic past. This awareness must constantly inform our inputting strategies, for these are influenced by expectations of output at a macro as much as at a micro level — the influence of accountability on the National Museums' work to date demonstrates that very convincingly. Certainly, it is vital that our initial input structures are fundamentally sound, but it would be a grave mistake to suppose that they do not subsequently need regular monitoring and a willingness to modify them in the light of changing output aspirations.

Bibliography

Almgren, B. 1971 [Source criticism], *Tor* 14 (1970–71), 5–6.
Atkinson, R. J. C. 1962 Fishermen and farmers, in Piggott, S. (ed) *The prehistoric peoples of Scotland*, London, 1–38.

Burnett, J. and Morrison, I. 1989 *Wimps, worms and Winchesters. A guide to documentation in museums*, Edinburgh.

Clarke, D. L. 1962 Matrix analysis and archaeology with particular reference to British beaker pottery, *Proc. Prehist. Soc.* 28, 371–82.

Clarke, D. L. 1970 *Beaker pottery of Great Britain and Ireland*, Cambridge.

Clarke, D. V. 1971 Small finds in the Atlantic Province: problems of approach, *Scottish Archaeol. Forum* 3, 22–54.

Davies, R. 1989 The creation of new knowledge by information retrieval and classification, *J. Documentation* 45, 273–301.

Merriman, N. 1985 Review of D. V. Clarke, T. G. Cowie and A. Foxon, 'Symbols of power at the time of Stonehenge', *Archaeol. Rev. Cambridge* 4, 253–55.

Miller, D. 1985 *Artefacts as categories. A study of ceramic variability in Central India*, Cambridge.

Moberg, C.-A. 1978 Some developments in North European prehistory in the period 1969–1976, *Norwegian Archaeol. Rev.* 11, 6–16.

Needham, C. D. 1971 *Organizing knowledge in libraries. An introduction to information retrieval*, (2nd edn) London.

Pearce, S. 1990 *Archaeological curatorship*, Leicester.

Popper, K. R. 1979 *Objective knowledge. An evolutionary approach*, (revised edn) Oxford.

Shanks, M. and Tilley, C. 1987 *Re-constructing archaeology. Theory and practice*, Cambridge.

SHIC Working Group 1983 *Social history and industrial classification (SHIC). A subject classification for museum collections*, Sheffield.

Society of Antiquaries of Scotland 1892 *Catalogue of the National Museum of Antiquities*, Edinburgh.

Swanson, D. R. 1986 Undiscovered public knowledge, *Library Quarterly* 56.2, 103–18.